ADOBE® PHOTOSHOP®
ELEMENTS 7

CLASSROOM IN A BOOK®

The official training workbook from Adobe Systems

www.adobepress.com

Adobe

Adobe Press books are published by Peachpit, a division of Pearson Education located in Berkeley, California. For the latest on Adobe Press books, go to www.adobepress.com. To report errors, please send a note to errata@peachpit.com. For information on getting permission for reprints and excerpts, contact permissions@peachpit.com.

Printed and bound in the United States of America

ISBN-13:   978-0-321-57390-2
ISBN-10:   0-321-57390-0

9 8 7 6 5 4 3 2

WHAT'S ON THE DISC

Here is an overview of the contents of the Classroom in a Book disc

Lesson files ... and so much more

The *Adobe Photoshop Elements 7 Classroom in a Book* disc includes the lesson files that you'll need to complete the exercises in this book, as well as other content to help you learn more about Adobe Photoshop Elements 7 and use it with greater efficiency and ease. The diagram below represents the contents of the disc, which should help you locate the files you need.

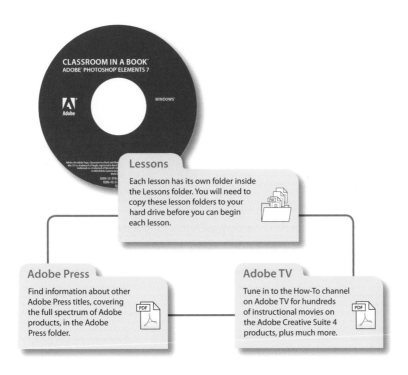

Lessons

Each lesson has its own folder inside the Lessons folder. You will need to copy these lesson folders to your hard drive before you can begin each lesson.

Adobe Press

Find information about other Adobe Press titles, covering the full spectrum of Adobe products, in the Adobe Press folder.

Adobe TV

Tune in to the How-To channel on Adobe TV for hundreds of instructional movies on the Adobe Creative Suite 4 products, plus much more.

CONTENTS

2 BASIC ORGANIZING

3 ADVANCED ORGANIZING

6   ADJUSTING COLOR IN IMAGES

9   WORKING WITH TEXT

10   COMBINING MULTIPLE IMAGES

11   ADVANCED EDITING TECHNIQUES

GETTING STARTED

Adobe® Photoshop® Elements 7 delivers image-editing tools that balance power and versatility with ease of use. Whether you are a home user, a professional photographer, a hobbyist, or a business user, Photoshop Elements 7 makes it easy to produce good-looking pictures and sophisticated graphics for the Web and for print.

If you've used an earlier version of Photoshop Elements, you'll find that this Classroom in a Book® will teach you advanced skills and covers the many new innovative features that Adobe Systems introduces in this version. If you're new to Adobe Photoshop Elements, you'll learn the fundamental concepts and techniques that will help you master the application.

About Classroom in a Book

Adobe Photoshop Elements 7 Classroom in a Book is part of the official training series for Adobe graphics and publishing software developed by Adobe product experts. Each lesson in this book is made up of a series of self-paced projects that will give you hands-on experience using Photoshop Elements 7.

The *Adobe Photoshop Elements 7 Classroom in a Book* includes a CD attached to the inside back cover. On the CD you'll find all the image files used for the lessons in this book, together with additional learning resources.

Prerequisites

Before you begin the lessons in this book, make sure that you and your computer are ready.

Requirements on your computer

You'll need about 380 MB of free space on your hard disk for the lesson files and the work files that you'll create as you work through the exercises.

Required skills

The lessons in this book assume that you have a working knowledge of your computer and its operating system. Make sure that you know how to use the mouse and the standard menus and commands, and also how to open, save, and close files. Do you know how to use context menus, which open when you right-click / Control-click items? Can you scroll (vertically and horizontally) within a window to see content that may not be visible in the displayed area?

If you need to review these basic and generic computer skills, see the documentation included with your Microsoft® Windows® software.

Installing Adobe Photoshop Elements 7

You must purchase the Adobe Photoshop Elements 7 software separately and install it on a computer running Windows Vista® or Windows® XP. For system requirements and complete instructions on installing the software, see the Photoshop Elements 7 Read Me file on the application CD and the accompanying documentation.

Copying the Classroom in a Book files

● **Note:** The files on the CD are practice files, provided for your personal use in these lessons. You are not authorized to use these files commercially, or to publish or distribute them in any form without written permission from Adobe Systems, Inc. and the individual photographers who took the pictures, or other copyright holders.

The CD attached to the inside back cover of this book includes a Lessons folder containing all the electronic files you'll need for the lessons. As you work through the exercises, you'll learn to organize these files using a catalog that is an essential part of many of the projects in this book. Keep the lesson files on your computer until you have completed all the exercises.

Copying the Lessons files from the CD

1   Create a new folder named **PSE7CIB** inside the *username/My Documents* folder on your computer.

2   Insert the *Adobe Photoshop Elements 7 Classroom in a Book* CD into your CD-ROM drive. If a message appears asking what you want Windows to do, choose Open Folder To View Files Using Windows Explorer, and then click OK.

If no message appears, open My Computer and double-click the CD icon to open it.

3   Locate the Lessons folder on the CD and copy it to the PSE7CIB folder you've just created on your computer.

4   When your computer has finished copying the Lessons folder, remove the CD from your CD-ROM drive and put it away.

Complete the procedures on the following pages before you begin the lessons.

Creating a work folder

Now you need to create a folder for the work files you'll create as you complete the lessons in this book.

1   In Windows Explorer, open the Lessons folder that you copied to your new PSE7CIB folder on your hard disk.

2   In the Lessons folder, choose File > New > Folder. A new folder is created in the Lessons folder. Type **My CIB Work** as the name for the new folder.

Creating a catalog file

The first time you launch Photoshop Elements, a catalog file is automatically created on your hard disk. Photoshop Elements uses this catalog file to store information about the images you import from your digital camera or your hard disk.

You will now create a new catalog to manage the image files for the lessons in this book. This will allow you to leave the default catalog untouched while working through the lessons, and to keep your lesson files together in one location where they will be easy to access.

1   Start Adobe Photoshop Elements 7. If Photoshop Elements opens without first displaying the welcome screen, click the Welcome Screen button (🏠) located at the left of the menu bar. You'll see a row of shortcut buttons across the top of the welcome screen. Click the Organize button to start Photoshop Elements in the Organizer mode.

Note: If this is the first time you have started the Organizer, an alert message may appear asking if you would like to specify the location of photos. If this alert message appears, click No.

Note: In this book, the forward arrow character (>) is used to refer to commands and submenus found in the menus at the top of the application window, for example, File, Edit, and so forth.

2   In Photoshop Elements (Organizer), choose File > Catalog.

3   In the Catalog Manager dialog box, click New. Do not change the location where the Catalog file is stored. *(See the illustration on the next page.)*

4   In the Enter A Name For The New Catalog dialog box, type **CIB Catalog** as the name for your new catalog, disable the Import Free Music Into This Catalog option, and then click OK.

5   In the Organizer, choose File > Get Photos And Videos > From Files And Folders. In the Get Photos From Files And Folders dialog box, click My Documents to open the My Documents folder. Double-click the PSE7CIB folder to open it; then click once to select the Lessons folder that you copied from the CD. Don't double-click—you do not want to open the Lessons folder.

6   In the Get Photos From Files And Folders dialog box, confirm that the Get Photos From Subfolders option is activated in the list of options above the Get Photos button. Disable the options Automatically Fix Red Eyes and Automatically Suggest Photo Stacks. You'll learn about these useful options as you work through the lessons but you won't use them just yet. *(See the illustration on the next page.)*

7   Click the Get Photos button. A window will open showing the photos being imported.

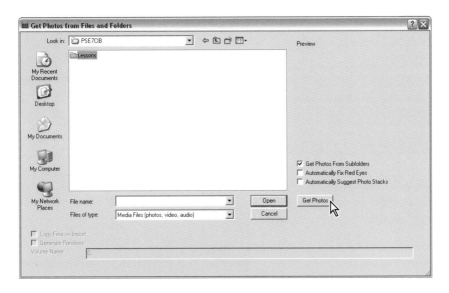

8 The Import Attached Keyword Tags dialog box opens. Click Select All below the Keyword Tags box, and then click OK.

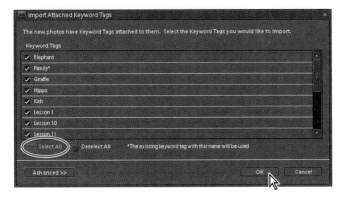

The images you are adding to the catalog contain additional information known as keyword tags, which have been applied to help you organize the images as you work through the lessons in this book. Once the image files have been imported into the catalog, the imported keyword tags are available in the Keyword Tags palette. You'll learn about using keyword tags in Lessons 2 and 3.

9   Photoshop Elements may display a dialog box informing you that the only items displayed in the Organizer are those you just imported. If this alert is displayed, click OK.

10 Click OK to close any other alert dialog box. The imported images are displayed in the Photo Browser in the main display area. Use the scrollbar at the right side to browse through the images.

11 Click the Show All button above the Photo Browser.

Reconnecting missing files to a catalog

● **Note:** To avoid missing files in your catalog, use the File > Move, File > Rename, and Edit > Delete From Catalog commands in Photoshop Elements to move, rename, or delete them, rather than doing so outside the application.

When you import a photo or video clip into Photoshop Elements, the name and location of the file is recorded in the catalog. If you move, rename, or delete a file outside Photoshop Elements after it has been added the catalog, Photoshop Elements may no longer be able to find it. If a file cannot be located, the missing file icon (❓) appears in the upper left corner of its thumbnail in the Photo Browser to alert you that the link between the file and your catalog has been broken.

If there are no files missing, you can now go on to the first lesson.

If Photoshop Elements alerts you that it cannot find an image file, you will need to carry out the following procedure to reconnect the file to your catalog.

1   Choose File > Reconnect > All Missing Files. If the message "There are no files to reconnect" appears, click OK, then skip the rest of this procedure.

2   If a message "Searching for missing files" appears, click the Browse button. The Reconnect Missing Files dialog box opens.

3 In the Browse tab on the right side of the Reconnect Missing Files dialog box, navigate to and open the moved folder.

4 Continuing to work in the Browse tab, locate and click once to select the folder that has the same name as the folder listed underneath the image thumbnail. The folder name is listed on the left side of the Reconnect Missing Files dialog box, directly under the image thumbnail.

5 After you select the appropriate folder and the correct thumbnail picture appears in the right side of the dialog box, click the Reconnect button.

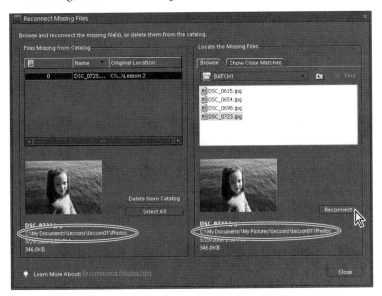

6 Repeat steps 4 and 5, continuing to select the appropriate folders and clicking the Reconnect button as you find matching files. When all the files are reconnected, click the Close button.

You can now use the Photoshop Elements Organizer to select and open files in the Photoshop Elements Editor.

Note: This procedure also eliminates error messages regarding missing files when you work with Creations, or print from the Organizer.

Additional resources

Adobe Photoshop Elements 7 Classroom in a Book is not meant to replace documentation that comes with the program, nor is it designed to be a comprehensive reference for every feature in Photoshop Elements 7. For additional information about program features, refer to any of these resources:

• Photoshop Elements Help, which is built into the Adobe Photoshop Elements 7 application. You can view it by choosing Help > Photoshop Elements Help. If you are connected to the Internet, you will be directed to the Photoshop

Elements Help and Support Center, your hub for community-based instruction, inspiration, and support that combines together the product Support pages, Design Center and Help Resource Center. If you are not connected to the Internet, you will access a subset of Help that installed with your product. For regular updates, it's best to connect to the Web for Help.

- Adobe TV, where you will find programming on Adobe products, including a How To channel. New movies are added regularly so be sure to check back if you don't find what you're looking for on your first visit to http://tv.adobe.com/.

1 A QUICK TOUR OF PHOTOSHOP ELEMENTS

Lesson Overview

This lesson will familiarize you with the Adobe Photoshop Elements 7 workspace and provide you with an overview of the tools and procedures you'll use to capture and edit your digital images.

As you work through the exercises in this lesson you'll be introduced to the following basic skills and concepts:

- Working with the Organizer and the Editor
- Attaching media
- Using the Photo Downloader
- Reviewing and comparing photos
- Sending photos in e-mail
- Using Photoshop Elements Help

 You'll probably need between one and two hours to complete this lesson.

Welcome to Adobe Photoshop Elements! Take a quick tour and get to know the Photoshop Elements workspace. You'll find all the power and versatility you'd expect from a Photoshop application in an easy-to-use, modular interface that will help you take your digital photography to a new level.

How Photoshop Elements works

Photoshop Elements has two primary workspaces: the Organizer and the Editor. You'll use the Organizer to locate, import, manage, and share your photos and media files, and the Editor for editing and adjusting your images and for creating presentations to showcase them.

About the Photoshop Elements workspaces

Once you've imported and selected a photo in the Organizer, you can open it in the Editor workspace by clicking the Editor button (▨) located near the top right corner of the Organizer window, and then choosing Quick Fix, Full Edit, or Guided Edit from the menu.

While you're working in the Editor, click the Organizer button (▦) located near the top right corner of the Editor window to open the Organizer workspace.

Use the buttons at the top of the work area to switch between the Organizer (shown in the background in the above illustration) and the Editor (shown in the foreground).

Once both the Organizer and the Editor windows are open, you can also move quickly between the two workspaces by clicking on the corresponding buttons in the Windows task bar at the bottom of your screen.

The Organizer workspace

In the Organizer workspace, the main work area is the Photo Browser pane where you can find, sort, and organize your photos and media files and preview the presentations you create to share them. At the right of the Organizer window is the Task pane, including the Organize, Fix, Create, and Share panels.

The Photo Browser pane can display a single photo or media file or show thumbnails of all the files in your catalog arranged in a variety of ways. Display your files sorted by import batch, folder location, or keywords—or if you prefer viewing your photos and media files by date, the Organizer includes a Date View workspace that lets you work with your files in a calendar format.

The Photo Browser makes it easy to browse through all the photos and assets in your catalog in one comprehensive window. It can even show previews of files that you keep stored remotely—on a CD or other removable media.

In the Organize panel of the Task pane you can sort and manage your photos by applying keyword tags and arranging them in albums. The Fix panel offers tools for the most common photographic editing tasks, such as color correction and red eye removal. (For more complex editing tasks, you'll switch to the Editor workspace by choosing Quick Fix, Full Edit, or Guided Edit from the Editor menu.) Use the Create panel to put together projects and presentations—from greeting cards to slide shows—and the Share panel to share your files with friends, family, clients or the world at large by burning a CD or DVD, sending your photos as e-mail attachments or photo mail layouts, or creating an online album.

The Editor workspace

In the Editor you'll focus on editing, adjusting, and correcting your images and creating projects and presentations to showcase them. You can choose between the Full Edit mode—with tools for color correction, special effects, and image enhancement—the Quick Fix mode with simple tools and commands to quickly fix common image problems, and the Guided Edit mode, which provides step-by-step instructions for editing tasks.

If you are new to digital imaging, the Quick Fix and Guided Edit modes make a good starting point for adjusting and correcting your photos.

If you've worked with image editing software before, you'll find that the Full Edit mode provides a more powerful and versatile image editing environment, with commands for correcting exposure and color and tools to help you make precise selections and fix image imperfections. The Full Edit tool bar also includes painting and text editing tools. You can arrange the Full Edit workspace to suit the way you prefer to work by moving, hiding, and showing palettes or arranging them in the Palette Bin. You can zoom in or out of a photo and set up multiple windows and views.

The Full Edit workspace.

Using the Palette Bin

In the Full Edit workspace, the Palette Bin of provides a convenient location to store and manage the palettes you use for image editing tasks. By default, only the Effects and Layers palettes are placed in the Palette Bin. Other palettes that you choose from the Window menu are opened in the work area. These are known as floating palettes. You can decide which palettes float and which will be stored in the Palette Bin.

To add floating palettes to the Palette Bin

1   Choose Window > [palette name] to open the palette you wish to place in the Palette Bin.

2   Drag the palette to the Palette Bin by its name tab. Dragging the palette by the bar across the top of the palette window simply repositions the palette without placing it in the Palette Bin.

Another way to add a floating palette to the Palette Bin is to choose Place In Palette Bin When Closed from the palette menu (accessed by clicking the triangle circled in the illustration below}, and then close the palette window.

To remove palettes from the Palette Bin or close palettes:

1   Remove a palette from the Palette Bin by dragging the it into the main work area by its title bar.

2   Open the palette menu and disable the option Place In Palette Bin When Closed.

3   To close a palette, choose Window > [palette name], or click the close box (■) in the top right corner of a floating palette. When a palette is visible, a check mark is displayed adjacent to the palette's name in the Window menu; selecting a palette name that shows a check mark causes the palette window to be closed.

Adjusting the size of palettes in the Palette Bin

Adjust the size of palettes in the Palette Bin by doing either or both of the following:

• Drag the triangle in the left border of the Palette Bin to adjust its width.

• Drag the separator bars between palettes up or down to adjust the height of a palette.

Workflow

A typical Photoshop Elements workflow follows these basic steps:

- Bring images and media into the Organizer from a digital camera, scanner, or digital video camera.

- Sort and group images and media by a variety of methods, including applying keyword tags and creating albums, in the Organizer.

- Edit, adjust, and correct images and media or add text in the Editor.

- Share your images and media by creating projects and presentations, using e-mail or an on-line sharing service, or by burning them to CD/DVD ROM.

Importing media

Bringing your digital files into Photoshop Elements is easy.

Getting photos

To view and organize your photos in Photoshop Elements, you first need to import them into your catalog. You can bring photos into Photoshop Elements from a variety of sources and in several different ways:

- Bring images from your camera or card reader directly into the Photoshop Elements Organizer using the Adobe Photo Downloader. Getting photos directly in this way will save you time and enable you to start working with them sooner.

- Download pictures to your hard disk using the software that came with your digital camera, and then bring them into Photoshop Elements using the Get Photos And Videos > From Files And Folders command. If you prefer to work with other software to import your files to your computer, you'll first need to disable Adobe Photo Downloader. To disable the Adobe Photo Downloader, click its icon (🖼) in the task bar, and then choose Disable. Do this only if you plan to use other software to import images to your computer.

* If your camera or card reader is displayed as a drive in Windows Explorer, you can drag the files to a folder on your hard disk, and then bring them into Photoshop Elements using the Get Photos And Videos > From Files And Folders command.

In most cases, you'll need to install the software drivers that came with your camera before you can download pictures to your computer. You may also need to set up the Photoshop Elements Camera or Card Reader Preferences. See "Getting photos" in Lesson 2, "Basic Organizing."

Creating a new catalog

Photoshop Elements stores information about your images in catalog files, which manage the photos on your computer but are independent of the image files themselves. As well as digital photographs, a catalog can include video and audio files, scans, PDF documents, and any presentations and layouts you might create in Photoshop Elements such as slide shows, photo collages, and CD jacket designs. When you sort and group your media in Photoshop Elements, all your work is recorded in the catalog. A single catalog can efficiently handle thousands of files, but you can also create separate catalogs for different types of work.

● **Note:** Before you start working on this lesson, make sure that you've installed the software on your computer from the application CD (see the Photoshop Elements 7 documentation) and that you have correctly copied the Lessons folder from the CD in the back of this book onto your computer's hard disk (see "Copying the Classroom in a Book files" on page 2).

1 Start Photoshop Elements, either by double-clicking the shortcut on your desktop or by choosing Start > All Programs > Adobe Photoshop Elements 7.

2 Do one of the following:

* If the Welcome Screen appears, click Organize in the row of shortcut buttons across the top of the Welcome Screen, and then wait until the Organizer has finished opening.

* If the Photoshop Elements Editor window opens without first displaying the Welcome Screen, click the Welcome Screen button (🏠) located at the left in the menu bar to display the Welcome Screen, and then click Organize. Or, click the Organizer button (▦) located at the right in the menu bar. Wait until the Organizer has finished opening.

* If the Photoshop Elements Organizer window opens without first displaying the Welcome Screen you are ready to continue with step 3.

3 In the Organizer window, choose File > Catalog.

4 In the Catalog Manager dialog box, click New.

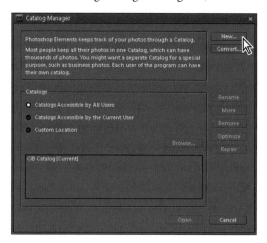

5 In the Enter A Name For The New Catalog dialog box, type Lesson1 for the catalog name, disable the option Import Free Music Into This Catalog, and then click OK.

Now you have a special catalog that you'll use just for this lesson. All you need is some pictures to put in it.

Using the Adobe Photo Downloader

The rest of this lesson is concerned with importing images into the Organizer. If you have a digital camera or memory stick reader at hand with images of your own, you can work through the steps in the next exercise; otherwise, simply follow the steps by reading through the exercise or skip to the section, "Getting photos from files and folders."

Getting photos from a digital camera or card reader

You can import image files from your camera directly into Photoshop Elements.

1 Connect your camera or card reader to your computer. For instructions on connecting your device, refer to the manufacturer's documentation that came with it.

2 Once your camera or card reader is connected to your computer, you're ready for the next step:

- If the Windows Auto Play dialog box appears, click Cancel.

- If the Photo Downloader dialog box appears automatically, continue with step 3.

- If the Photo Downloader dialog box does not appear automatically, choose File > Get Photos And Videos > From Camera Or Card Reader.

3 Under Source in the Photo Downloader dialog box, open the Get Photos From menu and choose the name of the connected camera or card reader.

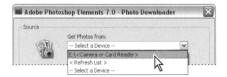

4 Under Import Settings, accept the folder location listed next to Location, or click Browse to choose a new location for the files.

5 Next to Create Subfolder(s), choose one of the date formats if you want the photos to be stored in subfolders named by capture or import date. You can also choose Custom Name to create a folder using a name you type in the text box, or choose None if you don't want to create any subfolders at all. Your selection is reflected in the pathname Location pathname.

6   From the Rename Files menu, choose Do Not Rename Files and from the Delete Options menu choose After Copying, Do Not Delete Originals. If the Automatic Download option is activated, click the check box to disable it.

You will learn more about customizing import settings and the advanced features of the Adobe Photo Downloader in Lessons 2 and 3.

7   Click the Get Photos button.

The photos are copied from the camera to the specified folder location.

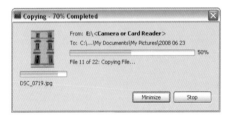

8   If the Files Successfully Copied dialog box appears, click OK.

The Getting Photos dialog box appears as the photos are imported into Photoshop Elements.

If the imported photos contain keyword metadata, the Import Attached Keyword Tags dialog box will appear. Select the keyword tags you wish to import.

The keyword tags you selected are added to the Keyword Tags palette when the photos are imported. If a keyword tag has an asterisk (*), you already have a keyword tag of the same name in your catalog and that keyword tag is attached to the photos.

9   Click OK to close any other alert dialog box.

The imported photos appear in the Photo Browser pane.

Getting photos from files and folders

Digital images stored on your computer can also be imported into Photoshop Elements.

1   Choose File > Get Photos And Videos > From Files And Folders.

2   In the Get Photos dialog box, navigate to the Lesson01 folder and click once to select the Photos folder that contains sample images.

3   Select the Get Photos From Subfolders check box. If selected, deselect the Automatically Fix Red Eyes and the Automatically Suggest Photo Stacks check boxes, and then click Get Photos. *(See the illustration on the next page.)*

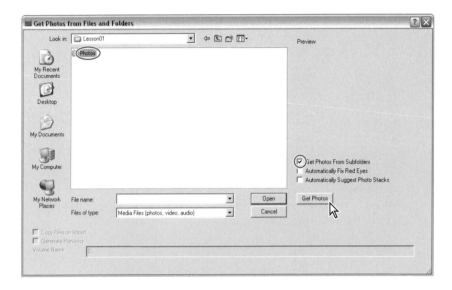

The Getting Photos dialog box appears and the photos are imported into Photoshop Elements. Since the imported photos contain keyword metadata, the Import Attached Keyword Tags dialog box appears. You will learn more about keyword tags in Lessons 2 and 3.

4 In the Import Attached Keyword Tags dialog box, click Select All, and then click OK. Click OK to close any other alert dialog box.

The imported photos appear in the Organizer.

Reviewing and comparing

Photoshop Elements provides several options to quickly and easily review and compare your images.

Viewing photos at full screen or side-by-side

The Full Screen View and Side by Side View let you review your images without the distraction of other interface items such as windows, menus and palettes.

About keyword tags

Keyword tags are personalized labels, such as "Vacation" or "Beach," that you attach to photos, video clips, audio clips and other creations in the Photo Browser to make it easier to organize and find them.

When you use keyword tags, there's no need to manually organize your photos in subject-specific folders or rename files with content-specific names.

In fact, both of the latter solutions confine a given photo to a single group. By contrast, you can assign multiple keyword tags to a photo, allowing it to be included in several different groupings. You can then easily retrieve the selection of images you want by clicking the appropriate keyword tags in the Keyword Tags palette.

For example, you could create a keyword tag called "Beach - Croatia" and attach it to every photo you took at that location. You can then instantly find all the photos with the Beach - Croatia keyword tag by clicking the Find box next to that tag in the Keyword Tags palette, even if the photos are stored in different folders on your hard disk.

You can create keyword tags to group your images any way you want. For example, you could create keyword tags for individual people, places and events in your life.

You can attach multiple keyword tags to your photos and easily run a search based on a combination of keyword tags to find a particular person at a particular place or event.

For example, you can search for all "Christine" keyword tags and all "John" keyword tags to find all pictures of Christine with her husband, John.

Or search for all "Christine" keyword tags and all "Beach - Croatia" keyword tags to find all the pictures of Christine vacationing at the beach in Croatia.

Use keyword tags to organize and find photos by their content or any other association. See Lessons 2 and 3 for more information on keyword tags.

1 Click the Display button (■) near the upper right corner of the Organizer window, and then choose View Photos In Full Screen from the menu.

In the Full Screen View Options dialog box, you can customize the slide show—for example, you can play an audio file as you view the images. You can also choose to display thumbnails of the selected files in a filmstrip along the right side of the screen, or add a fade between pictures.

2 Disable the Include Captions option and activate the Start Playing Automatically option; then click OK to start the slide show.

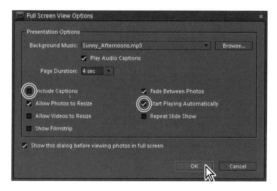

Your photos are displayed as a full-screen slide show—an enjoyable and efficient way to view a set of photos.

The control bar, which contains buttons for playing, rotating, and zooming disappears from view when you don't move the mouse for a couple of seconds.

▶ **Tip:** When you view images in full screen, you can quickly assign a rating. On the right end of the control bar, click a star to apply a rating. You can also apply the rating using the shortcut keys, 1 (for 1 star) through 5 (for 5 stars).

3 To make the control bar reappear, move the mouse.

4 Press the Esc key on your keyboard to return to the Organizer.

5 Click the Display button (■), and then choose Compare Photos Side By Side to display two photos simultaneously. Side by Side View is useful when you need to focus on details and differences between photos. You can select two or more photos to compare. When you click the Next Photo button (●) in the control bar, the selected image changes to the next image in your selection. By default, image # 1 (on the left or top) is selected. To select image #2 instead, click it.

Use the Side by Side View to analyze and compare composition and detail.

Note: The selected image has a blue border. If you have the filmstrip showing, you can click any image in the filmstrip to view it in place of the selected image.

Tip: Choose the photos to be compared in the Organizer by holding the Ctrl key and selecting the images. Then, choose View > Compare Photos Side By Side.

You can switch between views by clicking the Full Screen View button (▣) or the Side by Side View button (▣▣) in the control bar. While in either view, you can right-click an image and access further options from the context menu. For example, you can mark an image for printing, fix red eye, add a photo to an album, and delete or apply keyword tags.

6 Press the Esc key on your keyboard to return to the Organizer.

Choosing files

To select more than one photo in the Photo Browser, hold down the Ctrl key and click the photos you want to select. Ctrl-clicking enables you to select multiple non-consecutive files. To select a series of images that are in consecutive order, click the first photo, and then hold down the Shift key and click the last in the series. All the photos between the two images you Shift-clicked will be selected.

Sharing photos in e-mail

Have you ever had to wait long time for an incoming e-mail to download, and then found that the e-mail contained only a single photograph in an unnecessarily high resolution? You can avoid imposing this inconvenience on others by using the Organizer e-mail function, which exports a copy of the image that is optimized specifically for sending via e-mail.

1 In the Photo Browser, select the photo (or photos) you'd like to send by e-mail.

2   In the Share panel of the Task pane, click the E-mail Attachments button.

3   (Optional) Drag more photos from the Photo Browser to add to your selection.

4   Select Very Small (320 x 240 px) from the Maximum Photo Size menu and adjust the image quality using the Quality slider (the higher the quality the larger the file size and the longer the download time). The resulting file size and download time for a typical 56 Kbps dial-up modem are estimated and displayed for your reference. When you're done, click Next.

5 Under Message, select and delete the "Here are the photos…" text and type a message of your own.

6 Next to Select Recipients, click the Edit Contact Book button (🗐). In the Contact Book dialog box, click the New Contact button (🗐). In the New Contact dialog box, type in the name (or a nickname—our example uses Mom) and e-mail address of the person to whom you want to send the picture. Click OK to close the New Contact dialog box and click OK again to close the Contact Book dialog box.

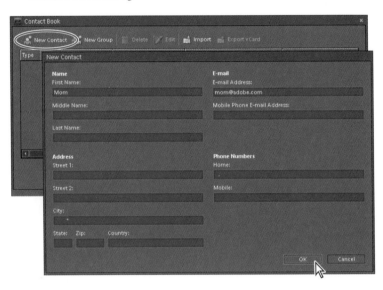

7 Under Select Recipients, click the check box next to Mom to select it, and then click Next.

Your default e-mail application immediately creates an e-mail message. You can edit the message and Subject line to say what you want. When you are finished and ready to send the e-mail, either make sure that you are connected to the Internet and click Send if you actually want to send the e-mail, or close the message without saving or sending it.

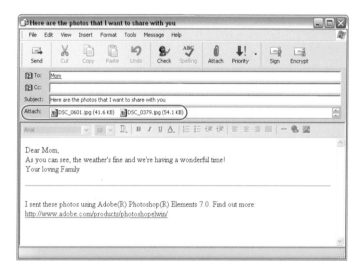

8   Switch back to Photoshop Elements (Organizer).

Creating a Photoshop.com account

Another way to share your photos and videos is by creating an online album. You'll learn how to do that in lesson 5, "Printing, Sharing and Exporting," but for now you can go ahead and create your free Photoshop.com account so that you're ready to take advantage of the exciting new Adobe-hosted Web-based services that extend the capabilities of Photoshop Elements.

With your free Photoshop.com membership you get your own personal web page, where you can not only share and showcase your images but also access your photos and videos anytime and anywhere that you can connect to the internet. You can use your Photoshop.com storage space to back up your Photoshop Elements albums and effortlessly safeguard your memories.

● **Note:** For Adobe Photoshop Elements 7, these services will be available to users in the United States only. Photoshop Elements users outside the United States will continue to share their Albums to third party sharing services via Photoshop Showcase (www. photoshopshowcase. com).

You'll also get access to the Photoshop.com Inspiration Browser, with regularly updated downloadable content such as sharing templates, page layouts, artwork, borders, frames, backgrounds, and more—as well as integrated tutorials offering tips and tricks related to whatever you're working on, providing a powerful way to advance your skill set with Photoshop Elements. (*See the illustration on the next page.*)

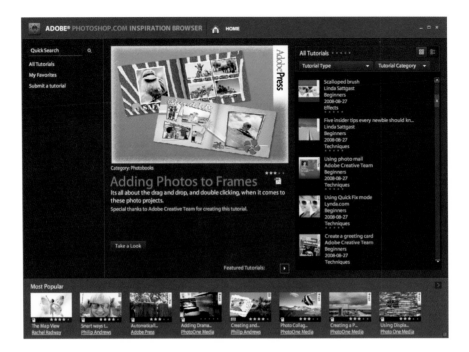

You can share your Photoshop.com web gallery with the world at large, or privately with friends, family, or clients to whom you chose to give the address. Check out http://bob.photoshop.com for an example of what your own sharing website could look like.

1   To sign up for your free Photoshop.com account, do one of the following:

   • In the Welcome screen, click the Join Now button.

   • In either the Organizer or Editor, click the Join Now link in the menu bar.

2   Fill out your personal details in the Photoshop.com Membership dialog box (*see the illustration on the next page*), and then click Create Account. Enjoy!

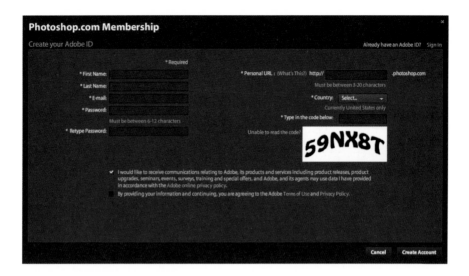

Using Help

Help is available in several ways, each one useful in different circumstances:

Help in the application The complete user documentation for Adobe Photoshop Elements is available as Help in the application, in the form of HTML content that you can access with your default browser. Help in the application provides easy access to summarized information on common tasks and concepts. Help in the application can be especially useful if you are new to Photoshop Elements or if you aren't connected to the Internet.

LiveDocs Help on the Web This is the most comprehensive and up-to-date version of Photoshop Elements Help. It is the recommended choice if you have an active Internet connection.

Help PDF Help is also available as a PDF that is optimized for printing; just go to http://www.adobe.com/go/learn_pse_printpdf to download the PDF document. The Help PDF file is about 30 MB in size and may take a considerable time to download when using a slow Internet connection.

Links in the application Within the Photoshop Elements application there are links to additional help topics, such as the "Tell me more" link at the bottom of the panel in each guided task.

Navigating Help in the application

Choose Help > Photoshop Elements Help, or press the F1 key. Your default Web browser will open and display the starting page of the Adobe Photoshop Help in the application. Do any of the following:

● **Note:** You do not need to be connected to the Internet to view Help in the application. However, with an active Internet connection, clicking the "This page on the Web" link on any page in the application's Help opens the corresponding page in LiveDocs.

- Click the Contents link in the top left corner of the window. Click a topic heading in the table of contents. Click the plus sign (+) to the left of a topic heading to see its sub-topics. Click a topic or sub-topic to display its content.

- Click the Index link in the top left corner of the window. Click on a letter to display index entries starting with that letter. Click the plus sign (+) to the left of an index header or click the index header to see its entries. Click the index entry to display its content on the right side of the window.

- Select the Search link in the top left corner of the window. Enter a search term, and then click Search. When the search has finished, click a search result in the list on the left side of the window to display its content on the right side of the window.

Search tips

Adobe Help Search works by searching the entire Help text for topics that contain all the words typed in the Search box. These tips can help you improve your search results in Help:

- If you search using a phrase, such as "shape tool," put quotation marks around the phrase. The search returns only those topics containing that specific phrase.

- Make sure that the search terms are spelled correctly.

- If a search term doesn't yield results, try using a synonym, such as "photo" instead of "picture."

Accessing LiveDocs Help on the Web

LiveDocs Help on the Web contains the most up-to-date version of Photoshop Elements Help. In addition, it enables you to search across multiple applications.

1 To access Photoshop Elements' LiveDocs Help on the Web, part of the Adobe Help Resource Center, do any of the following:

- Click the "This page on the Web" link, located at the bottom of any topic page in Adobe Help in the application.

- In your Web browser, open the Adobe Help Resource Center at http://www. adobe.com/support/documentation. Select Photoshop Elements from the list of products, and then click Go. On the Photoshop Elements resources page, click the LiveDocs link.

2 To switch to LiveDocs Help for a different product, select that product from the Browse menu, and then click Go.

3 To search for a topic, type the search term in the Search box, and then click Search. To search across all products, click Search All Products on the LiveDocs Search Results page, type in the search term, and then click Go.

Links to help in the application

There are some links to additional help within the Photoshop Elements application. Clicking these links will take you to the corresponding topic in either Help in the application or LiveDocs Help on the Web.

Hot-linked tips

Hot-linked tips are available throughout Adobe Photoshop Elements. These tips either display information in the form of a typical tip balloon or link you to the appropriate topic in the help file.

You've reached the end of the first lesson. Now that you know how to import photos, understand the concept of the catalog, and are familiar with the essentials of the Photoshop Elements interface, you are ready to start organizing and editing your photos in the next lessons.

Review questions

1 What are the primary workspaces in Adobe Photoshop Elements 7?

2 Define the typical Photoshop Elements workflow.

3 What is a catalog?

4 What are keyword tags?

5 How can you select multiple thumbnail images in the Photo Browser?

Review answers

1 Photoshop Elements has two primary workspaces: the Organizer and the Editor. You'll use the Organizer to locate, import, manage, and share your photos and media files, and the Editor for editing and adjusting your images and for creating presentations to showcase them. You can use the buttons on the top of the workspace windows to switch between the Organizer and the Editor.

2 A typical Photoshop Elements workflow follows these basic steps:

   • Bring images and media into the Organizer from a digital camera, scanner, or digital video camera.

   • Sort and group images and media by a variety of methods, including applying keyword tags and creating albums, in the Organizer.

   • Edit, adjust, and correct images and media or add text in the Editor.

   • Share your images and media by creating projects and presentations, using e-mail or an on-line sharing service, or by burning them to CD/DVD ROM.

3 Photoshop Elements stores information about your images in catalog files, which manage the photos on your computer but are independent of the image files themselves. As well as digital photographs, a catalog can include video and audio files, scans, PDF documents, and any presentations and layouts you might create in Photoshop Elements such as slide shows, photo collages, and CD jacket designs. When you sort and group your media in Photoshop Elements, all your work is recorded in the catalog. A single catalog can efficiently handle thousands of files, but you can also create separate catalogs for different types of work.

4 Keyword tags are personalized labels such as "House" or "Beach" that you attach to photos, creations, and video or audio clips in the Photo Browser so that you can easily organize and find them.

5 To select more than one photo in the Photo Browser, hold down the Ctrl key and click the photos you want to select. Ctrl-clicking enables you to select multiple non-consecutive files. To select a series of images that are in consecutive order, click the first photo, and then hold down the Shift key and click the last in the series. All the photos between the two images you Shift-clicked will be selected.

2 BASIC ORGANIZING

Lesson Overview

This lesson will get you started with the essential skills you'll need to import images and keep track of your growing photo library:

- Opening Adobe Photoshop Elements 7 in Organizer mode
- Creating a catalog of your images
- Importing photos from a digital camera
- Importing images from folders on your computer
- Switching between view modes in the Photo Browser
- Working with the Date view
- Creating, organizing, and applying tags to images
- Finding and tagging faces in photos

 You'll probably need between one and two hours to complete this lesson.

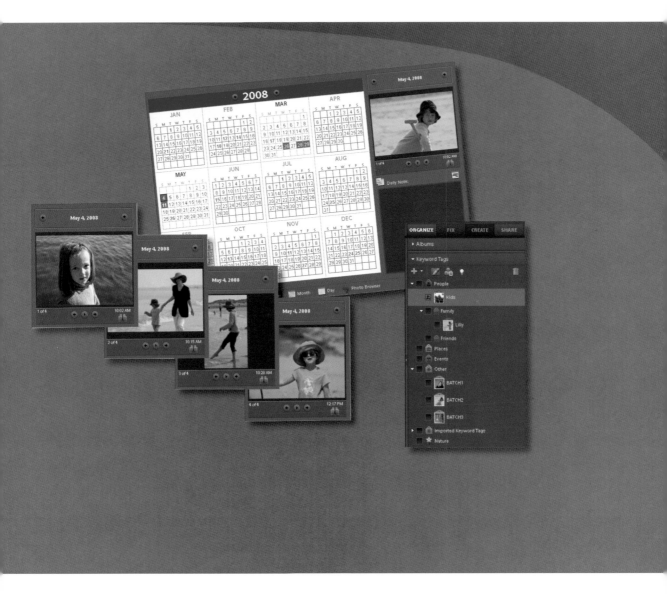

As you capture more and more images with your digital camera, it becomes increasingly important that you have ways to organize and manage your pictures on your computer so that your valuable memories are always accessible. Adobe Photoshop Elements makes it easy to import your photos from a variety of sources and provides powerful tools for sorting and searching your collection.

Getting started

● **Note:** Before you start working on this lesson, make sure that you've installed the software on your computer from the application CD (see the Photoshop Elements 7 documentation) and that you have correctly copied the Lessons folder from the CD in the back of this book onto your computer's hard disk (see "Copying the Classroom in a Book files" on page 2).

In this lesson, you'll be working mainly in the Photoshop Elements Organizer workspace.

1 Start Photoshop Elements, either by double-clicking the shortcut on your desktop, or by choosing Start > All Programs > Adobe Photoshop Elements 7.

2 Do one of the following:

• If the Welcome Screen appears, click Organize in the row of shortcut buttons across the top of the Welcome Screen.

• If the Editor window opens without first displaying the Welcome Screen, click the Welcome Screen button (⌂) located to the left in the menu bar, and then click the Organize button. Alternatively, click the Organizer button (⊞) located to the right in the Editor window menu bar, and then wait until the Organizer has finished opening.

• If the Organizer window opens without first displaying the Welcome Screen, you don't have to do anything more— you're all set to start with this lesson.

Getting photos

The Organizer component of Photoshop Elements provides a workspace where you can efficiently sort and organize your photos and perform some of the most common basic image editing tasks. Before you print your photographs, burn them to CD or DVD ROM, or share them by e-mail or on the Web, the first step is to assemble them in the Organizer, as you'll learn later in this lesson.

Creating a new catalog

Photoshop Elements stores information about your images in catalog files, which manage the photos on your computer but are independent of the image files themselves.

A catalog can include digital photographs, video and audio files, scans, PDF documents, and any presentations and layouts you might create in Photoshop Elements.

When you organize your files in Photoshop Elements, all your work is recorded in the catalog. A single catalog can efficiently handle thousands of files, but you can create as many catalogs as you wish to suit the way you work.

In this exercise you'll create a new catalog so that you won't confuse the practice files for this lesson with the files for the other lessons in this book.

1   In the Organizer, choose File > Catalog.

2   In the Catalog Manager dialog box, click New.

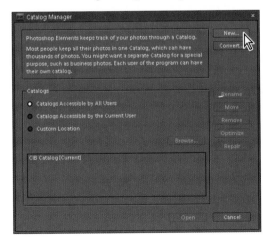

3 In the Enter A Name For The New Catalog dialog box, type Lesson2 as the catalog name, disable the option Import Free Music Into This Catalog, and then click OK.

You'll import the images for this lesson into your new catalog using a variety of different methods.

Dragging photos from Windows Explorer

Perhaps the easiest and most intuitive method of adding photographs to an Organizer catalog is by using the familiar drag-and-drop technique.

1 Minimize the Organizer by clicking the Minimize button (■) towards the right end of the Organizer window menu bar or by clicking the Organizer application button on the Windows taskbar.

2 Open the My Computer window in Windows Explorer by whatever method you usually use—double-click a shortcut icon on the desktop or use the Start menu or Windows Explorer.

3 Navigate through the folder structure to locate and open the Lesson02 folder you copied to your hard disk (see "Copying the Classroom in a Book files" on page 2).

You'll see three folders inside the Lesson02 folder: BATCH1, BATCH2, and BATCH3.

4 Drag and hold the BATCH1 folder icon over the Organizer application button on the Windows taskbar.

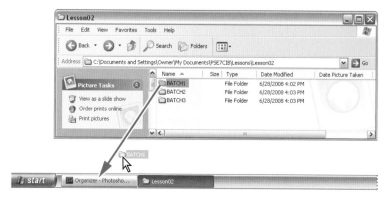

5 Wait until the Organizer becomes the foreground application, and then move the pointer with the BATCH1 over the Organizer application window and release the mouse button.

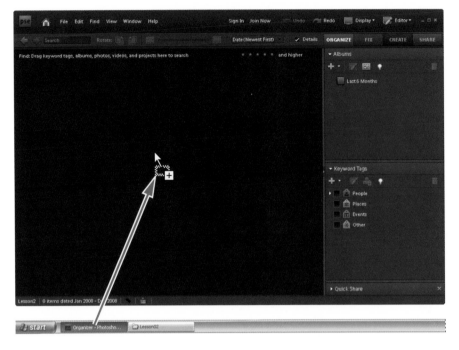

▶ **Tip:** If you can arrange the Windows Explorer window and the Organizer application window on your screen so that you can see both windows at the same time, you can also drag and drop the folder icon (or individual files) directly from the Windows Explorer window onto the Organizer application window.

The Organizer will briefly display a dialog box while searching inside the BATCH1 folder for files to import.

The files in the BATCH1 folder have keyword tags attached to them to help keep them organized, so the Import Attached Keyword Tags dialog box opens, giving you the opportunity to choose whether or not to import keywords with the images and to select which keywords to import.

6 In the Import Attached Keyword Tags dialog box, click Select All; then click OK.

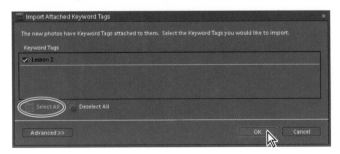

The Getting Photos dialog box appears briefly as the Organizer imports the image files from the BATCH1 folder.

7   If a message appears telling you that only the newly imported items will be visible in the Photo Browser, click OK.

▶ **Tip:** If you don't want to see this message each time you import new items, select Don't Show Again before clicking OK. To have it show again, click Reset All Warning Dialogs in the General section of the Preferences dialog box.

8   Click the Maximize button (▣) towards the right end of the menu bar in the Organizer window. This causes the window to expand and cover the entire screen.

▶ **Tip:** The timeline that you may expect to see above the Photo Browser if you're familiar with earlier versions of Photoshop Elements is now hidden by default. To toggle the visibility of the timeline, choose Window > Timeline. To toggle the visibility of the information displayed under the thumbnails in the Photo Browser, choose View > Details. If the View > Details option is active, you can show or hide File Names and Grid Lines using the View menu, where you can also choose to show or hide the borders around the thumbnails.

In the Photo Browser, you can now see thumbnails of the four images you've just added to your Lesson2 catalog. Don't drag the other two batches into the Organizer—you'll use different methods to import them into your catalog.

Getting photos from specific locations

Another technique for adding items to your catalog is to use a menu command rather than re-sizing and arranging windows on the desktop.

1   Choose File > Get Photos And Videos > From Files And Folders.

2   In the Get Photos From Files And Folders dialog box, navigate to your Lesson02 folder and open the BATCH2 folder.

3   Move the pointer over each of the four image files inside the BATCH2 folder. You'll see additional information about each image displayed in a Tooltip. Click once on the file and a thumbnail image will be displayed in the Preview area.

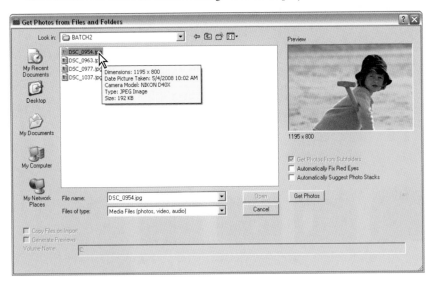

4   If the options Automatically Fix Red Eyes and Automatically Suggest Photo Stacks are activated, disable them by clicking their check boxes.

5   Press Ctrl+A or drag to marquee-select all four images in the BATCH2 folder, and then click the Get Photos button.

6   Select the keyword tag "Lesson 2" in the Import Attached Keyword Tags dialog box. You'll notice that by default the new batch of images will pick up the existing "Lesson 2" keyword tag that was already added to the catalog in the previous import.

▶ **Tip:** Select a folder icon in the Get Photos From Files And Folders dialog box, and then click Get Photos to import all items within that folder.
Activate the Get Photos From Subfolders option to import items from any subfolders.

7   Click the Advanced button in the lower left corner of the dialog box. You now have the option to either assign new name to the keyword tag found in the imported items, or to use the existing tag of the same name. For now, leave the settings unchanged. Click the Reset to Basic button, and then click OK. Click OK to close any other alert dialog box.

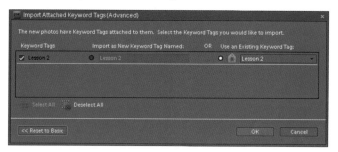

8   Click the Show All button above the Photo Browser to see all eight images.

9   Select the image of the girl with the red hat, named DSC_0977.jpg, and then click the Rotate Left button (▥) above the Photo Browser.

Searching for photos to import

This method is a good choice when you're not sure exactly where on your hard disk you've stashed your photographs and other resources over the years. You might run this search on your entire hard disk or for your My Documents folder. For this demonstration, you'll limit the search to a very restricted part of the folder structure on your computer.

1   In the Organizer, choose File > Get Photos And Videos > By Searching.

Automatically fixing red eyes

The term "red eye" refers to the common phenomenon in photos taken with a flash, where the subject's pupils are red instead of black. This is caused by the flash reflecting off the retina at the back of the eye.

While none of the images for this lesson require red eye correction, for photos taken with a flash you can have Photoshop Elements remove the red eye effect automatically while importing the images. To activate this option, click the Automatically Fix Red Eyes check box in the Get Photos From Files And Folders dialog box.

More ways to fix the red eye effect will be discussed in lessons 3 and 6.

2 Under Search Options in the Get Photos By Searching For Folders dialog box, choose Browse from the Look In menu.

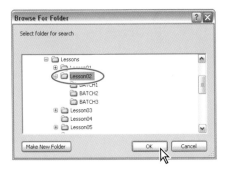

3 In the Browse For Folder dialog box, select the Lesson02 folder; then click OK.

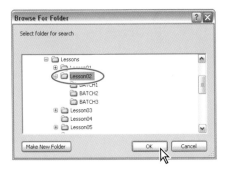

4 Under Search Options in the Get Photos By Searching For Folders dialog box, disable the Automatically Fix Red Eyes option.

5 Click the Search button located in the upper right corner of the dialog box.

6   In the Search Results box, select the BATCH3 folder and click Import Folders.

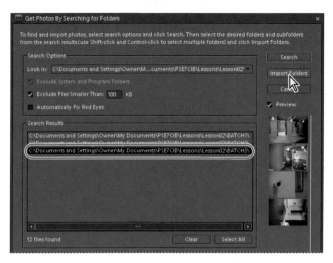

7   In the Import Attached Keyword Tags dialog box, click Select All, and then click OK. Click OK to close any other alert dialog box. Click the Show All button above the Photo Browser to see all 12 images in your Lesson2 catalog.

Importing from a digital camera

This exercise is optional and requires that you have a digital camera or memory card at hand with pictures on it. You can either step through this procedure now, or skip to the section "Viewing photo thumbnails" later in this lesson.

1   Connect your digital camera or card reader to your computer, following the manufacturer's instructions.

2   If the Windows Auto Play dialog box appears, click Cancel.

3   Do the following:

•   If the Photo Downloader dialog box appears automatically, continue with step 4.

- If the Photo Downloader dialog box does not appear automatically, choose File > Get Photos And Videos > From Camera Or Card Reader.

Tip: You can also launch the Adobe Photo Downloader by double-clicking its icon () in the system tray in the lower right corner of your screen.

4 Under Source in the Photo Downloader dialog box, choose the name of the connected camera or card reader from the Get Photos from menu.

5 Under Import Settings, accept the folder location listed next to Location, or click Browse to choose a new location for the files.

6 From the Create Subfolder(s) menu, choose Today's Date (yyyy mm dd) as folder name format. Your selection is reflected in the Location pathname.

7 Choose Do Not Rename Files from the Rename Files menu, and from the Delete Options menu choose After Copying, Do Not Delete Originals. If selected, deselect the Automatic Download check box.

8 Click the Advanced Dialog button.

The Advanced Photo Downloader Dialog displays thumbnail images of the photos on your camera's memory card.

9 (Optional) Click the check box below a thumbnail—removing the green check mark—to remove that photo from the selection to be imported.

10 (Optional) Select one or more photos to rotate. Click the appropriate Rotate button in the lower left corner of the dialog box.

11 Under Advanced Options, if the options Automatically Fix Red Eyes, Automatically Suggest Photo Stacks, and Make 'Group Custom Name' A Tag are activated, disable them by clicking their checkboxes, an then click Get Photos.

The selected photos are copied from the camera to the specified folder on your hard disk.

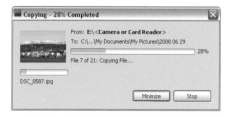

12 If the Files Successfully Copied dialog box appears, click OK.

The Getting Photos dialog box appears while the photos are being imported into Photoshop Elements.

13 Click OK to close any other alert dialog box.

The imported photos appear in the Photo Browser, already rotated where specified.

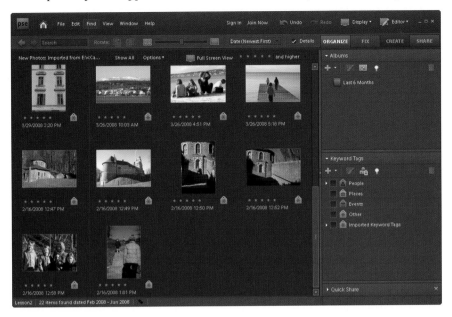

Using watched folders

You can specify any folder on your hard disk as a watched folder so that Photoshop Elements will automatically be alerted if a new photo is placed in (or saved to) that folder.

By default, the My Pictures folder is watched, but you can add additional folders to the Folders to Watch list.

You can choose to have new photos that are detected in a watched folder added to your catalog automatically or to have Photoshop Elements ask you before importing the new images. If you choose the latter option, the message "New files have been found in Watched Folders" will appear when new photos are detected. Click Yes to add the photos to your catalog or click No to skip them.

Now you'll add a folder to the watched folders list.

1 Choose File > Watch Folders.

2 Under Folders To Watch in the Watch Folders dialog box, click Add, and then browse to the Lesson02 folder.

3 Select the Lesson02 folder, and then click OK.

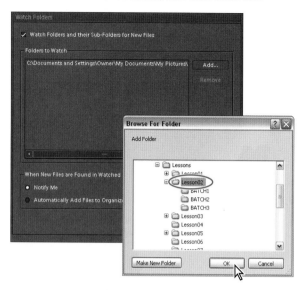

The folder name appears in the Folders to Watch list. To delete a folder name from that list, select it and then click Remove.

4 Leave the Notify Me option activated and click OK to close the Watch Folders dialog box.

This concludes this section on importing images into your catalog, but even more methods will be discussed in Lesson 3, "Advanced Organizing."

Viewing photo thumbnails in the Organizer

In the Organizer, there are several ways to view the images in your catalog. You can switch between the various viewing modes to suit different stages in your workflow or to make it easier and more efficient to perform specific organizing tasks.

Using the Photo Browser views

Up to this point, you've been working in the default Photo Browser view, the Thumbnail View, where your images are arranged by capture date and time. You can reverse the display order by choosing either Date (Oldest First) or Date (Newest First) from the menu to the right of the Thumbnail Size slider just above the Photo Browser pane.

Let's look at some of the other display options in the Organizer.

1 Use the Thumbnail Size slider to reduce the size of the thumbnails so that you can see all the images in your Lesson2 catalog.

2 Click the Display button () near the upper right corner of the Organizer window, and then choose Import Batch from the menu to see the thumbnails organized by their separate import sessions.

Notice the bar and film canister icons (▧) separating each row of thumbnails.

3 Try the following:

- Click the separator bar above any of the import batches (reading "Imported from hard disk on …") to select all the images imported in that session.

- Increase the thumbnail size by dragging the slider above the Photo Browser until only a few of the images in the catalog are visible in the Photo Browser.

- Choose Window > Timeline if the timeline is not currently visible above the Photo Browser. The timeline shows three frames representing the three import sessions that account for all the images in this catalog. Click each of the three frames in turn to jump to the first image imported in the corresponding session.

The view switches to the corresponding batch, the first image in the batch is temporarily surrounded by a green border and the capture date of that image flashes off and on.

4 Using the Display menu that you used in Step 1, select Folder Location to see the thumbnails organized according to the folders in which they are stored on your computer. Reduce the size of the thumbnails again so that you can see all the images. The divider bars between the groups now display a folder icon rather than the film canister.

● **Note:** To display the file names of the images in the Browser View, activate the menu option View > Details (or activate the Details checkbox in the bar above the Photo Browser), and then choose View > Show File Names.

5 Repeat the same steps you performed in Step 3. This time, the three frames in the timeline represent the three source folders.

6 As you click the different frames in the timeline the corresponding source folder is highlighted in the folder hierarchy displayed to the left of the Photo Browser.

Using the Date View

The Date View can be a great way to organize and access your images, particularly if you are working with a collection of photos that span a number of years.

1 Click the Display button (▣) near the upper right corner of the Organizer window, and then choose Date View from the menu.

2 Select the Year option under the calendar display. Use the right and left arrows on either side of the year heading at the top of the calendar to go to 2008, if it is not already selected.

3 Select May 4, 2008 on the calendar. A thumbnail preview of the first photograph taken on May 4, 2008 appears at the right of the Organizer window.

4 Use the Next Item On Selected Day button (⦿) under the thumbnail image on the right side of the Organizer window to see the other photographs taken on the same day.

You can view all the photos taken on the same day as a slide show by clicking the Start Automatic Sequencing button (⦿) under the preview.

5   Under the preview thumbnail, click the Find this photo in the Photo Browser
    button () to switch to the Photo Browser with the current photo highlighted.

6   In the Photo Browser, click the Back To Previous View button (◄) near the
    upper left corner of the Organizer window to return to the Date View.

7   Select the Month option below the calendar view.

8   Click the word May at the top of the calendar, and then choose March from the
    months menu. If you wished to move one month at a time, you could simply
    click the Previous Month button twice.

9 The March page opens with the 26th already selected, as that is the first date for which there are photos in your Lesson2 catalog. Click in the Daily Note box at the bottom right of the Organizer window and type **A grand day out** to add a note to the selected date. An icon appears on the thumbnail for March 26th indicating that there is a note attached.

Now you know how to access photos via the calendar you'll be able to return and use the Date view whenever you wish, but for the remainder of this lesson you'll work with the Photo Browser view. Choose Photo Browser from the Display menu.

Working with star ratings and keyword tags

Most of us find it challenging to organize our files and folders efficiently. Forgetting which pictures were stored in what folder is easy, and it can be tedious to have to open and examine the contents of numerous folders looking for the files you want.

Photoshop Elements provides powerful and versatile organizing, tagging, and search tools to make that kind of frustration a thing of the past. You learned earlier how you can use the Search feature in the Organizer to find and retrieve files from multiple locations on your computer. The next set of exercises will show you how a little time invested in applying star ratings and keyword tags can streamline the process of sorting through your pictures, regardless of where the image files are stored.

Applying keyword tags and rating photos

Applying keyword tags to your photos and grouping keyword tag in categories make it easy to quickly find exactly the images you're looking for. You can also apply star ratings to your photos, providing you with yet another way to refine your searches.

In this example, you'll apply a rating and a couple of keyword tags from the default set to one of the images you imported into your catalog.

1   Click the Display button (), and then choose Thumbnail View from the menu. Make sure the Details checkbox in the bar above the Photo Browser pane is activated.

2   In the Photo Browser, move the pointer slowly from left to right over the stars beneath the thumbnail image of the mother and daughter at the seaside. When you see four yellow stars, as in the illustration below, click to apply that rating.

3   Find images based on their assigned rating using the stars and the adjacent menu located in the top right corner the Photo Browser pane. For this example set the search criteria at 2 stars and higher. Only the image with the 4-star rating is displayed in the Photo Browser.

4   Click the Show All button.

5   in the Keyword Tags palette in the Organize palette bin, click the arrow next to the People category to expand it so that you can see the Family and Friends sub-categories.

Using Star ratings and the Hidden tag

Star ratings—Use *Star ratings* to rank your photos. You can attach only one star rating value per photo. If you assign 5 stars to a photo that already has 4 stars assigned, the 5 star rating replace the previous rating.

Hidden—The *Hidden tag* hides photos in the Photo Browser, unless you select the Hidden tag as one of the search criteria. Use the Hidden tag, for example, to hide items that you want to keep, but generally don't want to see.

—From Photoshop Elements Help

6   Drag the Family sub-category tag to the thumbnail of the mother and daughter at the beach.

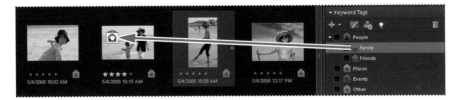

7   Allow the cursor to rest for a few seconds over the keyword tag icons under each thumbnail image until a Tooltip message appears identifying the keyword tags that are applied to the image.

Creating new categories and sub-categories

You can add or delete new keyword tag categories and sub-categories to group and organize your keywords tags.

1   Under Keyword Tags in the Organize pane, click the Create New button (➕) and choose New Category from the menu.

2 In the Create Category dialog box, type **architecture**, and then select the building icon from the Category Icon menu. Click OK.

3 In the Keyword Tags palette, click to select the People category, and then click the Create New button (➕) and choose New Sub-Category from the menu.

4 In the Create Sub-Category dialog box, type **Kids** in the Sub-Category Name box. Make sure that People is selected from the Parent Category or Sub-Category menu, and then click OK.

Your new keyword tag category and sub-category become part of this catalog.

Applying and editing category assignments

You can add keyword tags to several files at once, and—of course—remove keyword tag assignments.

1 In the Photo Browser, click to select any of the seven photos featuring children. Hold down the Ctrl key and click the other six photos with children to add them to the selection.

2 Drag the Kids keyword tag to any one of the selected thumbnails, as shown in the illustration on the next page. When you release the pointer, the keyword tag is applied to all seven images.

3   Keeping the same images selected, drag the architecture keyword tag to one of the un-selected images of the building interior. The keyword tag is applied to just this picture. Selecting the thumbnail or deselecting the other thumbnails is not necessary.

4   Choose Edit > Deselect, and then Ctrl-click the remaining three photos of the building interior. Drag the architecture keyword tag to any one of the selected images. The architecture keyword tag is applied to all three images at once.

5   Select the image of the mother and daughter at the beach—the one to which you applied the Family sub-category keyword tag. Then, choose Window > Properties to open the Properties palette.

6   Select the Keyword Tags tab (🏷) in the Properties panel to see which keyword tags are applied to this image.

Tip: You can also show or hide the Properties panel by holding down the Alt key, and then pressing the Enter key.

7 Remove the Family keyword tag from the image by doing one of the following:

- Right-click the blue keyword tag image underneath the thumbnail in the Photo Browser, and then choose Remove Family Sub-Category Keyword Tag from the menu.

- Right-click the thumbnail image and choose Remove Keyword Tag > Family from the context menu.

- In the Properties palette, right-click the Family, Kids listing, and then choose Remove Family Sub-Category Keyword Tag from the menu.

8 Close the Properties palette by clicking the Close button (⊠) in the upper right corner of the palette, or by choosing Window > Properties again.

Creating and applying new keyword tags

In the previous topic, you created new keyword tag categories and subcategories. In this topic, you'll create a new keyword tag and specify its location.

1 In the Keyword Tags palette in the Organize palette bin, click the Create New button (➕) and choose New Keyword Tag from the menu. The Create Keyword Tag dialog box appears.

2 In the Create Keyword Tag dialog box, choose Family (under People) for category and type Lilly for Name, and then click OK.

3   Drag the picture of the mother and child at the seaside from the previous
    exercise to the Lilly keyword tag under Keyword Tags.

The image becomes the icon for the new tag because it's the first image to have this
keyword applied. You will adjust the tag icon in the next steps, before applying the
new keyword tag to additional photos.

4   In the Keyword Tags palette in the Organize palette bin, select the Lilly
    keyword tag, and then click the Edit button (📝) above the list of keyword
    tags. Alternatively, right-click the Lilly keyword tag, and then choose Edit Lilly
    Keyword Tag from the context menu.

5   In the Edit Keyword Tag dialog box, click the Edit Icon button to open the Edit
    Keyword Tag Icon dialog box.

6   In the Edit Keyword Tag Icon dialog box, drag the corners of the boundary in the
    thumbnail so that it surrounds just the little girl with the blue hat in the center of
    the photo.

7   Click OK to close the dialog box and click OK again to close the Edit Keyword
    Tag dialog box.

You can update the keyword tag icon later when you find another photo that you
think works better as a keyword tag icon.

8 Drag the Lilly keyword tag to the picture of Lilly digging in the sand. The Lilly keyword tag is now applied to two images.

Converting keyword tags and categories

Changing the hierarchy of categories and keyword tags is easy. Doing this will not remove the keyword tags or categories from the images to which you've assigned them.

1 Click the Find box next to the Kids sub-category. A binoculars icon () appears in the Find box to remind you that it is now activated. Only the thumbnails tagged with the Kids keyword tag are displayed in the Photo Browser.

2 Click the Show All button above the Photo Browser to see all the images in the catalog.

3 Under the People category, right-click the Kids sub-category and choose Edit Kids Sub-Category from the context menu.

4   In the Edit Sub-Category dialog box, select None (Convert to Category) from the Parent Category or Sub-Category menu, and then click OK.

Now Kids is no longer a sub-category under People but a category on its own. Its icon has been inherited from its former parent category.

5   (Optional) Select a different category icon by choosing Edit Kids category.

6   Click the empty Find box next to the Kids category. Notice that the selection of images tagged with the Kids tag did not change. Click the Show All button.

7   Under Keyword Tags, drag the Kids category to the People category.

Now the Kids category appears as a sub-category under People. Because it's no longer a category, it has the generic sub-category icon.

8   Click the empty Find box next to the Kids sub-category. Notice that the selection of images tagged with the Kids tag did not change. Click the Show All button.

9   Under the Family category, right-click the Kids sub-category and choose Change Kids Sub-Category To A Keyword Tag from the context menu.

10 Under Keyword Tags, right-click the Kids keyword tag and choose Edit Kids Keyword Tag from the context menu. In the Edit Keyword Tag dialog box, click the Edit Icon button. In the Edit Keyword Tag Icon dialog box, select a different image for this tag by clicking on the arrows under the thumbnail image.

11 Click OK to close the Edit Keyword Tag Icon dialog box and click OK again to close the Edit Keyword Tag dialog box.

Applying more keyword tags to images

There are a few simple ways to automatically tag multiple images, as well as manual methods you can use for applying custom tags.

1 Click the Display button (▣) near the upper right corner of the Organizer window, and then choose Folder Location from the menu.

2 Click the Instant Keyword Tag icon on the right end of the separator bar above the thumbnails of BATCH1. That way you can quickly apply the same keyword tag to all items in that group.

3   In the Create And Apply New Keyword Tag dialog box, choose Other from the Category menu, leaving BATCH1 as the Name, and then click OK.

4   Repeat Steps 2 and 3 for the other folder groups, BATCH2 and BATCH3.

5   Switch back to Thumbnail View, using the same menu you used in Step 1.

Creating a keyword tag for your working files

You can create a keyword tag to apply to the files you create and save as you work through the lessons in this book.

1   Open the Organizer. If the Show All button is visible at the top of the Photo Browser pane, click it.

2   In the Keyword Tags palette, click the Create New button and choose New Category from the menu.

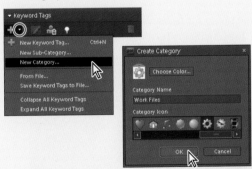

3   In the Create Category dialog box, type **Work Files** and select one of the Category icons. You can scroll to the right to see more icons. Click OK.

4   Apply this keyword tag to all the files you create and save to your My CIB Work folder as you complete the lessons in this book.

Automatically finding faces for tagging

When you use the Find Faces for Tagging feature, Photoshop Elements isolates faces in photos and displays them as individual thumbnails in the Face Tagging dialog box. This makes it quick and easy to tag faces of friends or family members. In the Face Tagging dialog box you can apply existing tags or create and apply new ones. When you tag a face in the Face Tagging dialog box, Photoshop Elements removes it from view, making it simpler to work with those remaining. You can activate the Show Already Tagged Faces option if you wish the thumbnails of the faces that you've already tagged to remain visible.

1   In the Photo Browser, select the file DSC_0698.jpg, an image of four girls at the seaside.

2   Choose Find > Find Faces For Tagging, or click the Find Faces For Tagging button ( ) at the top of the Keyword Tags palette.

Photoshop Elements searches the photo for faces. Thumbnails of the all the faces found are displayed in the Face Tagging dialog box.

As you can see, the Face Tagging dialog box is showing only three of the four girls' faces. Find Faces has missed one face. In the next exercise you'll find it.

Finding more faces

Occasionally the Find Faces feature misses a face due to unusual lighting or angle, or sometimes just because a photo is very busy or crowded with detail.

In this example, the angle of the taller girl's face combined with the strong sunlight and shadow are probably to blame, but don't worry—you can have Photoshop Elements find the missing face.

1   Click Done to dismiss the Face Tagging dialog box.

2   In the Photo Browser, make sure the file DSC_0698.jpg is still selected.

3   This time, hold down the Ctrl key on your keyboard as you choose Find > Find Faces For Tagging, or click the Find Faces For Tagging button (⬛) at the top of the Keyword Tags palette.

Once more, Photoshop Elements searches the photo for faces. This time the search is slower. While Find Faces is searching, a progress bar is displayed at the bottom of the Face Tagging dialog box. The missing face has been found and there are now four faces displayed in the Face Tagging dialog box. Photoshop Elements saves the data for the found faces in the catalog file.

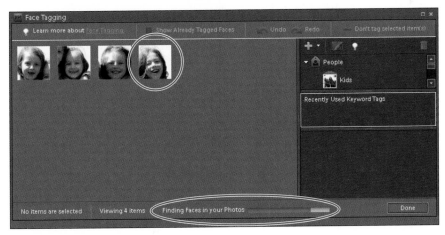

4   Click Done to dismiss the Face Tagging dialog box. In the next exercise you'll find the faces in all of the images in your Lesson 2 folder and apply some tags.

Tagging faces

Now that you know how to make sure Photoshop elements finds all the faces in your images, you can go ahead and apply the procedure to all of the photos in the Lesson 2 folder, and then you're ready to do some tagging.

1 Choose Edit > Select All to select all of the photos in the Photo Browser pane of the Organizer.

2 Just one more time, now—choose Find > Find Faces For Tagging, or click the Find Faces For Tagging button (🧑) at the top of the Keyword Tags palette. You won't need to hold down the Ctrl key—the data for the extra face you found in the last exercise is already recorded in the catalog.

Photoshop Elements searches your photos for faces. Thumbnails of the all the faces found are displayed in the Face Tagging dialog box. You can see that the problematic face from the last exercise has also been found.

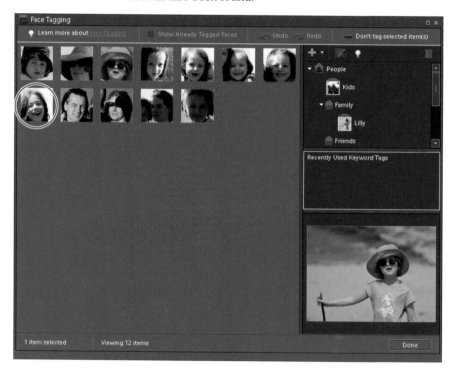

Remember: if you press Ctrl as you choose Find > Find Faces For Tagging, Photoshop Elements will produce more accurate results (for example, it will find more faces in the background of a busy photo), but it will take longer for the faces to appear. You can select your preferred searching method as default under Face Tagging in the Keyword Tags And Albums section of the Preferences dialog box (Edit > Preferences > Keyword Tags And Albums).

3 In the Face Tagging dialog box, Ctrl-click to select the three thumbnails showing Lilly's face, as shown in the illustration below. Drag the Lilly keyword tag onto any of the selected thumbnails, or drag the thumbnails onto the Lilly keyword tag. Once tagged, the thumbnails of Lilly disappear from the display.

4 Select the Show Already Tagged Faces option to show the faces already tagged.

5   Click Done to close the Face Tagging dialog box.

Using keyword tags to find pictures

Why create and apply all these keyword tags? Because they make it amazingly simple to find your pictures.

1   In the Organizer, click the empty Find box next to the Kids keyword tag. A binoculars icon appears in the Find box to remind you that it is selected. Only the thumbnails tagged with the Kids keyword tag are displayed.

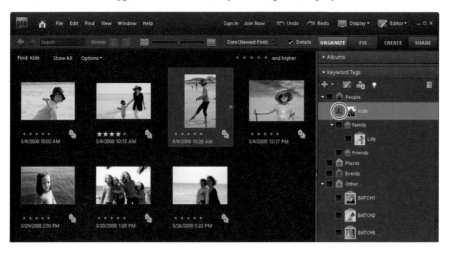

2   Leave the Kids keyword tag selected. Click the Find box for the BATCH2 keyword tag. Only four thumbnails appear: those tagged with both the Kids and the BATCH2 keyword tags.

3 From the Options menu above the Photo Browser, select Show close match results. The thumbnails display changes, also showing images that are tagged with some but not all of the selected keyword tags. These close matches are identified by a check mark in the upper left corner of the thumbnail images.

4 Click Show All to display all images.

Congratulations! You've finished the lesson and should be feeling pretty good about your accomplishment!

In this lesson, you've imported files into the Organizer using a variety of techniques and learned several different ways to view and access the images in your catalog. You've also created, edited, and applied keyword tags to individual photographs so that they'll be easy to find in future work sessions.

Review questions

1 How do you open the Organizer component of Adobe Photoshop Elements?

2 Name three methods to import photos located on your computer hard disk into your catalog.

3 What is a "watched folder"?

4 Explain the difference between the Photo Browser view and Date view in the Organizer.

Review answers

1 Click Organize in the row of shortcut buttons across the top of the Welcome Screen when you start Photoshop Elements. Alternatively, if the Editor window is already open, click the Organizer button located to the right in the menu bar.

2 This lesson demonstrated three different methods to import photos into Photoshop Elements:

- Drag-and-drop photographs from a Windows Explorer window into the Photo Browser pane in the Organizer window.

- In the Organizer, choose File > Get Photos And Videos > From Files And Folders, and then navigate to the folder containing your photos. You can import a whole folder, specify whether to include subfolders, or select just those images you want to add to your catalog.

- In the Organizer, choose File > Get Photos And Videos > By Searching, and then select the folder on the hard disk that you wish Photoshop Elements to search. This method will locate all images in that folder and its subfolders and offer you the opportunity to select which images to import.

3 A watched folder is a folders on your computer that automatically alerts Photoshop Elements when a new photo is saved or added to the folder. By default, the My Pictures folder is watched, and you can add additional folders to the list. New images added to these folders can be automatically added to the Organizer.

4 The default Photo Browser view in the Organizer lets you browse thumbnail images of your photos sorted in chronological order, by folder location, or by import batch. The Date view is organized in the form of a calendar where you can quickly find photos taken on a particular day, month, or year.

3 ADVANCED ORGANIZING

Lesson Overview

In this lesson, you'll learn a few new methods of importing images and some of the more advanced techniques for organizing, sorting, and searching your growing photo collection:

- Using advanced Photo Downloader options

- Acquiring still frames from video

- Importing pictures from a PDF document

- Importing pictures from a scanner

- Using Version sets and Stacks to organize photos

- Sorting photos by location using the Map view

- Finding photos by similarity, metadata, text search, and folder location

- Grouping photos in Albums and Smart Albums

 You'll probably need between one and two hours to complete this lesson.

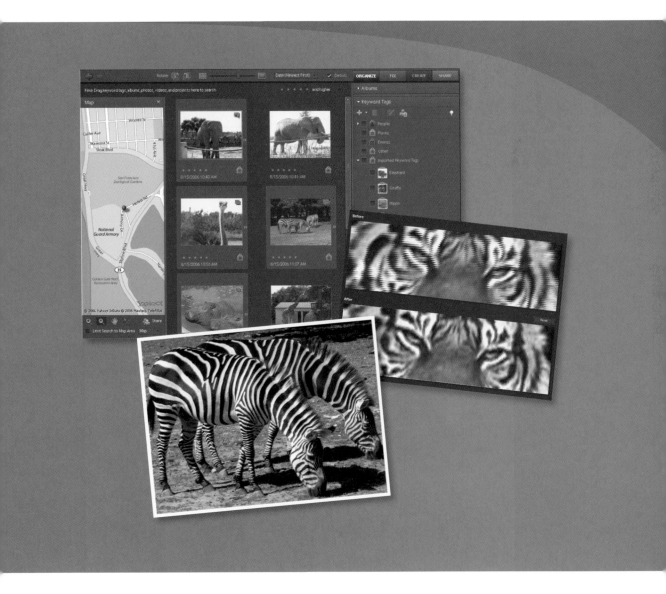

As your collection grows to hundreds or even thousands of images, keeping track of your photos can be a daunting task. Photoshop Elements 7 delivers advanced organizing tools that not only get the job done but in fact make the work quite enjoyable.

Getting started

Note: Before you start working on this lesson, make sure that you've installed the software on your computer from the application CD (see the Photoshop Elements 7 documentation) and that you have correctly copied the Lessons folder from the CD in the back of this book onto your computer's hard disk (see "Copying the Classroom in a Book files" on page 2).

In this lesson, you'll be working mainly in the Photoshop Elements Organizer workspace, though you will switch to the Editor to capture frames from video and import images from a PDF document. You'll also create a new catalog so that you won't confuse the practice files for this lesson with the files for the other lessons in this book.

1   Start Photoshop Elements, either by double-clicking the shortcut on your desktop or by choosing Start > Programs > Adobe Photoshop Elements 7.

2   Do one of the following:

- If the Welcome Screen appears, click Organize in the row of shortcut buttons across the top of the Welcome Screen.

- If the Editor window opens without first displaying the Welcome Screen, click the Welcome Screen button (⌂) at the left of the menu bar, and then click the Organize button. Alternatively, click the Organizer button (▦) located to the right in the Editor window menu bar, and then wait until the Organizer has finished opening.

- If the Organizer window opens without first displaying the Welcome Screen, you don't have to do anything more—you're all set to continue with step 3.

3   In the Organizer, choose File > Catalog.

4   In the Catalog Manager dialog box, click New.

5 In the Enter A Name For The New Catalog dialog box, type Lesson3 as the file name, disable the Import Free Music Into This Catalog option, and then click OK.

Now you have a special catalog that you'll use just for this lesson; all you need is some pictures to put in it.

Advanced import options

In Lesson 2 you learned various methods for importing images into the Organizer and how to apply tags manually to organize your photos once they are in your catalog. In the following exercise you will find out how you can use some advanced import options to make organizing your photos even easier by having Photoshop Elements tag and group them automatically during the import process. This way, your images will already be organized by the time they arrive in your catalog. You'll also learn how to import photos from some different sources—capturing a frame from a movie, extracting images embedded in a PDF document, and acquiring an image from a scanner.

Photo Downloader options

If you have a digital camera or memory card from your camera at hand with your own photos on it, you can step through this exercise using those images. For best results, you should have several batches of pictures taken at different times on a single day. Alternatively, you can simply follow the process by studying the illustrations in the book, without actually performing the exercise yourself.

1 Connect your digital camera or card reader to your computer, following the manufacturer's instructions.

2 Do the following:

- If the Windows Auto Play dialog box appears, click Cancel.

7   Use the slider under the Create Subfolder(s) menu to adjust the granularity of the subdivision to suit your needs. Move the slider to the left to generate fewer groups (or subfolders) or to the right to generate more groups. Scroll down the list of thumbnail images to review the grouping of the images. The number of groups chosen is displayed in the box to the right of the slider.

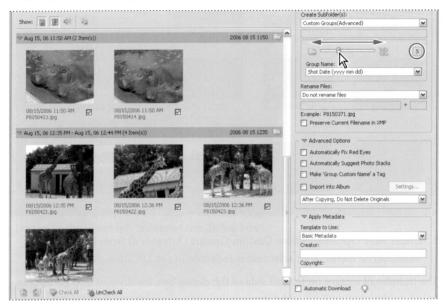

8   Choose Shot Date (yyyy mm dd) + Custom Name from the Group Name menu.

9   On the right end of the separator bar above the thumbnails of the first group, click the Custom Name field and type **Elephant** into the text box.

10 Repeat step 9 for the other groups in the thumbnail list, giving each group a distinct name (for this example, that could be **Ostrich**, **Zebra**, **Hippo**, and **Giraffe**).

11 Under Advanced Options, activate the option Make 'Group Custom Name' A Tag by clicking the check box. This will automatically create the appropriate tags and apply them to the pictures as they are imported in the Organizer. If the options Automatically Fix Red Eyes and the Automatically Suggest Photo Stacks are currently activated, disable them by clicking their checkboxes.

12 Click Get Photos.

The photos are copied from the camera to the specified folder locations.

13 If the Files Successfully Copied dialog box appears, click OK.

The Getting Photos dialog box appears and the photos are imported into your Lesson3 catalog.

The imported photos appear in the Photo Browser. You can see that Photoshop Elements has automatically created and applied tags for the groups during the import process.

The Advanced Photo Download dialog box also offers other options: you can choose to import only a specified selection of the images on your memory card, rotate images as they are imported, fix red eye effects automatically, have your photos grouped in stacks, change the file names, and add metadata such as copyright information.

The more of these import options you take advantage of when importing your photos into the Organizer, the less effort you will need to spend later on to sort and organize your files—and the easier it will be to find a specific photo months or even years after you added it to your catalog. Later in this lesson you'll learn more techniques for organizing your images, but first you'll look at some more methods of importing images into Photoshop Elements.

Acquiring still frames from a video

You can capture frames from your digital videos if they are saved in a file format that Photoshop Elements can open. Supported formats include: AVI, MPG, MPEG, WMV, ASF, and MLV. To capture frames from video, you'll need to open the Editor.

1   If you still have any image selected in the Organizer from the previous exercise, choose Edit > Deselect.

2 Click the Editor button () located near the top right corner of the Organizer window, and then choose Full Edit from the menu; then wait until the Editor has finished opening.

3 In the Editor, choose File > Import > Frame From Video.

4 In the Frame From Video dialog box, click the Browse button. In the Open dialog box, navigate to the Lesson03 folder and select the file Video.avi, and then click Open.

5 To start the video, click the Play button (▶). Click the Pause button (⏸) after 3 or 4 seconds, and then use the arrow keys on your keyboard to move forward or backward one frame at a time until you find a frame you want to capture.

6 To capture a frame of the video as a still image, click the Grab Frame button or press the spacebar when the frame you want is visible on the screen.

● **Note:** Some video formats don't support rewinding or fast-forwarding. When this is the case, the Rewind (◀◀) and Fast Forward (▶▶) buttons are dimmed.

7 (Optional) You can continue to move forward and backward in the video to capture additional frames.

8 When you have all the frames you want, click Done.

Depending on your video footage and which frames you captured, you might notice artifacts in the still image resulting from the fact that a video picture consists of two interlaced half-pictures. The odd-numbered scanlines of the image, also called odd fields, constitute one half of the picture, and the even-numbered scanlines, or even fields, the other. Since the two halves of the picture were recorded at slightly different times, the captured still image might look distorted.

In Photoshop Elements you can remedy this problem by using the De-Interlace filter. With the De-Interlace filter you can remove either the odd or even fields in a video image and replace the discarded lines by duplication or interpolation from the remaining lines.

For the purposes of this exercise, it's worthwhile to deliberately choose a frame with this kind of distortion, which is most easily identified as a 'zigzag' effect that is particularly noticeable on vertical detail. *(See the illustration on the next page.)*

9 Choose the captured image with which you wish to work for this exercise. You can discard the others by clicking the Close button in the top right corner of each image window. Click No in the alert dialogs that appear to ask if you wish to save the images.

10 With your chosen image still visible in the Edit work area, switch from the Full Edit mode to the Quick Edit mode by clicking the Quick button.

11 From the View menu in the lower left corner of the image display window, choose Before & After - Vertical.

12 Click the number in the Zoom value box in the lower left corner of the image display window, type **300**, and then press Enter. Use the Hand tool to move the image in either the Before or After pane so that you can see the Tiger's eyes. (When you're working with a tiger, it's *always* a good idea to watch the eyes!)

13 Choose Filter > Video > De-Interlace. Position the De-Interlace dialog box so that you can see both the Before and After views, and then choose either Odd Fields or Even Fields under Eliminate and either Duplication or Interpolation under Create New Fields By, and then click OK. The combination of options that will produce the best results depends on the image at hand. You can Undo after each trial and repeat this step until you are satisfied with the result.

14 Return to the Full Edit mode, save the image (File > Save) in your My CIB Work folder, and then close the image window in the Editor.

Importing from a PDF document

Photoshop Elements enables you to import whole pages or just selected images from a PDF document.

1 In the Editor, choose File > Open.

2 In the Open dialog box, navigate to the Lesson03 folder and select the file ZOO. pdf, and then click Open. If you can't see the file ZOO.pdf, in the Open dialog box, choose either All Formats or Photoshop PDF (*.PDF,*.PDP) from the Files Of Type menu.

In the Import PDF dialog box, you can choose to import entire pages or just the images from the PDF file.

If you choose to import whole pages from a multiple-page PDF file, you can Ctrl-click the page thumbnails to select those pages you wish to import. Pages are rasterized according to your choice of image size, resolution, and color mode. The imported result will be an image of the page similar to that acquired by scanning a printed document.

If you choose to import just the images from the PDF file rather than full pages, you can use the same method to select the images you want.

3 Under Select in the Import PDF dialog box, choose Images.

4 Select Fit Page from the Thumbnail Size menu to see the image previews at the largest possible size. Use the scrollbar at the right of the preview pane to scroll down to the last image.

5 Select Large from the Thumbnail Size menu. This enables you to see all 4 of the images in this file. Click to select an image you wish to import. Ctrl-click any additional images you would like to add to the selection to be imported, and then, click OK.

6 If any alert dialogs appear to let you know that the image files use an unsupported color mode, click Convert Mode.

Each imported image opens in its own document window in the Editor, ready for further processing.

7 For each imported image choose File > Save As, navigate to your My CIB Work folder, and save the file with a descriptive name in Photoshop (*.PSD,*.PDD) file format. Select the option Include In The Organizer before you click Save, if you wish to add the files to your catalog.

Scanning images

This exercise is optional and requires that you have a scanner available.

● **Note:** Photoshop Elements 7 also allows you to scan images using a video input source—such as a web camera—attached to your computer.

1 To prepare for acquiring images from a scanner, choose Edit > Preferences > Scanner, and then do the following:

   • If you have more than one scanner or an additional video input source installed, make sure that the correct device is selected in the Scanner menu.

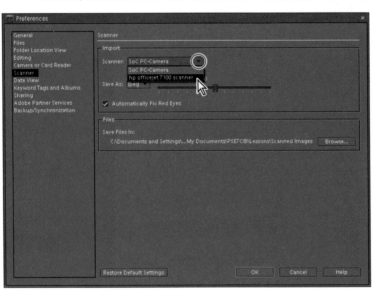

   • Either accept the default settings for Save As (jpeg), and Quality (6 Medium) or, if you prefer different settings, change them now.

   • Disable the Automatically Fix Red Eyes option. You will learn how to fix red eye in the Organizer in Lesson 8, "Repairing and Retouching Images."

   • If you want to change the location to which the scanned files will be saved, click Browse, and then find and select the folder you want to use.

   • Click OK to close the Preferences dialog box.

2 Place the picture or document you want to scan on the scanner bed and make sure your scanner is turned on.

3 If the scan dialog box does not appear automatically, go to the Organizer and choose File > Get Photos And Videos > From Scanner.

4 In the scan dialog box, click the Preview button and examine the resulting image.

● **Note:** The general appearance of the dialog box and the options available for your scanner may differ from what you see in the illustrations.

▶ **Tip:** When you scan several photographs at once, Photoshop Elements can crop the scan into individual photos automatically and will also straighten them for you. For more information on the Divide Scanned Photos feature, see Photoshop Elements Help.

5 (Optional) If you are not satisfied with the preview, change the settings as preferred.

6 Click Scan.

When the scan is complete, the image thumbnail appears in the Organizer.

7 Click Back To All Images to see your entire catalog.

Organizing photos

Organizing your files and folders efficiently can be challenging. It's easy to forget which pictures are stored in what folder, and being forced to open and examine the content of numerous folders to find files or images can be time consuming and extremely frustrating.

The Organizer can make the whole process much simpler and more enjoyable. The next set of exercises will show you how investing a little time in organizing your pictures can streamline the process of sorting through your image files, regardless of where they are stored.

Working with Version sets

A version set groups the original imported image file with any edited versions. In the Photo Browser, you'll see all versions of the image in a single stack rather than scattered amongst the rest of the images in your catalog—making it much easier for you to find the version you want.

For this exercise you'll use Auto Smart Fix to edit an image in the organizer and create a version set containing the original and the edited version. To prepare, for the exercise, you'll clear any images you've added to your Lesson3 catalog since the beginning of this lesson.

1   In the Organizer make sure the Lesson3 catalog is open. If the Show All button is visible above the Photo Browser, click it. Choose Edit > Select All, and then choose Edit > Delete Selected Items From Catalog. If you see the options Delete All Photos In Collapsed Stacks and Delete All Items In Collapsed Version Sets in the Confirm Deletion From Catalog dialog box, activate both options by clicking their checkboxes, and then click OK.

2   Choose File > Get Photos And Videos > From Files And Folders.

3   In the Get Photos From Files And Folders dialog box, navigate to the Lesson03 folder and select the Photos folder. Select the Get Photos From Subfolders check box. If the options Automatically Fix Red Eyes and Automatically Suggest Photo Stacks are activated, disable them by clicking their check boxes, and then click Get Photos.

4   In the Import Attached Tags dialog box, click Select All, and then click OK. Click OK to close any other alert dialog box. Click the Show All button above the Photo Browser.

In the Photo Browser, you can now see thumbnails of all the images you just added to your Lesson 3 catalog.

5   In the Keyword Tags palette, click the triangle next to Imported Keyword Tags to see the newly added keyword tags.

6   In the Photo Browser, select the first photo of the Elephant (taken at 10:40 am) and choose Edit > Auto Smart Fix. The Auto Smart Fix command corrects the overall color balance and improves shadow and highlight detail, if necessary. The edited copy of the photo is automatically grouped with the original photo in a version set, with the edited version topmost. A version set can be identified in the Photo Browser by the version set icon in the upper right corner of the thumbnail.

7   Click the expand button on the right side of the thumbnail image, to see the original and edited images in a version set.

8   To see only the topmost photo in a version set, click the collapse button on the right side of the last thumbnail image in the expanded set, or right-click any of the thumbnail images in the set, and then choose Version Set > Collapse Items In Version Set from the context menu. Notice the other commands available from the same context menu—as well as from the Edit menu—such as Version Set > Convert Version Set To Individual Items.

About stacks

You can create stacks to group a set of related photos in the Photo Browser, making them easier to manage. Stack photos that make up a series or multiple images of the same subject to help reduce clutter in the Photo Browser.

For instance, you might create a stack for several photos of your family taken in the same pose until you have a chance to pick the best shot, or for photos taken at a sports event using your camera's burst mode or auto-bracket feature. Generally, when you take photos this way, you end up with many variations of the same photo, but you only want the best one to appear in the Photo Browser. Stacking the photos lets you easily access them all in one place instead of having them scattered across rows of thumbnails.

1   Click the empty Find box next to the Zebra tag in the Imported Tags category.

2   To marquee-select all three images, click below the first thumbnail image and drag to the top and right. When you release the pointer, all images intersected by the selection marquee are selected.

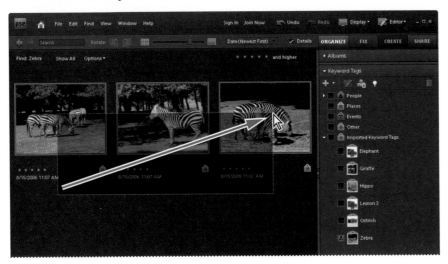

3   Choose Edit > Stack > Stack Selected Photos.

All three Zebra photos are now grouped in a stack. You can expand and collapse stacks in the Photo Browser the same way you expand and collapse version sets.

A stack can be identified in the Photo Browser by the stack icon in the upper right corner of the thumbnail.

4 Click the Show All button above the Photo Browser, and then click the empty Find boxes next to the Hippo and Ostrich tags in the Imported Tags category.

5 Choose Edit > Select All, and then choose Edit > Stack > Automatically Suggest Photo Stacks.

The Automatically Suggest Photo Stacks dialog box appears. The two photos of the hippopotamus have been successfully placed in a group already, but the ostrich photos, which have less visual similarity, will need to be grouped manually.

6 In the Automatically Suggest Photo Stacks dialog box, scroll down to the bottom of the thumbnail list. Click the image of the ostrich in the last group and drag it up to place it in the same group as the other ostrich photo.

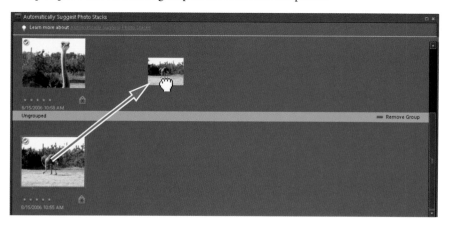

7   To split one group into two, position the cursor between two images in the group. When the cursor changes to the scissors icon, click to divide the group.

8   To exclude all photos in a group from being stacked, click the Remove Group button. Alternatively, select individual photos, and then click the Remove Selected Photo(s) button in the lower left corner of the dialog box.

9   If you change your mind about a photo excluded from being stacked, make sure the Show Removed Photos option at the bottom of the dialog box is activated, and then drag the thumbnail image from the removed photos bin to add it to a group in the main thumbnail area.

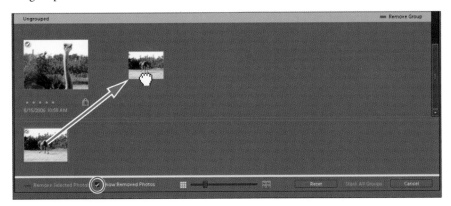

10 When you're done, click Stack All Groups to stack the photos in each group and close the Automatically Suggest Photo Stacks dialog box. Click Show All in the Photo Browser.

A stack can be identified in the Photo Browser by the stack icon in the upper right corner of the thumbnail.

Tips for working with stacks

● **Note:** If you edit a photo that's already in a stack, the photo and its edited copy are put in a version set that is nested inside the stack.

Keep these points in mind when working with stacks:

- By default, the most recent photo is placed on top of the stack. As you create the stack, you can specify a new image as the topmost by right-clicking it and choosing from the context menu.

- Combining two or more stacks merges them to form one new stack, with the most recent photo on top of the stack. The original groupings are not preserved.

- Many actions applied to a collapsed stack, such as editing, printing, and e-mailing, are applied to the topmost item only. To apply an action to multiple images in a stack, expand the stack and select the individual images or un-stack them.

- If you apply a keyword tag to a collapsed stack, the keyword tag is applied to all items in the stack. When you run a search on the keyword tag, the top photo in the stack appears in the search results marked with the stack icon. If you want to apply a keyword tag to only one photo in a stack, expand the stack and apply the keyword tag to just that photo.

- You can access stack commands by right-clicking or by using the Edit menu.

Creating Albums

Another way of grouping photos is to organize them into albums. You can create a new album to group shots from a special occasion such as a wedding or vacation, or to assemble the images that you want to use in a project such as a presentation to a client or a slideshow. Add pictures to the album the same way you would add them to a group of pictures with the same keyword tag. The main difference between albums and keyword tags is that in an album you can rearrange the order of the photos into any order you want. Smart albums automatically search your catalog and collect the images that match any search criteria that you have specified. You'll learn about using smart albums later in this lesson in the section "Viewing and finding photos."

1 If the Albums palette is collapsed in the Organize palette bin, click the triangle in the header of the palette to expand it.

2 To create a new album, click the Create New button (➕) in the header of the Albums palette, and then choose New Album from the menu.

3 In the Create Album dialog box, type **Animals** as the name of the new album, and then click OK.

4 Ctrl-click to select two or three photos in the Photo Browser, and then drag the group onto the Animals album icon.

Note: If you add a collapsed version set or a collapsed stack to an album, only the topmost picture of the version set or stack will be visible in the album. To add a different picture to the album, first expand the version set or stack.

Note: You can only view the contents of one album at a time.

5 To see the contents of an album, click the album icon, or drag and drop the album icon onto the Find bar above the Photo Browser. Notice the number in the top left corner of each photo, representing its order in the album.

6 To change the order of the images in an album, select one or more photos in the Photo Browser, and then drag the selection to the desired position. The photos are reordered when you release the pointer.

7   (Optional) To remove a picture from an album, right-click the picture in the album view, and then choose Remove from Album > [album name] from the menu.

8   Click Show All above the Browser View to see all the photos in your catalog.

9   To delete an album, right-click its icon in the Albums palette, and then choose Delete [album name] album from the menu.

10 Click OK in the Confirm Album Deletion dialog box.

The Map View

In the Map view of the Organizer, you can arrange and search for photos by geographic location. Associate an image with a location by simply dragging its thumbnail from the Photo Browser directly to a location on the map.

1   In the Organizer, right-click the second thumbnail image of the elephant, and then choose Place on Map from the context menu.

2   In the Photo Location On Map dialog box, type **1 Zoo Road, San Francisco, CA** in the text box, and then click Find.

3   In the Look Up Address dialog box, click OK to confirm 1 Zoo Rd San Francisco, CA, 94132-1027 US.

Tip: You can group related albums in an album group, as you group keyword tags in a category. Change an album's properties and icon by clicking the Edit album button.

Note: Deleting an album does not delete the photos in the album from your catalog. Albums store only references to the actual photos.

Note: You must have an active Internet connection to use this feature.

4   The Map view opens to the left of the Photo Browser. You can use the Hand tool to drag the map in any direction. The red pin indicates the location for your photo.

5   Select Hybrid from the menu in the lower right corner of the Map panel, beside the Zoom, Hand, and Move tools.

6   Use the Zoom In tool and the Hand tool in combination to magnify the view on the San Francisco Zoological Gardens. Use the Move tool to reposition the red pin to exactly where you want it to appear on the map.

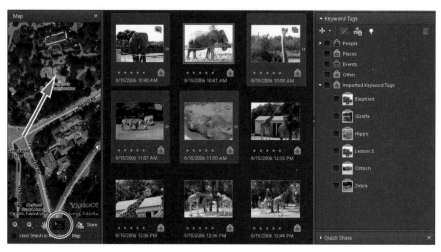

7 To place additional photos on the map, drag them from the Photo Browser to the Map view. If you get too close to an existing pin, the photos will be grouped under one pin location—which may or may not be what you want.

▶ **Tip:** You can drag a keyword tag—for example, a keyword tag in the Places category —to the Map view to position all photos tagged with that keyword tag on the map.

8 Select the Limit Search To Map Area check box in the lower left corner of the Map View. Only photos mapped to the currently visible map area are displayed in the Browser View.

9 Click the Close button (🞩) in the upper right corner of the Map panel to close the Map view. Click the Show All button above the Photo Browser. Right-click the second thumbnail of the elephant, and then choose Show on Map from the context menu. The Map view will open, displaying the location to which the photo was mapped.

10 Close the Map view.

This concludes the section on organizing your photos. You've learned about version sets and stacks, how to group photos in albums, and how to arrange them by geographic location. In the next section, you'll learn how you can easily find photos in your catalog—even when you haven't spent a lot of time organizing them.

Viewing and finding photos

In the Organizer, Photoshop Elements offers several methods to find photos:

- **The Timeline** If necessary, choose Window > Timeline to display the timeline above the Browser View. Then, click a month or set a range to find photos and media files by date, by import batch, or by folder location.

- **The Find bar** Drag and drop a photo, keyword tag, creation, or album onto the find bar to locate similar or matching photos and media files.

- **The Find menu** Use the commands in this menu to find photos by date, caption or note, file name, history, media type, metadata, or color similarity. Commands are also available for finding photos and media files that have unknown dates, are un-tagged, or are not in an album.

Finding photos by visual similarity

You can search for photos containing similar images, color, or general appearance.

1　In the Organizer, choose Edit > Select All. Choose Edit > Stack > Unstack Photos, and then choose Edit > Version Set > Revert To Original. Click OK to close any alert dialog box that might appear.

2　Choose Edit > Deselect. Then, drag the first image with the zebras to the find bar.

The images in the Photo Browser are now displayed in decreasing order of similarity in visual appearance to the selected image. A similarity percentage appears in the bottom left corner of each image.

3   Click the Show All button.

Finding photos using details and metadata

You can search for your images by file details or metadata. Searching by metadata is useful when you want to narrow a search by using multiple criteria. For example, if you want to find all photos captured on a certain date that are also marked with a specific keyword tag, you can search using both capture date and keyword tags in the Find By Details (Metadata) dialog box.

Searchable metadata includes file name, file type, keyword tags, albums, notes, author, map location, and capture date, as well as camera model, shutter speed, and F-stop—to name just a few of the many available search criteria.

For this exercise you will search for photos taken near a specific location using the Find By Details (Metadata) dialog box.

1   Choose Find > By Details (Metadata) in the Organizer. The Find By Details (Metadata) dialog box appears.

2   Under Search Criteria, click the first menu, and then use the scrollbar to scroll down towards the end of the list. While scrolling, notice the many options available as search criteria.

Some metadata is generated automatically by your camera when you capture an image, some is added when you spend time organizing your catalog. For this exercise, choose the last entry in the list, Map Location.

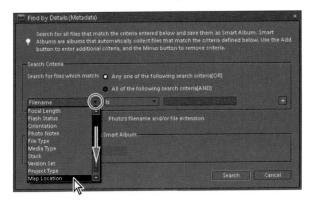

3   From the menu next to Map Location, choose Within.

4   Click the magnifying glass icon to open the Photo Location On Map dialog box. In the Photo Location On Map dialog box, type **1 Zoo Road, San Francisco, CA**, and then click Find. Click OK to close the Photo Location On Map dialog box.

5   In the Find By Details (Metadata) dialog box, type **1** as distance and choose Miles from the menu at the right.

● **Note:** To include more metadata values in your search, click the plus (+) button and specify new values using the menus that appear. To remove criteria from your search, click the minus (-) sign to the right side of the item you wish to remove. If you specify multiple search criteria, click the appropriate radio button to search for files matching any or all of the search criteria.

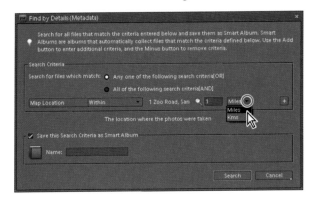

6   If it's activated, disable the option Save This Search Criteria As Smart Album by clicking its check box. You'll learn about using smart albums in the last part of this lesson. Click the Search button. Only images that match the specified criteria are displayed.

7 (Optional) To modify the search, click Options in the find bar, and then choose Modify Search Criteria from the menu. This will open the Find By Details (Metadata) dialog box with the current search criteria set. Make your changes, and then click Search to display the new search results in the Photo Browser.

8 Click the Show All button in the find bar.

Find photos using a text search

You can quickly find the photos you want using a text-based search. Type a word in the Text Search box at the left of the Find bar just above the Photo Browser, and the Organizer will display images that match the text across a wide range of criteria.

Matches can include items such as author, captions, dates, filenames, keyword tags, metadata, notes, album names, album groups, and camera information—Photoshop Elements will look for the search term in any type of text that is associated with the file.

You can use a text search as a convenient shortcut—for example, type the name of a tag, rather than navigating to the Keyword Tags palette.

Text search also supports the operators: "and," "or," and "not" if they are preceded and followed by a space. For example, you could type "vacation and kids" to find only images with both words in their metadata, not just either one.

Some words can be processed by Photoshop Elements as special instructions, not as specific search criteria. For example, you may want to search for a file tagged "Birthday," but only among your video files. You can use the Media "Type" and "Video" keywords. So, you would type "Type: Video Tag: Birthday."

For more information on using Text Search, and for a list of supported operators and special tags, please refer to Photoshop Elements Help.

Metadata support for audio and video files

Photoshop Elements 7 provides improved metadata support for audio and video files in the Organizer.

In the Properties - Metadata panel, metadata information is categorized into separate audio and video sections. For video, you'll find information such as pixel aspect ratio in the Brief view, while the audio section includes artist, album name, etc.—if that information is present in the file.

The File Properties section displays the filename, document type, creation and modification dates, and—if you activate the Complete view—the file size for your audio and video files.

1   Right-click on the audio file Temple of the Moon.wav and choose Show Properties to open the Properties - Metadata panel. Click the Info button (●) at the top of the panel, and select Complete from the view options below the Info pane to view all metadata.

2   Repeat step 1 for the video file Video.avi.

● **Note:** You cannot edit the metadata for audio and video files in Photoshop Elements.

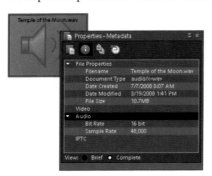

3   Close the Properties panel by clicking the close button in the top right corner.

Viewing and managing files by folder location

The Folder Location view in the Organizer splits the Photo Browser into three sections: a folder hierarchy pane on the left, an image thumbnail pane in the center, and the Palette Bin on the right. From this view you can manage your folders, add files to your catalog, automatically tag files using their folder name as the keyword tag, and add or remove folders from Watched Folder status.

By default, the left pane displays all the folders on your hard disk, and the center pane displays only the thumbnails of the managed files in the selected folder. Folders containing managed files have a Managed folder icon (▤). Watched folders have a Watched folder icon (▦).

1 Click the Display button (⬛) near the upper right corner of the Organizer window, and then choose Folder Location from the menu.

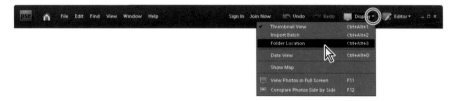

The folder hierarchy appears on the left side of the Photo Browser.

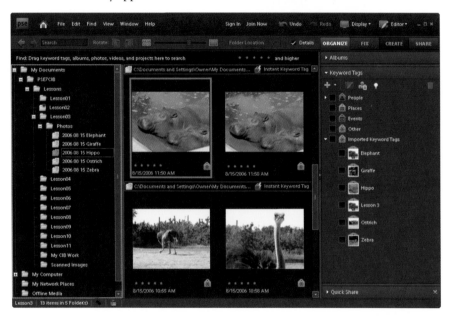

The contents of a selected folder are displayed in the Photo Browser when using Folder Location view.

● **Note:** You can change the default view for each panel by choosing Edit > Preferences > Folder Location View and selecting your preferred options.

2 Do one of the following to specify which files appear in the center panel:

• To view only the managed files in the selected folder, right-click in the left panel and disable the menu option Show All Files.

• To view all your managed files in the center panel grouped by folder location, right-click in the left panel and activate the menu option Show All Files.

• If you want to search all your managed files while in Folder Location view, select Show All Files.

• To find the folder location of a file, click the file's thumbnail in the center panel. The file's folder is highlighted in the left panel.

• To find files in a specific folder, click the folder in the left panel. Thumbnails for the files in that folder appear in the center panel, grouped under the folder name.

- To instantly tag files by their folder locations, click the Instant Keyword Tag icon in the Photo Browser pane. In the Create And Apply New Keyword Tag dialog box you can attach keyword tags simultaneously to all images in that folder.

3 To manage files and folders, select a folder and do any of the following:

- To move a file to a different folder, drag the file's thumbnail from the Photo Browser pane to a folder in the left panel.

- To view the folder in Windows Explorer, right-click in the left panel and choose Reveal in Explorer.

- To add or remove the folder from watched-folder status, right-click in the left panel and choose Add to Watched Folders or Remove from Watched Folders.

- To add a file in the folder to your catalog, right-click in the left panel and choose Add Unmanaged Files To Catalog.

- To rename the folder, right-click in the left panel and choose Rename Folder. Then, type a new name.

- To delete the folder, right-click in the left panel and choose Delete Folder.

4 Click the Display button (⬛), and then choose Thumbnail View from the menu. In the Photo Browser, click Show All.

Hiding files

You have already learned that you can simplify the process of working with your growing catalog by creating stacks and version sets to help reduce clutter in the Photo Browser, effectively reducing the number of images on view by stacking similar or related shots and grouping edited versions with their originals. With a stack or a version set you can choose the image in which you are most interested as the topmost in the collapsed grouping and the other images are tucked out of view until you choose to work with them.

In many cases it may be more effective to hide those images from view entirely. Once you have settled on the best shot from a stack of similar images, or the best of several edited versions in a version set, you can hide the other images from view so that they will no longer appear in search results, distract you when making selections, or need to be considered when applying commands.

Hiding photos does not delete them from their folders on your hard disk or remove them from your catalog or even from an album—you can always un-hide them if you start a new project where they might be useful or find that you could make use of a differently edited version.

1   Ctrl-click to select both of the photos of the elephant. Choose Edit > Auto Smart Fix Selected Photos. Auto Smart Fix is applied to both images and both are grouped in separate version sets with the edited versions topmost.

2   Ctrl-click to select both version sets and choose Edit > Version Set > Convert Version Set To Individual Items. There are now 4 images of the elephant in the Photo Browser: 2 originals and 2 edited copies.

3   Ctrl-click to select both of the originals of the elephant photos; then add to the multiple selection by Ctrl-clicking the first ostrich photo, the second zebra photo, the second hippo photo and the third giraffe photo. You should have six images selected. Choose Edit > Visibility > Mark As Hidden.

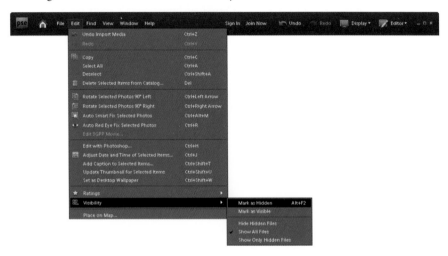

4   The Hidden File icon now appears on all six Thumbnails. Now choose Edit > Visibility > Hide Hidden Files. The six images marked as Hidden are removed from the Photo Browser view. Expand the Keyword Tags palette, if necessary, and then expand the Imported Keyword Tags category so that you can see all the imported tags.

5   Click the empty Find box beside each keyword tag in turn. The 6 hidden files do not appear in any of the search results.

6   In the Photo Browser, click Show All. Choose Edit > Visibility > Show Only Hidden Files, and then choose Edit > Visibility > Show All Files. Finally Ctrl-click to select all six thumbnails with the Hidden File icon. Choose Edit > Visibility > Mark As Visible. The Hidden File icon is removed from all 6 files.

7   Ctrl-click to select both of the edited images of the elephant and press the choose Edit > Delete from Catalog. In the Confirm Deletion From Catalog dialog box, activate the option Also Delete Selected Items From The Hard Disk, and then click OK.

Working with smart albums

Note: You cannot change the order of photos in a smart album, as you can for other albums. Nor can you add photos to a smart album by dragging them onto the album's icon; you need to modify the album's search criteria to change the content. The content of a smart album may change over time even without modifying the search criteria if photos matching the search criteria are added or removed from the catalog; for example, a smart album may be set up to contain photos captured within the last six months from the current date. Photos included in the album today may not fall within that date range tomorrow.

All albums, including smart albums, contain photos of your choosing. However, instead of manually selecting individual photos as you do for ordinary albums, you only need to specify search criteria to create a smart album. Once you set the criteria for a smart album, any photo in a catalog that matches the specified criteria will appear automatically in that smart album. As you add new photos to the catalog, those photos matching a smart album's criteria will appear automatically in that smart album. Smart Albums keep themselves up-to-date.

1   To set up search criteria for a new smart album, choose Find > Find by Details (Metadata). In the Find By Details (Metadata) dialog box, select the search criteria for the smart album. Click the plus sign (+) to add a criterion, click the minus sign (-) to remove a criterion.

2   If necessary, activate Save this Search Criteria as Smart Album. Enter **My first smart album** as the name, and then click Search.

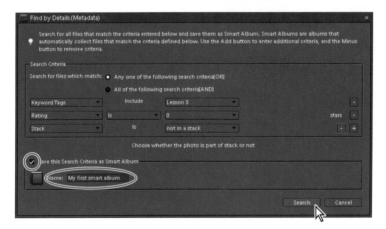

3   To display the photos in a smart album in the Photo Browser, select the smart album from the Albums palette.

4   To change the name of a smart album, do the following:

   •   Select the smart album from the Albums palette.

   •   Click the Edit button () in the Albums palette.

   •   Enter a new name in the Edit Smart Album dialog box, and then click OK.

5 To change the search criteria of a smart album, do the following:

- Select your new smart album from the Albums palette.

- Click Options in the find bar, and then choose Modify Search Criteria from the menu.

6 Modify the search criteria in the Find By Details (Metadata) dialog box, and select to save it as smart album. Provide a new name for the smart album, and then click Search.

7 To delete the smart album, right-click its icon in the Albums palette, and then choose Delete *[smart album name]* album from the menu. Click OK to confirm.

⬤ **Note:** You can save the modified search criteria using the same name, but this is not recommended. A second smart album with the same name will be created, rather than the first smart album being over-written. A dialog box will alert you about the duplicate file name. Click OK if you want to go ahead and create a second smart album with the same name anyway.

Congratulations! You've reached the end of Lesson 3. In this lesson, you've learned about advanced import options in the Photo Downloader, how to acquire still frames from a video, and how to import images from a PDF file or acquire them from a scanner. You've organized images in version sets, stacks, and albums, placed photos on a map, and learned some advanced methods for finding and managing the photos in your catalog.

Before you go on to the next lesson you can review what you've learned and test your command of the concepts and techniques presented in this lesson by working through the following questions and answers.

Review questions

1 How can you automatically create and apply tags to images while importing them from a digital camera or card reader?

2 What does the Photoshop Elements De-Interlace filter do?

3 What does the Auto Smart Fix command do?

4 What are Version Sets and Stacks?

5 What is the main difference between grouping pictures using tags and grouping them in an album?

Review answers

1 In the Advanced Photo Downloader dialog box, choose Custom Groups (Advanced) from the Create Subfolder(s) menu. Next, choose an option including Custom Name from the Group Name menu. Enter a Group Name in the Custom Name field in the separator bar above each group of thumbnails. Finally, select the Make 'Group Custom Name' A Tag check box before clicking Get Photos.

2 The Photoshop Elements De-Interlace filter can improve the appearance of still frame images acquired from a video by removing artifacts caused by the fact that a video picture consists of two interlaced half-pictures taken at slightly different times. The De-Interlace filter removes either the odd or even fields in a video image and replaces the discarded lines by duplication or interpolation from the remaining lines.

3 The Auto Smart Fix command corrects the overall color balance and improves shadow and highlight detail, if necessary. The Auto Smart Fix command groups the edited copy of the photo automatically with the original photo in a version set.

4 A version set groups an original photo and its edited versions. Stacks are used to group a set of similar photos, such as multiple shots of the same subject, or photos taken using your camera's burst mode or auto-bracket feature. A version set can be nested inside a stack: if you edit a photo that's already in a stack, the photo and its edited copy are put in a version set that is nested inside the original stack.

5 The main difference between albums and keyword tags is that in albums you can rearrange the order of the photos.

4 CREATING PROJECTS

Lesson Overview

Photoshop Elements makes it easy to create stylish, professional-looking projects to showcase your photos. Choose from preset themes and layouts—or create your own designs from scratch. Put together a range of creations from greeting cards and photo collages to animated slide shows and online albums.

This lesson will familiarize you with the Create mode by stepping you through a few basic techniques and simple projects:

- Creating a greeting card
- Animating your photos in a Slideshow
- Producing a Photo Collage
- Using the Artwork library
- Working with layers

 You'll probably need between one and two hours to complete this lesson.

Use your own images in personalized CD or DVD jackets and labels, calendars, photo books, and digital flip-books. Combine images, text, animation, and even music and narration, to produce unique multimedia creations. Whether you're sharing your photos online, designing your own coffee table book, or making special greeting cards for your family or friends, Photoshop Elements unleashes your creativity.

Getting started

Note: Before you start working on this lesson, make sure that you've installed the software on your computer from the application CD (see the Photoshop Elements 7 documentation) and that you have correctly copied the Lessons folder from the CD in the back of this book onto your computer's hard disk (see "Copying the Classroom in a Book files" on page 2).

While you're working on the projects in this lesson, you'll use the CIB Catalog you created in the "Getting Started" section at the beginning of this book. To open your CIB Catalog, follow these steps:

1   Start Photoshop Elements and click the Organize button in the Welcome Screen. Wait until the Organizer has finished opening.

2   Choose File > Catalog.

3   In the Catalog Manager dialog box, select the CIB Catalog, and then click Open.

If you don't see the CIB Catalog file, review "Copying the Lessons files from the CD" on page 2 and "Creating a catalog" on page 3 in the "Getting Started" section at the beginning of this book.

Creating a Greeting Card

Eye-catching personalized greeting cards based on your own photos are a sure way to impress family and friends—a really attractive card can spend many months on a loved one's mantelpiece, or may even get framed and displayed with pride.

As with the other photo project options, you can include one or more photos on each page of a greeting card and either print it on your home printer, order prints online, or sent it via e-mail.

The Photo Projects panel in Adobe Photoshop Elements offers you a variety of templates to help you create sophisticated designs quickly and easily.

This exercise will show you how easy it is to choose a theme and format to present a photo in a creative and professional-looking manner. When you're finished, you'll have transformed your photo into a delightful greeting card.

1   In the Organizer, use the Keyword Tags palette to isolate the photos in your CIB catalog that are tagged with the keyword Lesson 4. Sselect the portrait of a little girl with the file name 4_Zoe.jpg.

▶ **Tip:** If you don't see the names of the image files displayed below the thumbnail images in the Photo Browser pane, choose View > Show File Names.

2   Click to select the purple Create tab in the Task pane to the right of the Photo Browser.

3   Choose Greeting Card from the More Options menu below the project buttons in the Create panel.

4 The Editor workspace opens. In the Photo Projects panel, scroll down to see all the options in the Choose A Theme menu. Select the "Wedding Classic" template (the third design from the end) featuring worn grey paper with pale flowers scattered across the bottom.

5 From the Choose A Layout menu, select the template "1 Tilted" (the design in the center of the second row), a horizontal layout with a single landscape format photo frame placed on an angle. Activate the option Auto-Fill With Project Bin Photos and disable the Include Captions option; then, click Done.

To move the photo, click inside its bounding box and drag it to a new position. To re-size the image, move the pointer over any one of the corner handles of the bounding box and drag the handle with the diagonal double-arrow cursor. By default, the photo will be scaled proportionally. Move the pointer close to a corner handle, outside the bounding box—when the pointer becomes a curved double-arrow cursor, drag in either direction to rotate the photo around its center point.

6 You'll see a preview of your greeting card in the Editor panel with a bounding box surrounding the photo. You can move, rotate and re-size the photo if you wish.

▶ Tip: To move the photo, click inside its bounding box and drag it to a new position. To re-size the image, move the pointer over any one of the corner handles of the bounding box and drag the handle with the diagonal double-arrow cursor. By default, the photo will be scaled proportionally. To rotate a photo around its center point, move the pointer close to any handle, staying outside the bounding box; when the pointer becomes a curved double-arrow cursor, drag to rotate the image in either direction.

7 When you're done re-sizing and repositioning the photo, click the green Commit button (✔) at the bottom of the bounding box to commit the changes.

▶ Tip: When the Move tool is active, you can use the arrow keys on your keyboard to move the elements of a selected layer in small increments instead of dragging them using your pointer. Similarly, when one of the selection tools is active you can use the arrow keys to nudge a selection.

That was quick! Composing your photo with an appropriate theme and layout can make a really distinctive card.

8　Choose File > Save. In the Save As dialog box, navigate to the My CIB Work folder and name the file 4_Greeting_Card.psd. Make sure that the option Include In The Organizer is activated. Click Save.

9　Choose File > Close. Congratulations; you've created your first photo project!

● **Note:** Frames occupy the same layers as the images they contain, though they appear to be overlaid.

Adjusting a photo inside a frame

The theme template you used for your greeting card consists of a background and an image frame. The image frame and the photo it surrounds are on the same layer—when you scale or move the photo, the frame is scaled or moved with it.

In this case, the frame crops the edges of the photograph slightly (notably at the top and back of the girl's head) so you may want to scale, move, or even rotate the image slightly within the frame. To do this, first double-click the photo; then you can drag it to reposition it inside its frame and scale or rotate it using the handles.

Working with multiple pages

You can create multiple-page layouts with Photoshop Elements, which are perfect for projects such as photo albums where you want consistency from page to page. In the Edit menu you'll find options for adding either blank pages or pages using the same layout. The example shown below also uses the same theme that you used for the greeting card but applies a different layout template.

Animating your photos in a slide show

A Photoshop Elements slide show is a digital project that makes a dynamic, fun way to present and share your photos. You can add and edit slide transitions and zoom or pan effects, choose from an array of graphic extras and frames, add text and even music or narration.

Using the Slide Show Editor

1   In the Organizer, select the four photos with the little girls playing on a sculpture in a park. These images are tagged with the Lesson 4 keyword and are named 4_Slideshow1.jpg through 4_Slideshow4.jpg.

2 Click the purple Create tab in the Task pane, and then click the Slide Show button.

3 In the Slide Show Preferences dialog box, choose 3 sec for Static Duration, Gradient Wipe as Transition, and 2 sec for the Transition. Disable all the option checkboxes except for Landscape Photos beside Crop to Fit Slide, as in the illustration below. Click OK and your project will automatically open in the Slide Show Editor window.

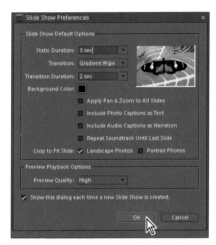

4 Click the Play button (▶) below the preview panel or press the spacebar to start the slide show. The timing of the transitions needs adjustment, and the flow could be improved by changing the display order of the four images.

Adding Music and Narration to a slide show

Sound adds another dimension to the animation of your images and complements your presentation. You can add an ambitious full-scale sound track or record a simple voice narration.

Import music from your Photoshop Elements catalog or from any folder on your hard disk. In the Slide Show Editor window, click the Add Media button above the preview pane; then, choose Audio From Organizer or Audio From Folder and navigate to your music files.

In the Add Audio dialog box, you can listen to an audio file before adding it by selecting the clip and clicking Play.

To align the pace of the slide show with the music, select Fit Slides To Audio; the length of each slide will be updated in the film strip. You can also drag the audio file to begin playing at a specific slide.

If you have a microphone attached to your computer, you can record voice narration for a selected slide. You can also attach your narration to a photo as an audio caption. You'll find the narration button in the Extras palette of the Slide Show panel. Click the button to see the recording controls.

For more information on adding music and narration to your project, please consult Photoshop Elements Help.

Refining your Slide Show

In the next steps, you'll tweak the timing of the slideshow, change the style of the transitions, and rearrange the slides to make for smoother playback.

1 From the menu bar in the Slide Show Editor window, choose Edit > Select All Transitions.

Note: The overall duration set for a slide (in this case, you specified 3 seconds as the Static Duration setting in the Slide Show Preferences) includes the time for the transition to the next slide.

For this example, this means that each slide was showing for only 1 second before the 2 second transition to the next slide started. Changing the transition duration to one second will mean that each slide will be displayed for 2 seconds before the next transition begins.

2   In the Properties panel, choose 1 sec from the Multiple Transitions menu. To change the style of the transitions, choose Fade from the Transition menu.

3   Press the spacebar to play your slideshow, which looks more fluid with the new settings applied. However, there is still room for improvement: the first image would fit much better at the end of the show.

4   Drag the first thumbnail in the filmstrip to the right and release the mouse button when the blue line appears at the end of the series. The other three images move back one position. To work with the thumbnail images in a larger panel, which can be helpful if you are producing a slideshow with more than just a few images, click the Quick Reorder button (⏏), located above the thumbnail images at the left end of the filmstrip. When you're done in the Quick Reorder panel, click Back.

Adding Extras

Once you're happy with the image order and slide transitions, you can increase the impact of the slide show and have some fun by including a few graphic elements. First, let's add a message with a speech bubble and text.

1   In the Slide Show Editor window, select the third thumbnail image in the filmstrip—the photo of the girl in orange sitting alone on the sculpture.

2   In the Extras panel to the right of the Slide Editor pane, select the graphics category, and then scroll down to Thought & Speech Bubbles. If necessary, click the triangle next to the name to see the choice of shapes. Drag the first speech bubble close to the little girl's head. *(See the illustration on the next page.)*

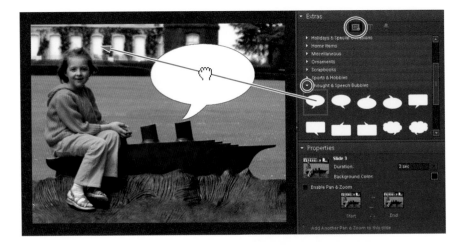

3 Position the pointer over one of the six handles around the bounding box of the graphic; when the cursor becomes a double arrow, you can drag the handle to scale the bubble or alter its shape. Try to size and shape the speech bubble as show in the illustration below. Move the pointer inside the white area and drag the graphic to move it to a new position on the image.

4 Under Extras, select the type category, and then locate the second T in the third row—a narrow black letter representing the font Myriad Pro Condensed.

5 Drag the T onto the speech bubble in the Slide Editor pane.

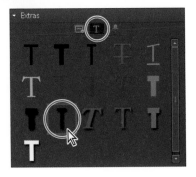

6   Choose 30 pt from the text size menu beside the font name, and then click the
    Edit Text button in the Properties panel. Type **BON VOYAGE!** in the Edit Text
    dialog box; then click OK.

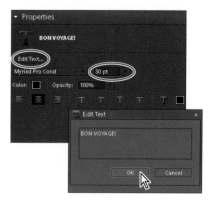

7   Drag the text box to center the message in the speech bubble.

▶ **Tip:** Explore the
Graphics options in the
Extras panel. You can
liven up your slides
with costumes, frames,
holiday and sports
motifs, or ornamental
embellishments—but
remember: in design
terms, less can be more!

8   Now the first slide has a prominent message, but there is so much more you
    could do. For example, you could add a flower behind the girl's ear and a rabbit
    or two to set off this slide with some fun touches. Collapse the Extras panel.

Adding a Zoom effect

Press the spacebar to preview the slide show once more.

The first three images are all framed quite closely around the group of girls playing, but the final image has a wider focus, bringing the whole of the sculpture and much more of the background into view. This creates the feeling that we are pulling back as a farewell to the scene.

As a finishing touch, we can capitalize on this impression by adding a zoom effect to the last slide.

1   Select the last slide in the filmstrip. In the Properties panel, click the checkbox beside Enable Pan & Zoom and change the Duration for this slide from 3 to 4 seconds, to allow a little extra time for the zoom effect.

2   Click the Start view (the thumbnail with the blue border) and drag the handles at the corners of the green frame to arrange the view for the beginning of the zoom as shown on the left below. Now click the End view (the thumbnail with the blue border) and drag the handles at the corners of the red frame to arrange the view for the end of the zoom as shown on the right. The green and red frames also appear on the thumbnail of the last slide in the filmstrip.

3 Click the Full Screen Preview button above the Slide Editor pane.

4 When you're done previewing your slide show, choose File > Save As. In the Adobe Photoshop Elements dialog box, type **4_Slideshow_work** as the file name, and then click Save.

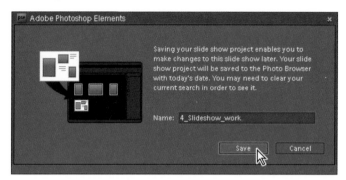

5 The Slide Show Complete dialog box appears to inform you that your project has been saved and is selected at the top of the Photo Browser. Click OK.

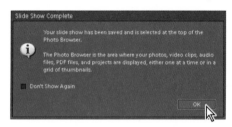

6 Note that the saved project has automatically been tagged with the Lesson 4 keyword and that it is identified as a slide show in the Photo Browser by the slide show icon in the top right corner of its thumbnail.

Done! You've completed another project and learned about some fun features along the way. There are a number of ways to share your slide show: you can publish it as a PDF or movie file, as a video CD or DVD, or in Adobe Premiere Elements for use in a video project. For more detail on sharing your presentation, please refer to Photoshop Elements Help.

Assembling a photo collage

In the next few exercises you'll create another photo project—this time, a photo collage. You can print a photo collage on your home printer, order prints on-line, or save it to your hard drive to send by e-mail or use in another digital document.

Using the Photo Projects panel

1   In the Organizer, find the items in your CIB catalog that are tagged with the Lesson 4 keyword by clicking the find box beside the Lesson 4 tag in the keyword Tags palette. Ctrl-click to select the two images of flowers, named banana_bloom.jpg and blackwater_lily.jpg.

2   Click the purple Create tab at the top of the Task pane, and then click the Photo Collage button.

3   The Editor window opens in Create mode, with thumbnails of your selected photos visible in the Project Bin at the bottom of the workspace. In the Photo Projects panel at the right, choose Letter (8.5 inch x 11 inch) from the Paper Size menu. Move the pointer over the theme swatches; a Tooltip appears with the name of each theme. Locate and select the No Theme swatch in the top row.

As you saw when you created a greeting card earlier in this lesson, a theme consists of a preset combination of background artwork and photo frame style. The background and frame style can be changed later in the Editor, but for this exercise you'll start without any theme preset, and then explore the Photo Projects panel and the Artwork library to choose your own options.

Tip: Even if you chose a layout with more or fewer images, you could change it later in the Editor, adding or removing images, repositioning them in the layout, changing their orientation, or rotating them to appear at an angle on the page.

4   Scroll about half-way down the Layout menu. As you move the pointer over each layout thumbnail a Tooltip appears with the name of that layout. Locate and select the 2 Portrait vertical layout. This is a layout preset to accommodate two portrait-format images, each on its own layer.

5   Activate the Auto-Fill With Project Bin Photos option to automatically place the two photos you selected from the Photo Browser into the selected layout template. Click Done.

6   Your images are placed in the selected template and your photo project opens in its own window in the work area. *(See the illustration below.)*

7   Choose View > Fit On Screen to see the layout displayed as large as possible.

Exploring the Artwork library

Photoshop Elements makes it quick and easy to create distinctive photo projects by providing an extensive collection of themes, backgrounds, frames, text styles, and clip-art shapes and graphics in the Artwork library. In this series of exercises, you'll choose a background for your collage and add graphics as you explore the options.

1   Click the Artwork button at the top of the Photo Projects panel. If necessary, expand the Content palette and collapse the Favorites palette, as shown in the illustration below, so that you can see as many of the sample swatches as possible.

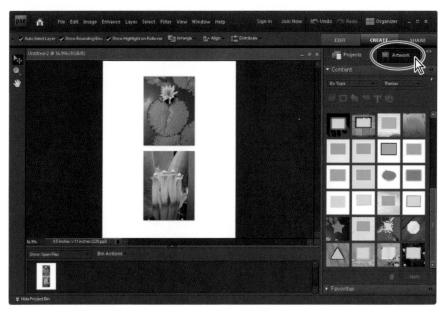

What you see displayed in the Content palette depends on the options you choose from the sorting menus above the sample swatches.

2   In the Content palette, choose By Type from the menu on the left to see the content of the artwork library sorted by functional category. In the menu on the right, the options are Backgrounds, Frames, Graphics, Shapes, Text, Themes, and Show All. Choose each option in turn and scroll the sample swatch menu to see the options available.

3   Set the content sorting menus to By Type and Show All, and then click the double arrow button at the top right of the Artwork panel to expand the Artwork panel to full screen view.

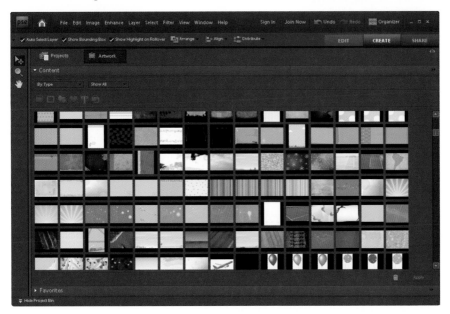

Scroll down to see the many backgrounds, frames, graphics and themes available in the library. In Show All mode, the number of choices may seem overwhelming, but

Photoshop Elements provides several options that make it easy to sort the library and locate the items you need. One of these is the Favorites palette.

4   Expand the Favorites palette at the bottom of the Artwork panel. Drag a small assortment of the items that interest you from the Content palette into the Favorites palette.

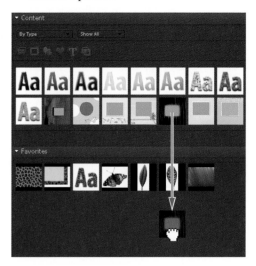

5   Click the double arrow button at the top right of the Artwork panel to collapse the Artwork panel and return to the to full Create workspace.

6   For now, collapse the Favorites palette once more so that you can see as much of the Content palette as possible.

Adding a background

In this exercise you'll choose a background from the Content palette and add it to your photo collage.

1   In the Content palette, open the sorting menu on the left. Note the options in the menu; the content in the Artwork library has been tagged with keywords that allow you to search it intuitively by activity, mood, season, and many other associations. For now, choose By Color. From the other sorting menu, choose Green.

The Content palette now displays all the items in the artwork library that are tagged with the key-word "green". This is reflected by the active state of all the Content Filter buttons above the sample

swatches. From left to right, these six buttons filter the items in the Content palette for Backgrounds, Frames, Graphics, Shapes, Text Effects, and Themes, providing another means for finding what you want in the artwork library.

2 Starting from the Filter For Themes button at the right, click to disable each of the content filters except Filter For Backgrounds. The Content palette now displays only the backgrounds in the Artwork library that are tagged with the keyword "green". Scroll down in the sample swatches menu to locate the background "Leaves 02". Click to select the Leaves 02 thumbnail, and then click Apply. Alternatively, simply double-click the Leaves 02 thumbnail to apply the background.

▶ **Tip:** If you had started the process of creating your photo collage by choosing a theme that included a preset background, you could use the same technique to change it.

The new background appears behind the photos in your photo collage. The background layer is selected and the background image is surrounded by a bounding box. The bounding box shows that the image is considerably wider than your photo collage page.

3 Choose View > Zoom Out. Move the pointer close to one of the handles around the bounding box for the background. When the curved double arrow cursor appears, drag to rotate the background image 90° counter-clockwise. Hold down the Shift key as you drag to constrain the rotation to 15° increments.

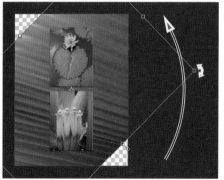

4 Drag the background image up and to the left to align the lower right corner of the bounding box with the lower right corner of the photo collage page. The bounding box snaps to the page edges to assist you in placing it precisely.

5 Click the Commit button () at the bottom of the page preview to commit the changes.

6 Choose Select > Deselect Layers. Click the Hide Project Bin button in the lower left corner of the workspace, and then choose View > Fit On Screen.

7 Click inside the photo of the water lily, and then click one of the corner handles on its bounding box. Width (W) and height (H) values appear in the bar above the work area. Ensure that the Constrain Proportions option is activated, and then double-click or swipe to select the 100% value in the width text box. Type **120**, and press the Enter key on your keyboard. The new scaling value is applied to the height box and the water lily image is scaled proportionately. Click the Commit button to accept the change.

8 Repeat step 7 for the photo of the banana flowers. Click the Commit button to accept the change, and then choose Select > Deselect Layers.

Adding graphics

1 Choose the option By Word from the sorting menu in the Content palette and type **leaf** in the text box beside it. Click to activate the Filter For Graphics button and make sure that all the other content filters that are disabled.

2 Drag Leaf 04, Leaf 08, and Leaf 11 onto your Photo collage page as shown in the illustration below: each overlapping the last, along the edge of the photograph of the water lily.

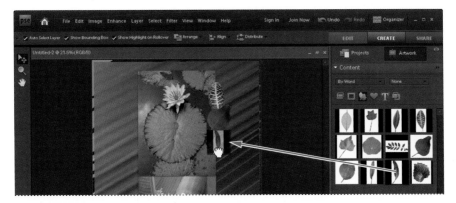

3 Choose Select > Deselect Layers.

Working with layers

Each element in your photo collage occupies its own layer. The background is at the bottom with the other images overlaid in successive layers in the order in which they were added to the project. The two photographs from the Organizer were added in the order of their capture date and time, so that the oldest is on the layer directly above the background.

● **Note:** Backgrounds chosen from the Artwork library will always appear on the bottom layer, even when they are added to the layout after the photographs—as was the case in this project. You can use your own image as a background by converting its layer.

1 Click the yellow Edit button above the Artwork panel. Collapse the Effects palette and expand the Layers palette if necessary so that you can see all the layers in your photo collage project.

Layers are like transparent overlays on which you can paint or place photos, artwork, vector graphics or text. The checkerboard grid areas in the layer thumbnails represent the transparent parts of the layers through which you can see the layers below.

2 Experiment by clicking the eye icons beside the layer thumbnails to hide and show each layer in turn.

3 Click the layer names to select each layer in turn. The selected layer is highlighted in the Layers palette and its contents are surrounded by a bounding box in the editor pane to indicate their selected state.

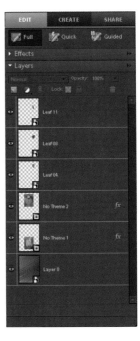

● **Note:** As well as photos and graphics from the artwork library layers can contain text, fills, gradients, or even saved photo projects. You can apply filters or special effects to any layer and specify the way those effects will affect other layers in the project. You can specify a layer's opacity and blending mode and create adjustment layers that allow you to tune the images on the layer or layers below.

4   Click the top layer "Leaf 11" (the last layer added) to select it. Use the corner handles of the bounding box surrounding the leaf to rotate and scale it, and then click the image and drag to position it on the page as shown in the illustration below. Click the Commit button to commit the changes.

5   Click the third layer from the top "Leaf 04" and use the same techniques to achieve the result shown in the next illustration; then, click the Commit button.

6 Ctrl-click to select both of the layers you just edited, and then click the Link Layers button (⬚) just above the top layer in the Layers palette. Both layers are marked with the Linked Layer icon. Drag the Leaf 04 layer down over the border between the background layer, Layer 0, and the layer above it, No Theme 1, and release the mouse button when the border is highlighted. The linked layers move to the second and third positions and the other layers move up to accommodate them.

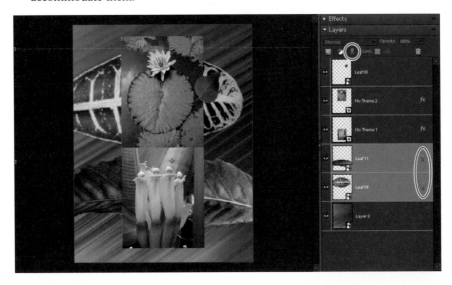

7 Select each of the two linked layers in turn and change their opacity to 40%, either by using the Opacity slider at the top of the Layers palette or by typing the new value directly into the Opacity text box and pressing Enter on your keyboard.

8 Double-click the layer name of each of the layers No Theme 1 and No Theme 2 in turn and type **banana bloom** and **blackwater lily** respectively to rename the layers.

9 Select each of the top three layers in turn and drag the images to position them as shown in the illustration on the next page. You will also need to rotate the image Leaf 08 and make it slightly larger.

● **Note:** For more detailed information about understanding and working with layers, please refer to Photoshop Elements Help.

Applying effects

● **Note:** For more detailed information about applying effects and working with layer styles, refer to Photoshop Elements Help.

As a finishing touch you can apply a drop shadow effect to the top three layers.

1   Select the layer "banana bloom."

2   Expand the Effects palette, click the Layer Styles button (the second button from the left at the top of the Effects palette), and choose Drop Shadows from the effects menu.

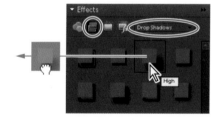

3   Locate the "High" drop shadow style. Simply drag the sample swatch from the Effects palette and drop it onto the photo of the banana flower.

4   In the Layers palette, double-click the *fx* icon at the right of the banana bloom layer. In the Style Settings dialog box, set the Lighting Angle to 135° and the Size, Distance, and Opacity values to 50, 60, and 60 respectively. Click OK.

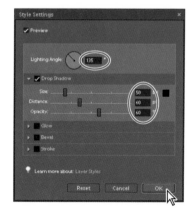

5   Choose Layer > Layer Style > Copy Layer Style; then, select the layer "blackwater lily" in the Layers palette and choose Layer > Layer Style > Paste Layer Style.

6 In the Layers palette, double-click the *fx* icon at the right of the banana bloom layer. In the Style Settings dialog box, set the Lighting Angle to 135° and the Size, Distance, and Opacity values to 70, 100, and 55 respectively. These settings will help with the illusion that the leaf is higher above the background than the two photographs. Click OK, and then choose Select > Deselect Layers.

7 Save your photo collage to your My CIB Work folder.

Congratulations! You've completed the last project in this lesson. You've learned about using the preset Theme and Layout templates, explored the Artwork library, and become familiar with a variety of methods for locating the items you need. You've also learned the basics of working with layers and applying layer styles. Before you move on to the next lesson, "Printing, Sharing, and Exporting," take a moment to refresh your new skills by reading through the review on the next page.

Review questions

1   How do you begin a new project such as a greeting card, photo collage, or slide show?

2   How do you scale and reposition a photo in a photo project?

3   How do you change the order of slides in a slide show?

4   How can you find the items you want amongst all the choices in the Artwork library?

5   What are layers, how do they work, and how do you work with them?

Review answers

1   To create a project in the Organizer, select a project option in the Create panel of the Task pane by clicking one of the project buttons or choosing from the More Options menu. The Projects panel offers prompts to guide you through choosing theme and layout presets and the Artwork panel provides access to frames, graphics and more.

2   Once you've selected and applied a theme and a layout, an edit window opens with a bounding box around the photo. You can scale or rotate the photo by dragging the bounding box handles and move it on the page by dragging the image itself. To scale, rotate, or move a photo within its own frame you need to double-click the image before using the same techniques, so that the changes affect the photo independently and are not applied to the photo and its frame together.

3   You can change the order of slides in a slideshow by dragging them to new positions in the filmstrip below the Slide Editor pane. When you are working on a slideshow with too many slides to display at a convenient size in the filmstrip, click the Quick Reorder button located above the slide thumbnails to open the Quick Reorder window, where there is plenty of room to display, select, and manipulate a large number of slides.

4   You can sort and search the items in the Artwork library by using the menus and buttons at the top of the Content palette. From the first menu you can choose options to sort the content by type, activity, mood, season, color, keywords and other attributes. Once you have set up the first menu, you use the other menu to narrow the search—to specify which type, color, or mood you want. Use the Filter buttons to limit the search results to display only backgrounds, frames, graphics, shapes, text styles, or themes with the attributes you've specified. Use the favorites palette to assemble a collection of the items you're most likely to use, rather than looking through the entire library every time you want to add an artwork item to a project.

5 Layers are like transparent overlays on which you can paint or place photos, artwork, or text. Each element in a photo project occupies its own layer—the background is at the bottom and the other elements are overlaid in the order in which they are added to the project. Photos from the Project Bin are placed in the order of their capture date, so that the oldest is on the lowest layer. You work with layers in the Layers Palette, where you can toggle their visibility and change their order. The checkerboard grid areas in the layer thumbnails represent the transparent parts of the layers through which you can see the layers below.

5 PRINTING, SHARING, AND EXPORTING

Lesson Overview

In previous lessons you imported photos, learned how to organize and search your catalog, and created projects to showcase your images. Now you'll learn how you can output your images and creations to share them with family, friends, or the world at large:

- Printing at home and ordering prints online

- Sharing photos by e-mail and Photo Mail

- Setting up a Quick Share flow

- Signing up for a Photoshop.com account

- Creating your own Online Album

- Using an online sharing service

- Burning your photos and projects to CD or DVD

- Exporting images for use on the Web

 You'll probably need between one and two hours to complete this lesson.

Now that you've learned how to find your way around the Photoshop Elements workspace, how to organize and find the photos and other media that you've brought into your catalog, and how to create photo projects and digital presentations, you're ready to share your images and creations with the world as printed output, by e-mail, or online.

Getting started

Note: Before you start working on this lesson, make sure that you've installed the software on your computer from the application CD (see the Photoshop Elements 7 documentation) and that you have correctly copied the Lessons folder from the CD in the back of this book onto your computer's hard disk (see "Copying the Classroom in a Book files" on page 2).

If you have already created a catalog for your own photos you can use that for the purposes of this exercise; otherwise, use the CIB Catalog you created at the start of the book. To open the catalog you wish to use, follow these steps:

1   Start Photoshop Elements. In the Welcome Screen, click Organize in the row of shortcut buttons across the top of the Welcome Screen.

2   The name of the currently active catalog is displayed in the lower left corner of the Organizer window. If the catalog you plan to use for this lesson is already open you can skip to the next section, "About printing." If the catalog you want is not already open, continue to step 3.

3   Choose File > Catalog.

4   In the Catalog Manager dialog box, select the catalog of your choice in the Catalogs list, and then click Open.

If you do not see the CIB Catalog file listed, review "Getting Started," the first chapter in this book. See "Copying the Lessons files from the CD" on page 2, and "Creating a catalog" on page 3.

About printing

Photoshop Elements offers several options for printing your photos or Photo Projects, such as photo albums, greeting cards, and calendars. You can order professional prints from online providers through Adobe Photoshop Services, or use your home printer. You can print your photos individually, as contact sheets (thumbnails of a selection of photos arranged in a grid layout), picture packages (one or more photos repeated at a variety of sizes on the same page), or print photo labels on commercially available label paper.

Printing individual photos

The Organizer helps you minimize wastage of expensive photographic paper by giving you the option of printing either single or multiple images on the same page, arranged on the page in the sizes you want.

1   In the Organizer, select the thumbnails of the image or images you wish to print. Ctrl-click to select more than one image.

2   Choose File > Print.

3   In the Print Photos dialog box, specify the following settings:

- Choose a printer from the Select Printer menu.

- Choose Individual Prints from the Select Type Of Print menu.

- From the Select Print Size And Options menu, choose 3.5" x 5." If you're using the lesson files in the CIB Catalog for this exercise, you may see a warning about print resolution, as some of the sample files are provided at low resolution. Click OK to dismiss this warning.

- If the One Photo Per Page option is active, click the checkbox to disable it.

4 (Optional) Do any of the following:

- Select one of the thumbnails in the menu on the left side of the dialog box, and then click the Remove button (➖) below the thumbnails to remove that image from the selection to be printed.

- Click the Add button (➕) under the column of thumbnails. Activate the Entire Catalog option, and then click the check box beside any image you'd like to add to the selection to be printed. Click Done.

- If you have selected more pictures than will fit on one page, you can see the other pages by clicking the arrows buttons below the Print Preview.

Note: You can only print images from Photoshop Elements if they are part of the currently active catalog. If you want to add pictures to the printing batch that are not in the currently active catalog, you must first import them using one of the methods described in chapters 1, 2 and 3.

5 Do one of the following:

- If you'd prefer to save your ink and paper for your own prints, click Cancel to close the dialog box without printing.

- If you'd like to go ahead and try printing with these sample images, click Print.

Printing a contact sheet

Contact sheets make it easy to assess a multiple selection of images by printing them at thumbnail size, arranged on the same page in a grid layout.

● **Note:** If you choose the Print command without first selecting any images, Photoshop Elements will ask if you want to print all the images currently visible in the Photo Browser.

1 In the Photo Browser, select the photos you'd like to see printed on a contact sheet. If you wish to select a consecutive series of thumbnails, click the first image in the series, and then Shift-click the last; the images in-between will be selected. If you wish to select non-consecutive images, Ctrl-click their thumbnails.

2 Choose File > Print.

3 In the Print Photos dialog box, choose a printer from the Select Printer menu.

4 Choose Contact Sheet from the Select Type Of Print menu. By default, the contact sheet layout includes all the photos in the thumbnail menu column at the left of the Print Photos dialog box. To remove a photo from the contact sheet, select its thumbnail in the menu and click the Remove button.

5 You can alter the contact sheet layout by changing the number of columns under Select A Layout. Click the arrow buttons beside the Columns number or type a number between 1 and 9 in the text box.

The thumbnail size and number of rows are adjusted according to your choice for the number of columns. If the number of photos selected for printing exceeds the capacity of a single page, more pages will be added to accommodate them.

● **Note:** Some words in the text label may be truncated, depending on the page setup and column layout.

6 To print image information labels below each image on the contact sheet, activate any or all of the Text Label options:

- Date, to print the capture date recorded in the images' metadata.

- Caption, to print any caption text embedded in the file's metadata.

- Filename, to print the filename for each photo.

- Page Numbers, to print a page number at the bottom of each page if there are more images than will fit on a single page for the specified column layout.

7 Click Print or Cancel.

Printing a Picture Package

In a Picture Package layout you can print one or more photos repeated at a variety of sizes on the same page. You can choose from a variety of layout options with an assortment of image sizes to customize your picture package print.

1 Select one or more pictures from the browser, and then choose File > Print.

2 In the Print Photos dialog box, choose a printer from the Select Printer menu.

3 Choose Picture Package from the Select Type Of Print menu. If a Printing Warning dialog box cautioning against enlarging pictures appears, click OK. For this exercise you'll print multiple images at smaller sizes.

4 Choose a layout from the Select A Layout menu, and activate the Fill Page With First Photo option. This will Result in a printed page with a single photo repeated at a variety of sizes, according to the layout you have chosen. If you selected more than one photo in the Photo Browser, a separate Print Package page will be printed for each photo selected; you can see the previews for each page by clicking the page navigation buttons below the print preview.

5 (Optional) Choose Icicles (or another border of your preference) from the Select A Frame menu. You can select only one border style per picture package print.

● **Note:** The options available in the Picture Package Layout menu depend on the paper size specified in the page setup or printer preferences. To change the paper size, click either the Page Setup button at the lower left of the Print Photos dialog box or the Show Printer Preferences button (▤) to the right of the printer menu and select your preferred paper size. Depending on your printer, you may need to look for the paper size options in the Advanced preferences settings.

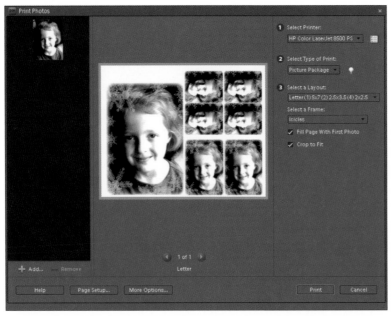

The images in a Picture Package layout are oriented to produce the optimum coverage of the printable area for the layout you have chosen. This feature is automatic and cannot be overridden. You cannot manually rotate the images in a picture package layout.

6 If your photo is of non-standard proportions, the Crop To Fit option may fit the multiple images more closely to the layout and fill the printable area better.

7 (Optional) To add more photos from your catalog to the picture package, click the Add button, select the photos you want in the Add Photos dialog box, and then click Done. The selected photos are added to the thumbnails column. To replace a photo in the layout with another, drag an image from the thumbnails menu column over an image in the print preview and release the mouse button.

8 Click Print or Cancel.

Ordering professionally printed photos online

● **Note:** You need an active Internet connection to order prints online.

If you want high quality prints of your photos—for your own enjoyment or to share with others—you can order professionally printed photos online. In this exercise you will learn how to order individual prints from the Organizer (a service available in the US, Canada, and Japan).

1 In the Organizer, select one or more pictures that you would like to have printed professionally.

2 If the Quick Share palette is not already open in the Organizer palette bin, choose Window > Quick Share to open it.

3 Drag the selected photos from the Browser view onto the *Drag photos here to create an order* target in the Quick Share palette.

The New Order Prints Recipient dialog box appears. *(See the illustration on the next page.)*

4 In the New Order Prints Recipient dialog box, enter all the required information for the person who is to receive the printed photos. For this exercise, you can enter your own name, address, and home phone number, and then click the checkbox beside This Is My Home Address. If you would prefer to import contact information from an existing contact book entry, click the Choose Existing Contact button, select a contact from the list, and then click OK.

5 Click OK to close the New Order Prints Recipient dialog box.

A new target entry appears in the Quick Share palette. If you clicked the This Is My Home Address check box in the New Order Prints Recipient dialog box in step 4, you'll see a home icon next to the new target entry. The number in brackets next to the target name indicates the number of photos selected for this print order.

6 In the Quick Share palette, double-click the new target entry or click the View Photos In [Recipient's Name] button () above the list of recipients in the Quick Share panel to open the Order Prints for [Recipient's Name] dialog box. *(See the illustration on the next page.)* Do any of the following:

- Use the slider to increase or decrease the size of the thumbnail images.

- Select one or more photos and click Remove Selected Photo(s) to remove the selected photos from the current order.

- Click Remove All to remove all photos from the current order.

7 When you're done, click Close to close the dialog box without confirming the order.

8 (Optional) Add additional photos to the order by dragging thumbnails from the Photo Browser onto the same target entry in the Quick Share palette.

9 In the Quick Share palette, click the Order button on the right side of the target entry. The Welcome To Adobe Photoshop Services dialog box appears.

10 In the Welcome To Adobe Photoshop Services dialog box, do one of the following:

- If you are already an Ofoto or EasyShare Gallery member, enter your e-mail address and password and click Next to log in.

- If you are not an Ofoto or EasyShare Gallery member, click Join Now.

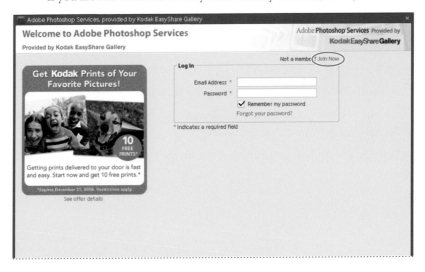

11 If you chose Joint Now in the previous step, create a new account by entering your first name, e-mail address, and a password of at least six characters. If you agree with the Terms of Service click the respective check box under Create Account, and then click Next.

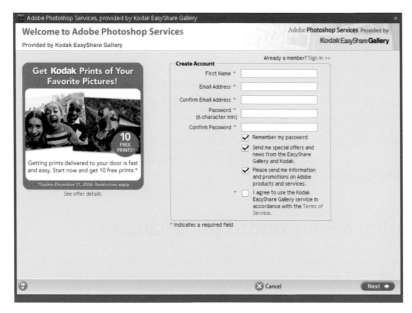

12 In the Review Order dialog box, do any of the following:

- Click Change Quantities Or Sizes for any of the photos in your order.

- Click Remove under a thumbnail image in the list on the left side of the dialog box to remove that print from your order.

- Review the Order Summary and Delivery Information.

13 When you're done reviewing your order, click Checkout.

14 If you wished to proceed with your order, you would now provide your credit card details in the Billing Information dialog box and review the information under Billing Address and Order Summary. Clicking Place Order would initiate the processing of your order and your credit card would be charged. For this exercise, click Cancel unless you want to go ahead and order prints. A dialog box appears to ask if you want to stop using this service. Click OK.

15 Right-click the target entry in the Quick Share palette and choose Cancel Order from the context menu. Click Yes in the alert dialog box to confirm the cancellation of the order.

Creating a Photoshop.com account

Note: At this stage, Photoshop.com services are available only to Photoshop Elements users in the United States.

U.S.-based users of Photoshop Elements users can sign up for a free Photoshop.com membership and take advantage of exciting new Adobe-hosted Web-based services that extend the capabilities of Photoshop Elements.

Photoshop.com offers several different membership levels. The Basic membership is free and gives you your own storage space, where you can not only share and show-case your images but also access your photos and videos anytime and anywhere that you can connect to the internet. You can also use your Photoshop.com storage space to back up your Photoshop Elements albums and effortlessly safeguard your photos and creations.

Basic membership also gives you access to the Photoshop.com Inspiration Browser, with regularly updated downloadable content such as project templates, and extras such as backgrounds, frames, graphics, and more to keep your projects fresh and appealing. The Inspiration Browser also offers integrated tutorials with tips and tricks related to whatever you're currently working on, providing a powerful way to advance your skill set and helping you make the most out of your photos and creations.

You can upgrade your membership to the Premium level if you need more storage space or if you wish to access more of the special content.

Signing up from the Welcome screen

1 Start Photoshop Elements.

2 In the Welcome screen, click Join Now and follow the instructions to create your Adobe ID. An e-mail message confirms the creation of your account.

3 Follow the instructions in the e-mail to activate your account.

Signing up from the Organizer or Editor

1 In either the Organizer or Editor, click the Join Now link in the menu bar.

● **Note:** You don't have to open a Photoshop.com membership account when the Welcome screen appears. You can open an account anytime you want. Links for joining and signing in are conveniently located throughout the Photoshop Elements workspace.

2 Fill out your personal details in the Photoshop.com Membership dialog box, and then click Create Account.

Signing in to your Photoshop.com account

1 Make sure, your computer is connected to the Internet, and then start Adobe Photoshop Elements.

2 In the Welcome screen, enter your Adobe ID and password, and click Sign In.

If you didn't sign in at the Welcome screen, you can always click the Sign In link at the top of either the Organizer or Editor windows.

About sharing

In Lesson 1 you learned how to use the E-mail Attachments feature to create copies of your photos optimized as e-mail attachments (see "Sharing photos in e-mail" on page 25). Another option is to use the Photo Mail feature, which embeds your photos in the body of an e-mail within a colorful custom layout. To share items other than photos—such as slide shows, photo collages, or flipbooks—you are offered a choice of output options during the creation process.

Using Photo Mail

1 In the Organizer, select one or more photos in the Photo Browser and click the Photo Mail button in the Share panel of the Task pane.

If this is the first time you have accessed an e-mail feature in Photoshop Elements you will be presented with the E-mail dialog box. Choose your e-mail service from the menu, enter your name and e-mail address, and then click Continue. You can review or change your settings later by choosing Edit > Preferences > Sharing.

2   Activate the Include Captions option beside Items, and then click Next.

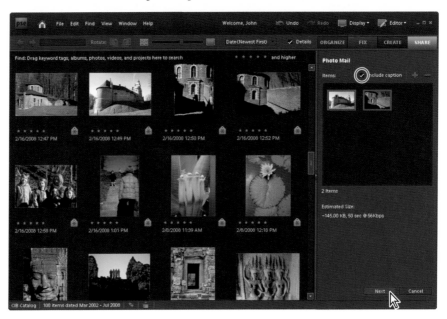

3   In the Message text box, delete the default text "Here are the photos…" and type a message of your own.

4   Select a recipient from the list in the Select Recipients pane. (If you didn't work through Lesson 1 and your recipient list is still empty, click the Edit Contact Book button (📖) and create a new entry in the Contact Book dialog box.

5   Click Next. The Stationery & Layouts Wizard dialog box appears.

6   In the Stationery & Layouts Wizard dialog box, click on each category in the list at the left of the dialog box to see the range of designs available. (See the illustration on the next page.) Select a stationery style appropriate to your selected photos. A preview of your photo e-mail will appear on the right side of the dialog box.

7   Click Next Step.

8   Customize the layout by choosing from the Photo Size and Layout options. Choose a font from the menu under Text. Click the color swatch beside the font menu and choose a text color from the color palette. To edit the message text, click the message in the preview to make it active, and then edit the text as you would usually do. Use the same technique to edit the caption text.

9   Click Next.

Photoshop Elements opens your default e-mail application and creates an e-mail message with your design embedded in the body of the message. You can send Photo Mail through Outlook Express, Outlook, or Adobe E-mail Service.

10 Switch back to the Photoshop Elements Organizer.

Creating a Quick Share Flow

If you find yourself sending the same kind of documents to the same group of people on a regular basis, then setting up a Quick Share Flow can help you automate the process, minimizing your effort considerably. For example, if you frequently (or even only occasionally) send your family e-mail messages with vacation or holiday season photos, you need only set up such information as the mailing list and your preferred image size for the attachments once, and then reuse these settings by simply dropping photos on the Quick Share target.

While you can create a new print order by clicking the New button in the Quick Share palette, you can only create a Quick Share Flow only from within the respective workflow. In the following steps you will set up a Quick Share Flow to send photos as e-mail attachments to a specified group of recipients.

1 Select several photos in the Photo Browser and click the Share tab in the Task pane; then, click the E-mail Attachments button.

2 From the Maximum Photo Size menu, select Very Small (320 x 240 px), which will result in a relatively small file size for an e-mail with several images attached. Use the Quality slider to adjust the image quality, remembering that a higher quality setting will equate to a longer download time.

Photoshop Elements will calculate the file size and display the estimated download time for a typical dial-up modem at 56 Kbps. When you're satisfied with the settings, click Next.

3   In the Message text box, delete the default "Here are the photos...." text and type a message of your own.

4   Choose the recipients you wish to include in this Quick Share target from the Recipients list by clicking the check boxes beside their names.

5   Under Save As Quick Share Flow?, click the radio button for Yes. Type a descriptive name for this quick share target, and then click Next.

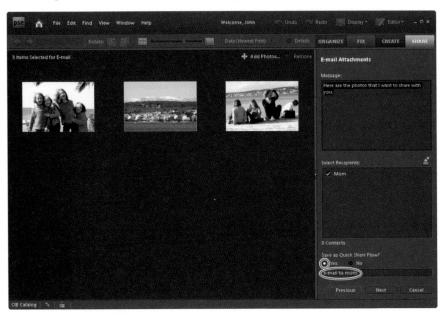

Your default e-mail application opens and creates an e-mail message with the selected photos attached at the specified image size and quality. You can still edit the message and subject line if you wish. If you intend to send this e-mail, first make sure that you are connected to the Internet, and then click Send; otherwise, close the message without saving it.

6   Switch back to the Photoshop Elements Organizer. You'll notice the new e-mail attachments Quick Share target in the Quick Share palette. Select one or more photos in the Photo Browser; then, drag and drop your selection onto the new target.

7 (Optional). Drag and drop additional photos onto the Quick Share target. The number in brackets next to the target name indicates the number of photos selected for this Quick Share target.

8 When you're done, click the E-mail button in the Quick Share target.

With just one click your default e-mail application opens and creates an e-mail message with the selected photos attached at the specified image size and quality, ready to be sent.

9 Close your e-mail application, and then switch back to the Photoshop Elements Organizer.

Creating an Online Album

● **Note:** At this stage, Photoshop.com membership will be available to users in the United States only. Photoshop Elements users outside the United States will continue to share their Albums to third party sharing services via Photoshop Showcase.

 Another way to share and showcase your photos is by creating an Online album. You can choose from a variety of interactive layout templates that are optimized for viewing photos on the Web. Photoshop Elements guides you through the process of adding and arranging photos, applying templates, and sharing your files.

1 In the Organizer, choose View > Show File Names, if necessary, to see the file names below the thumbnails. Type **jungle** in the Text Search box at the upper left of the workspace, and then press Enter on your keyboard to find the images for this exercise. The Photo Browser shows 12 photos named "5_jungle_ruins_1.jpg" to "5_jungle_ruins_12.jpg."

2 In the Image Browser, Ctrl-click to select the top 4 photos.

3 Click the Share tab at the top of the Tasks pane, and then click the Online Album button. The 4 selected photos are added to the album and their thumbnails are displayed in the Items pane.

4 In the Album Details panel, type **Jungle Ruins** in the Album Name text box.

Adding photos to your Online Album

1 In the Photo Browser, Ctrl-click to select the next 4 photos, and then click the Add Items Selected In Photo Browser button (✚) above the Items pane. The selected photos are added to the album and appear in the Items pane.

2 Ctrl-click to select the last 4 images in the Photo Browser and drag them into the Items pane. All 12 photos are now included in the Jungle Ruins album.

To add a photo to the album, select a thumbnail in the Photo Browser and click the Add Items Selected In Photo Browser button (✚) above the Items pane as shown in the illustration on the left. To remove an image from the album, select a thumbnail in the Items pane and click the Remove Selected Items button (➖) above the Items pane as shown in the illustration on the right.

Changing the order of photos in an Online Album

To change the order in which the photos will be displayed, simply drag the thumbnails to rearrange them in the Items pane. If you wish, you can arrange them in the order in which they were intended to be displayed by referring to the numbering in their file names.

1   When you're satisfied with the order of the images, click Share. The 12 photos are displayed in an animated Online Album preview, using the default template.

2   Click any of the image thumbnails across the bottom of the preview to see an enlarged view of that image. Click the navigation buttons above the enlarged photo to cycle through the images in the album.

3   Click the Change Template button to see the options available. You can experiment with the templates later, but for now leave the template as it is. Click Cancel.

Choosing a sharing option for your Online Album

1   Click the radio button beside one of the options under Share To:

   •   Choose Photoshop.com if you are a US resident and have already signed up for Photoshop.com membership.

   •   Choose Export To CD/DVD if you wish to make a backup of your album, if you don't have access to an online sharing service, or if you wish to share your album with someone who does not have an internet connection.

   •   Choose Export To FTP if you plan to upload your album to a web server.

2   Click Next.

3   Type **Angkor** as the on-screen title for your online album, type **Cambodia** for the subtitle, and then click Next.

4   Depending on your choice of sharing option, do one of the following:

- If you chose Export To CD/DVD, choose a destination drive from the menu, type a name for the disc, and then click Export. When the process is complete, skip the rest of the steps in this exercise and move on to the next section, "Sharing an existing album."

- If you chose Export To FTP, type the server name for your web server, your user name and password for that server, and a folder name for the folder into which you want to upload your files, and then click Export. When the process is complete, skip the rest of the steps in this exercise and move on to the next section, "Sharing an existing album."

- If you chose Export To Photoshop.com, you can move on to step 5.

5 Click a radio button to specify whether you wish to share your album publicly for everyone to see or privately with only those friends to whom you choose to send an invitation.

6 Type a message to be e-mailed with your invitation in the Message text box.

7 Under Send E-mail To, select those contacts to whom you wish to e-mail an invitation by clicking the checkboxes beside their names in the list.

8 Specify whether you wish to allow viewers to download photos or order prints, and then click Share.

Photoshop Elements informs you that the album is now being shared and will be available online as soon as the upload is complete.

9 Return to the Organizer. In in the Albums palette, the Jungle Ruins album is marked with an Online Album icon (icon). Click the entry for the new online album. The Stop Sharing button (icon) to the right of its name indicates that the Jungle Ruins album is currently being shared.

Sharing an existing album online

If you have a Photoshop.com account it's easy to convert any Photoshop Elements album into an Online Album.

1 In the Organizer, click Show All above the Photo Browser pane.

Note: This feature is currently only available to Photoshop Elements users in the US who have signed up for Photoshop.com membership.

2   In the Keyword Tags panel, click the Find box beside the Lesson 1 tag.

3   Select the four images of New York buildings.

4   Click the Create New Album Or Album Group button (✚) at the top of the Albums palette and choose New Album from the menu.

5   In the Album Details dialog box, type **New York** as the name for the new album, click the checkbox to disable the Backup/Synchronize option, and then click Done.

The entry for the new album in the Albums palette is marked with the standard Album icon (▪). In the Image Browser, the thumbnails if the images included the new album are also marked.

6   In the Albums palette, click the entry for the New York album, and then click the Share button (▣) to the right of the album name.

7   The Album Details dialog box appears. You can change the template if you wish, and follow steps 5, 6, and 7 from the previous exercise to specify sharing options and invite your friends to view your album by e-mail.

8   Specify whether you wish to allow viewers to download photos or order prints, and then click Share.

9   Return to the Organizer. In in the Albums palette, the New York album is now marked with an Online Album icon (▣). Click the entry for the new online album. The Stop Sharing button (◉) to the right of its name indicates that the New York album is currently being shared.

Backing up and synchronizing albums

● **Note:** This feature is currently only available to Photoshop Elements users in the US who have signed up for Photoshop.com membership.

If you have signed up for Photoshop.com membership, you can choose to synchronize the files in your Photoshop Elements catalog and your Photoshop.com account, making your photos and videos available to you from any web browser through Photoshop.com and Photoshop Express.

You can manage your media from any web browser: add, delete, edit, or re-organize items at home or on the road. Any changes you make online will be synchronized back to Photoshop Elements on your desktop. Don't worry; the Synchronization feature will not overwrite anything on your base computer—Photoshop Elements creates a Version Set on your computer, so you will still have the original. If you delete something online, a copy is kept on your computer unless you confirm that you really do want it deleted from your Photoshop Elements Catalog.

Only Albums can be backed up and synchronized in this way. If you wish to protect photos from your catalog you must first place them in an album.

1   In the Organizer, click Show All above the Photo Browser pane.

2   In the Keyword Tags panel, click the Find box beside the Lesson 1 tag.

3   Select the six images of flowers.

4   Click the Create New Album Or Album Group button (➕) at the top of the Albums palette and choose New Album from the menu.

5   In the Album Details dialog box, type **Flowers** as the name for the new album, make sure that the Backup/Synchronize option is activated, and then click Done.

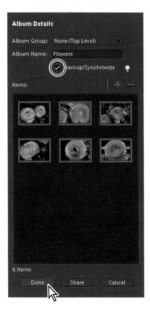

The entry for the new album in the Albums palette is marked with the Synchronized Album icon (⬛). The Share button (⬛) to the right of the album name indicates that the album is not being shared.

▶ **Tip:** You can also access the Backup/ Synchronization Preferences by choosing Edit > Preferences > Backup/ Synchronization.

6   Click the entry for the Flowers album, and then click the Backup/ Synchronization Preferences button (⬛) at the top of the Albums palette.

The Backup/Synchronization Preferences dialog box opens.

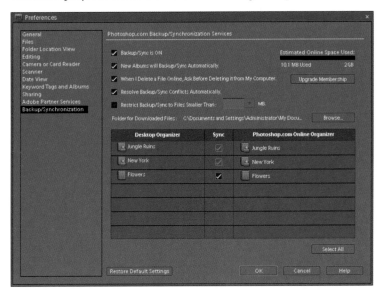

7   Notice the settings in the Backup/Synchronization Preferences:

•   Backup/Synchronization is active and new albums are set to backup and synchronize by default.

•   By default, when you delete a file online Photoshop Elements will ask before deleting it from your computer.

•   You can choose whether conflicts between the data in your catalog and your backed-up data online will be resolved automatically, or whether you wish to control which data is changed, and you can restrict backup to exclude large (time and CPU intensive) files.

There is also a status bar showing how much online space you've used, a button for upgrading your Photoshop.com membership, and a setting to specify a folder for downloads.

8   Now look at the table below the preferences settings. Synchronization is enabled for all three albums. The Sync checkboxes for the Jungle Ruins and New York albums are greyed out—the settings cannot be changed because both are Online Albums that are currently shared and therefore enabled for synchronization by default. To disable synchronization for an Online Album, you first need to stop sharing that album.

9   Click OK to close the Backup/Synchronization Preferences dialog box.

You can also set Backup/Synchronization preferences from the Welcome Screen (once you log in to your Photoshop Express account) and even from within Photoshop.com's Photoshop Express. For more detailed information on backup and synchronization options, please refer to Photoshop Elements Help.

Using an online sharing service

From within Photoshop Elements you can use Adobe Photoshop Services to upload your images and creations to online sharing service providers. You can also use these services to download photos.

1   In the Organizer, select the photos you wish to share from the Photo Browser.

2   In the Share panel of the Task pane, click the More Options button, and then choose Share With Kodak Easyshare Gallery from the menu to access the Kodak® EasyShare Gallery service.

3   If the Welcome to Adobe Photoshop Services dialog box appears, do one of the following:

   •   If you are already an Ofoto or EasyShare Gallery member, click Sign in, and then use the e-mail address and password associated with your existing online account to sign in.

   •   Create a new account by entering your first name, e-mail address, and a password of at least six characters. If you agree with the Terms of Service, select the respective check box under Create Account, and then click Next.

● **Note:** If you are still signed in to Adobe Photoshop Services from the previous exercise, you don't need to sign in again. Just click Next to continue.

4 In the Share Online dialog box, click Add New Address.

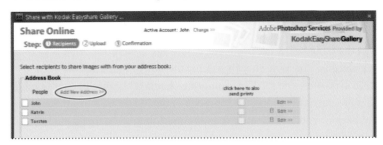

5 In the Add Address dialog box, complete the address information for the person with whom you wish to share your photos, and then click Next.

6 In the Share Online dialog box, select the newly added address book check box. Under Message, type **Photos** in the subject field and **Enjoy!** in the message field; then, click Next and your photos will be uploaded.

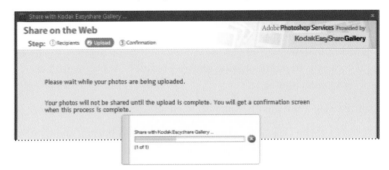

7 In the Share Online Confirmation dialog box, click Done. Alternatively, if you wish to purchase prints of your photos click Order Prints, and then follow the on-screen directions.

An e-mail will be sent to the recipient you specified in step 6, containing a Web link to the photos which can be viewed as an online slide show.

About exporting

Even though Photoshop Elements offers a variety of ways to share your photos and creations, there may be situations where you wish to export copies of your files for use in another application. In the Organizer, you can move or copy your files to CD or DVD. In the Editor, you can export you photos optimized for use in a web page design application.

Burning photos to CD or DVD

Choose File > Make A CD/DVD in the Organizer to copy a set of photos to a CD or DVD. You might do this in order to share a large number of photos at full size with a friend, or when you want to backup only selected images. Alternatively, use the Copy/Move to Removable Disk command to copy or move photos to any removable storage device—an external hard disk, USB memory stick, network drive, or CD/DVD writer—connected to your computer.

1 In the Photo Browser, select the items you want to burn to CD or DVD. Make sure you have a blank writable disc in the CD or DVD drive connected to your computer, and then choose File > Make A CD/DVD.

If you haven't selected any files, you'll see a dialog box giving you the option of copying all the files currently visible in the Photo Browser.

2 In the Make A CD/DVD dialog box, select a destination drive, and then click OK. If you'd prefer to stop now, without copying any files, click Cancel.

3 In the Photo Browser, select the items you want to copy or move, and then choose File > Copy/Move To Removable Disk. The Copy/Move To Removable Disk wizard appears.

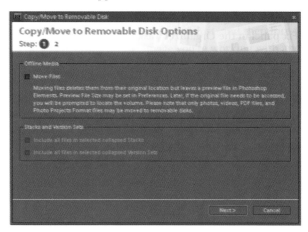

Review questions

1 How do you print multiple images on a single sheet of paper?

2 What is Photo Mail?

3 What is a Quick Share Flow?

4 What command can you use to backup all photos in your catalog to a CD or DVD?

5 How do you convert an existing album to an Online Album?

6 Is synchronization only possible for shared Online Albums?

7 Is the Save For Web command also available in Quick Fix mode?

Review answers

1 In the Organizer, select the photos you want to print and choose File > Print. Choose Individual Prints as the Type Of Print, select a print size that's small enough for multiple images, and then deselect the One Photo Per Page check box. Alternatively, choose Picture Package or Contact Sheet from the Select Type Of Print menu and experiment with different layout options.

2 The Photo Mail feature embeds selected photos in the body of an e-mail within a colorful custom layout. You can tweak the layout and image size, choose backgrounds, frames, and effects, and add text messages and captions. You can send Photo Mail through Outlook Express, Outlook, or Adobe E-mail Service.

3 A quick share flow can help you automate sharing tasks you perform frequently. Save your settings within a sharing workflow—such as attaching photos to an e-mail to be sent to all the members of your family—as a Quick Share Flow, and then perform the same task by simply dropping photos onto your new target in the Quick Share palette.

4 In the Organizer, choose File > Backup Catalog. After the first full backup, you can choose to perform only an incremental backup. To copy or move only selected files in your catalog, use the File > Copy/Move Offline command.

5 You need a Photoshop.com account to be able to convert any album into an Online Album. In the Albums palette, click the entry for the album, and then click the Share button to the right of the album name. You can select a template if you wish, and specify sharing options.

6   No. Synchronization is enabled for shared Online Albums by default, but you can choose whether or not you wish to enable backup and synchronization to Photoshop.com for any album in your catalog. You can either specify that an album is synchronized when you create it, or change it's status later in the Backup/Synchronization Preferences dialog box.

7   Yes, the Save For Web command is available in all three modes of the Editor, Quick Fix, Full Edit, and Guided Edit.

6 ADJUSTING COLOR IN IMAGES

Lesson Overview

This lesson introduces you to a variety of tools and techniques for fixing color problems in your photos:

- Correcting color in Guided Edit mode
- Auto-correcting in Quick Fix and Full Edit mode
- Using automatic options to improve images
- Adjusting skin tones
- Correcting an image using Smart Fix
- Using Color Variations to correct color balance
- Whitening teeth and removing red eyes effects
- Selecting and saving selections
- Adjusting color in selected areas
- Troubleshooting color printing
- Working with color management

 You'll probably need about two hours to complete this lesson.

Explore the many powerful and versatile tools and
options available in Photoshop Elements for correcting color problems in your photos—starting with a
few of the easy-to-use, one-step image correction
features, and then experimenting with some of the
more advanced features and adjustment techniques
that can be mastered easily.

Getting started

Note: Before you start working on this lesson, make sure that you've installed the software on your computer from the application CD (see the Photoshop Elements 7 documentation) and that you have correctly copied the Lessons folder from the CD in the back of this book onto your computer's hard disk (see "Copying the Classroom in a Book files" on page 2).

For the exercises in this lesson you'll be working in the Editor in Full Edit mode, Quick Fix mode, and Guided Edit mode. You'll be using the CIB Catalog you created in the "Getting Started" section at the beginning of this book.

1 Start Photoshop Elements and click the Organize button in the Welcome Screen. The name of the currently active catalog is displayed in the lower left corner of the Organizer window.

2 If your CIB Catalog is not already open choose File > Catalog and select the CIB Catalog in the Catalog Manager dialog box. If you don't see the CIB Catalog file listed, see "Creating a catalog" on page 3.

3 Once you have loaded your CIB Catalog, click the Editor button (⬛) near the top right corner of the Organizer window and choose Full Edit from the menu.

Before you begin the exercises, you can set up the Editor workspace so that what you see on screen corresponds to the illustrations in this section.

Note: You cannot add or remove palettes in Quick Fix mode. For detailed instructions on adding palettes to (and removing them from) the Palette Bin in Full Edit mode, see "Using the Palette Bin" in Lesson 1, "A Quick Tour of Photoshop Elements."

4 In Full Edit mode, choose from the Window menu to show the Tools palette, the Palette Bin, and the Project Bin. In both Full Edit and Quick Fix modes, you can expand or collapse palettes in the Palette Bin by clicking the arrow beside the palette name on the palette title bar.

The Editor workspace in Full Edit mode.

Each of the three Edit modes offers a different set of tools, controls and views. In the Guided Edit mode, the Palette Bin is replaced by a list of guided tasks.

The Editor workspace in Quick Fix mode.

The Editor workspace in Guided Edit mode.

Correcting color problems

You may have noticed that not all the photographs used for the lessons in this book are of professional quality. Many of the pictures were selected to illustrate common image faults—the kind of challenges that people typically face when attempting to make the most of their photographs.

Artificial light sources, unusual shooting conditions, and incorrect camera exposure settings can all cause tonal imbalances and unwelcome color casts in an image. In the following exercises we'll look at some of the ways Photoshop Elements can help you correct such problems.

In the Editor, you can make adjustments using the simple controls in the Quick Fix mode or be stepped through a wide range of editing tasks in Guided Edit mode. You can have Photoshop Elements apply corrections automatically, processing your photos in batches, or work in Full Edit mode to perform sophisticated edits selectively.

Fixing files in batches

Photoshop Elements allows you fix multiple photographs with one command by processing them as a batch. In this exercise, you'll apply automatic fixes to all the image files to be used in this lesson.

You'll save the auto-adjusted files as copies so that at the end of each project you can compare these automatic results to the edits you have made to the original files using various other techniques.

1   In the Editor, choose File > Process Multiple Files. The Process Multiple Files dialog box opens.

2   In the Process Multiple Files dialog box, set the source and destination folders as follows:

   •   Choose Folder from the Process Files From menu.

   •   Under Source, click the Browse button. Find and select the Lesson06 folder in the Lessons folder. Click OK to close the Browse For Folder dialog box.

   •   Under Destination, click Browse. Then, find and select the My CIB Work folder that you created at the start of the book. Click OK to close the Browse For Folder dialog box.

3   Under File Naming, select Rename Files. Select Document Name from the menu on the left and type **_Autofix** in the second field. This adds the appendix "_Autofix" to the existing document name as the files are saved.

4   Under Quick Fix on the right side of the dialog box, select all four options: Auto Levels, Auto Contrast, Auto Color, and Sharpen.

5   Review all the settings in the dialog box, comparing them to the illustration below. Make sure that the Resize Images and Convert Files options are disabled.

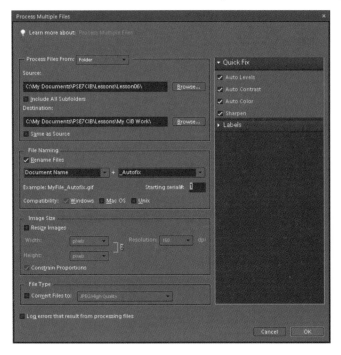

6   When you are sure that the settings are correct, click OK.

Photoshop Elements goes to work, automatically opening and closing image windows. All you need to do is sit back and wait for the process to finish, then move on to the next exercise.

To see the how the images look after the Quick Fix operations, you can either use Windows Explorer, or import them into your catalog (as you will do in the next exercise) where you can view them in the Photo Browser. For more information on the Photo Browser, see Photoshop Elements Help.

An error message warning that files are missing indicates that the Lessons folder has been moved or was not expanded correctly. See "Copying the Classroom in a Book files" on page 2 and redo that procedure, following the instructions exactly.

Note: If an error message appears warning that some files couldn't be processed, you can ignore it. This error is often caused by a hidden file that is not an image, so it has no effect on the success of your project.

Adding the corrected files to the Organizer

For most files modified in the Editor, the Include In Organizer option is activated in the Save, Save As, and Save Optimized As dialog boxes by default.

However, when you batch-edit files with the Process Multiple Files feature, this option isn't part of the process—you must add the edited files to the Organizer manually.

1 In the Editor, click the Organizer button (⊞) to open the Organizer workspace.

2 In the Organizer, choose File > Get Photos And Videos > From Files And Folders.

3 In the Get Photos From Files And Folders dialog box, locate and open your My CIB Work folder.

4 Ctrl-click or marquee-select all six files with the _Autofix suffix.

5 Activate the Automatically Fix Red Eyes option, disable the Automatically Suggest Photo Stacks option, and then click Get Photos.

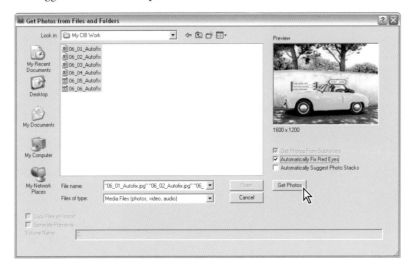

6 The Import Attached Keyword Tags dialog box opens. Click OK without selecting any keyword tags—you'll be adding keyword tags manually in the next few steps.

7 If the Auto Red Eye Fix Complete dialog box appears, click OK.

8 If a message appears reminding you that only the new photos will appear in the Photo Browser, click OK.

The files are imported to your CIB Catalog and the Organizer displays thumbnails of the newly added images in the Photo Browser.

9 Choose Edit > Select All, or press Ctrl+A.

10 If necessary, click the triangle beside the Imported Keyword Tags category in the Keyword Tags palette to expand the category entry so that you can see the imported keyword tags. Drag the Lesson 6 keyword tag to any of the selected image thumbnails to apply it to all selected images. *(See the illustration on the next page.)*

11 Click the Show All button above the Photo Browser.

In this lesson you saw how easy it is to have Photoshop Elements apply Quick Fix corrections to a batch of image files automatically. In the next exercises you'll explore some other methods for correcting color.

Using Guided Edit

If you are new to digital photography, the Guided Edit mode in Photoshop Elements is a great place to start when it comes to learning how to fix many common image problems. Even more experienced users can enjoy the ease and simplicity of performing editing tasks using the Guided Edit mode, and may just pick up some new tricks!

Removing a color cast using Guided Edit

One of the photos in the Lesson 6 folder, an image of three glass vases, has a very obvious color cast—a result of inadequate artificial lighting. In this exercise, you'll correct that color problem using the Guided Edit mode in the Editor.

1 If you are not still in the Organizer from the last exercise, switch to it now.

2 In the Keyword Tags palette, click the Find box for the Lesson 6 keyword tag.

The Image Browser is updated to show twelve images tagged with the Lesson 6 keyword: each of the six original photos from the Lesson06 folder is displayed beside the edited copy of the same image from your My CIB Work folder.

> **Note:** As you gain advanced skills in Photoshop Elements 7, you might require additional information to solve any problems you may encounter. For help with common problems you might have while working through the lessons in this book, see "Why won't Photoshop Elements do what I tell it to do?" later in this lesson.

3 Select the original photo of the three vases, 06_01.jpg, to make it active. Make sure not to confuse the original file with the copied file 06_01_Autofix.jpg, to which color correction—among other Quick Fix adjustments—has already been applied.

▶ **Tip:** To see the file name below each thumbnail image in the Photo Browser, choose View > Show File Names.

4 Click the Editor button () near the top right corner of the Organizer window, and then choose Guided Edit from the menu.

5 Wait until the Editor workspace has loaded and the image of the three vases has opened in Guided Edit mode.

6 If necessary, click the triangle beside the Color Correction entry in the guided tasks menu so that you can see the nested options. Choose Remove A Color Cast from the Color Correction submenu.

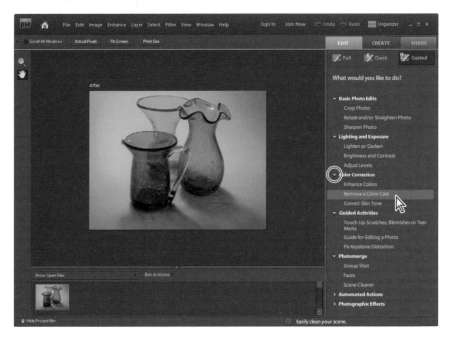

7   Click the display mode button near the bottom of the Guided Edit task panel to change the display to the Before & After - Horizontal view.

8   Read the instructions under Correct Color Cast. Then, using the Color Cast Eyedropper tool, click near the top left corner of the Before image to remove the color cast. Notice the change in the After image.

9   (Optional) If you are not satisfied with the result, click the Undo button () in the menu bar at the top of the organizer window, and then click a different area in the Before image with the Color Cast Eyedropper tool. To clear the Undo/Redo history and start all over with the original version of the image, click the Reset button in the Guided Edit panel.

10 When you are satisfied with the result of the color correction in the After image, click the Done button near the bottom of the Guided Edit task panel.

Adjusting lighting using Guided Edit

As is often the case with poorly exposed photos, this image has more than just one problem. After the color cast has been removed, the image looks as if it could benefit from some lighting adjustments.

1   If necessary, click the triangle beside the Lighting And Exposure entry in the guided tasks menu so that you can see the nested options, and then choose Lighten Or Darken from the submenu of Lighting And Exposure tasks.

2 In the Lighten Or Darken A Photo task panel, click the Auto button. Notice the substantial improvement in the appearance of the image.

3 Use the Lighten Shadows, Darken Highlights, and Midtone Contrast sliders to fine-tune the lighting for this image. We set a value of 30 for Lighten Shadows, left the Darken Highlights slider at 0, and set a value of 32 for Midtone Contrast. Your choices may vary, depending on the results of your color correction and your preferences for the look of the final image.

4 When you are satisfied with the results of the lighting adjustment as they are shown in the After image, click the Done button near the bottom of the Guided Edit task panel.

● **Note:** To avoid the image artifacts that can result from over-sharpening, sharpening is best applied at a magnification of 100%. Use the display mode button near the bottom of the Guided Edit task panel to change the display to the After Only view, and then choose View > Actual Pixels.

5 (Optional) In the guided tasks menu, choose Sharpen Photo from the Basic Photo Edits submenu. Click the Auto button near the top of the Sharpen Photo task panel. Use the slider to manually fine-tune the sharpening to your liking, and then click Done.

6 Choose File > Save As. In the Save As dialog box, navigate to and open your My CIB Work folder. Leaving the JPEG file format selected, name the file **06_01_Guided**, activate Include In The Organizer, disable Save in Version Set with Original, and then click Save.

7 In the JPEG Options dialog box, click OK without making any changes.

8 In the Editor, choose File > Close, and then switch back to the Organizer.

9 In the Organizer, type the word **guided** in the Text Search text box above the Photo Browser. The Photo Browser is updated to display only the newly added image 06_01_Guided.jpg. Drag the Lesson 6 keyword tag from the Keyword Tags palette onto the image thumbnail in the Photo Browser.

10 Click the Show All button above the Photo Browser.

With just a few clicks you have improved the appearance of the photo dramatically. You don't need to have prior experience using an image editor to get good results in Guided Edit mode. Try the Guided Activities ("Touch Up Scratches, Blemishes Or Tear Marks", "Guide For Editing A Photo", and "Fix Keystone Distortion") that each step you through several image editing tasks in the recommended order to get professional results. In the exercise to follow, you'll move on to the next level in editing—working in the Quick Fix mode.

Using Quick Fix for editing

The Quick Fix workspace conveniently assembles many of the basic photo fixing tools in Photoshop Elements. If one control doesn't work for your image, click the Reset button and try another one. Whether you've used the Quick Fix mode before or not, the intuitive slider controls make adjusting your image easy.

Applying automatic adjustments separately

When you apply a combination of automatic fixes to a set of images using the Process Multiple Files feature, the process happens too fast for you to see the changes made to each image at each stage of processing.

In this exercise, you'll apply some of the same automatic fix options separately, one at a time. This enables you to see how each editing step affects an image, and provides the opportunity to fine-tune the correction process by adjusting the default settings to optimize the results.

Opening image files for Quick Fix editing

Once again, you can use the Keyword Tags palette to find the sample image you want, and then open it in Quick Fix mode from the Organizer.

1 If the Organizer is not currently active, switch to it now.

2 In the Keyword Tags palette, click the Find box next to the Lesson 6 keyword tag.

3 Select the original version of the image with three glass vases, 06_01.jpg.

4 Click the Editor button (◪) near the top right corner of the Organizer window and choose Quick Fix from the menu.

● **Note:** To see the file names for images in the Photo Browser, choose View > Show File Names.

5   Choose Before & After - Horizontal from the View menu in the lower left corner of the image window. If you prefer the before and after images one above the other rather than side-by-side, choose the Before & After - Vertical view.

Using Smart Fix

In the Quick Fix workspace the Palette Bin at the right contains five palettes—General Fixes, Lighting, Color, Sharpen, and Touch Up. In the General Fixes palette, the first option available is the Smart Fix feature, which corrects overall color balance and improves shadow and highlight detail in your image. As with the other editing features in Quick Fix mode, you can click the Auto button to apply corrections automatically or you can use the slider controls to fine-tune the adjustments. You can even combine these methods, as you will in this exercise.

1   In the General Fixes palette, click the Smart Fix Auto button. Notice the immediate effect on the image.

2   Now, move the Amount slider to change the color balance and highlight and shadow detail settings for your image. Experiment to find the setting you prefer. In our example the slider has been moved to the middle position.

3   Click the Commit button (✓) in the title bar of the General Fixes palette to commit the changes.

Applying other automatic fixes

More automatic fixes are available in the Lighting, Color, and Sharpen palettes.

1 In the Lighting palette, click the Auto button for the Levels feature. Depending on the adjustment you made to the Smart Fix edit, you may or may not see a big shift in the lighting of this image.

2 Click the Auto buttons for Contrast, Color, and Sharpen in turn, noticing the affects of each of these adjustments on the After image.

3 Experiment with the slider controls in each palette. When you're satisfied with an adjustment, click the Commit button (✔) in title bar of the respective palette to commit the changes.

4 If you wish to undo your modifications and start again using the original version of the image, click the Reset button above the After view.

5 When you have achieved the results you want, choose File > Save As. In the Save As dialog box, navigate to and open your My CIB Work folder, rename the file **06_01_Quick** and select the JPEG format. Select Include In The Organizer. If Save In Version Set With Original is selected, deselect it. Click Save.

6 When the JPEG Options dialog box appears, select High from the Quality menu, and then click OK.

7 In the Editor, choose File > Close, and then switch back to the Organizer.

8 In the Organizer, type the word **quick** in the Text Search text box above the Photo Browser. The Photo Browser is updated to display only the newly added image 06_01_Quick.jpg. Drag the Lesson 6 keyword tag from the Keyword Tags palette onto the image thumbnail in the Photo Browser.

9 Click the Show All button above the Photo Browser.

Using the Touch Up tools

The last palette in the Quick Fix Palette Bin is the Touch Up palette. The four tools in the Touch Up palette all enable you to apply corrections and adjustments selectively to specific parts of an image:

- The Red Eye Removal tool removes red eye effects in flash photos of people and red, green, or white eye effects in flash photos of pets.

- The Whiten Teeth tool brightens smiles.

- The Blue Sky tool can bring new life to an image.

- The Black And White - High Contrast tool simulates the high-contrast image effects that black and white film photographers produce by placing a red filter over the camera lens.

Except for Red Eye Removal, all Touch Up adjustments are applied on a separate adjustment layer; they do not discard or permanently edit any information on the image layer. You can always change adjustment settings without degrading the original image.

Note: The Whiten Teeth, Blue Sky, and Black And White - High Contrast tools in Quick Fix mode are all variants on the Smart Brush tool in Full Edit mode. For more information on the Smart Brush, see "Using the Smart Brush" later in this lesson or refer to Photoshop Elements Help.

Brightening a smile

We'll be looking closer at the Red Eye Removal feature in a later exercise. For now, let's try the Whiten Teeth tool.

1 If the Organizer is not currently active, switch to it now.

2 In the Keyword Tags palette, click the Find box next to the Lesson 6 keyword tag.

3 Select the original version of the image 06_02.jpg, showing a couple photographed in bright sunlight. Take care not to select the "_Autofix" file.

4 Click the Editor button (■) near the top right corner of the Organizer window and choose Quick Fix from the menu.

Note: To see the file names for images in the Photo Browser, choose View > Show File Names.

Setting up the Quick Fix workspace

1 Collapse all the palettes in the Palette Bin except for the Touch Up palette.

2 To maximize the space available for editing, hide the Project Bin by clicking the triangle in the lower left corner of the Editor window.

3 From the View menu at the left below the Quick Fix editing preview, choose Before & After - Vertical.

4 Set the Zoom level to 200%. Either use the slider or type **200** in the text box.

5 Use the hand tool to drag either the Before or After image within the preview window. The images will move together. Position them so that you can see the man's teeth.

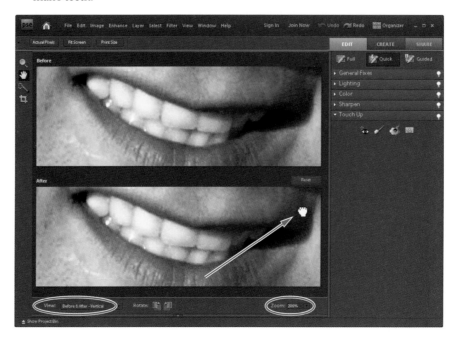

Using the Whiten Teeth tool

Now it's time for a little dental magic. With the Whiten Teeth tool, as with the other Touch Up tools, you'll work directly into the After image—the tools have no effect on the Before image.

1 Click to select the Whiten Teeth tool (![icon]) in the Touch Up palette.

2 Notice that settings and controls for the Whiten Teeth tool are now available at the top left of the Editor window, just above the Tools palette.

3   In the Whiten Teeth tool settings, click the triangle to open the Brush picker. As the image you're using for this exercise is of a fairly low resolution, you'll need a small brush—set the Diameter to 5 px. Set the Hardness value to 50%, and then click the triangle again to close the Brush picker.

4   Move the pointer over the After image. A small cross-hair cursor indicates the brush size set for the Whiten Teeth tool: Notice that in the tool settings at the top left of the Editor window, the brush icon on the left is highlighted to indicate that the tool is in New Selection mode. Drag the cross-hair across two of the brightest teeth as shown below, and then release the mouse button.

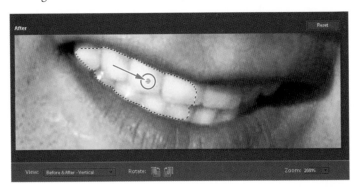

Adding to and subtracting from an adjustment selection

The Whiten Teeth tool, like the Blue Sky and Black And White Touch Up tools, is both a selection tool and an image adjustment tool. You have just used the tool to create a selection through which the tooth whitening adjustment is applied once. While this selection is active, you can add to or subtract from it, without re-applying the adjustment.

The Whiten Teeth selection and edit is being made on an adjustment layer separate from the original image. The edit remains active on its adjustment layer—so you can always alter the selection area or the way the adjustment is being applied without degrading the original image.

1 Notice that in the tool settings at the top left of the Editor window, the brush icon in the center is now highlighted. Now that there is already an active selection, the brush has automatically switched to Add To Selection mode.

2 To add the shadowed teeth on the right to the selection, drag with the Add To Selection brush as shown below, and then release the mouse button. Don't worry if parts of the lips are also selected—you'll deal with that in the next step.

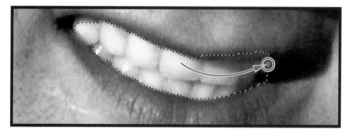

3 Hold down the Alt key. The cursor changes to that of the Subtract From Selection brush. Notice that in the tool settings at the top left of the Editor window, the brush icon on the right is now highlighted. Sill holding down the Alt key, carefully drag with the Subtract From Selection brush to remove the lip areas from the adjustment selection as shown below.

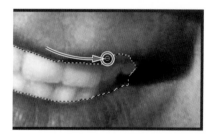

4 Release the Alt key. The brush returns to Add To Selection mode. Drag carefully as shown below to include the shadowed tooth on the left corner.

The selection is complete. The Whiten Teeth adjustment has been applied to the selected area on an adjustment layer separate from the original image. Although the adjustment has had a noticeable effect, you can improve the image by using the Whiten Teeth feature again.

5 With the Whiten Teeth tool still active, choose Select > Deselect to deselect the current adjustment. Using the Whiten Teeth tool on the After image now will create a new adjustment selection on a new layer—applying a second instance of the adjustment.

6 Use the brush picker to change the Hardness of the brush to 10%. Drag using very short strokes as shown in the illustration on the left below, to create an irregular selection area including only the brighter areas of the smile. Avoid shadowed teeth—the whitening will look unnatural if applied too evenly. Alternate between the Add To Selection and Subtract From Selection brushes.

7 With the Whiten Teeth tool still active, choose Select > Deselect to deselect the current adjustment. Create a third adjustment layer by dragging in the After image, using short strokes to make a small selection as shown in the illustration on the right below. choose Select > Deselect to deselect the current adjustment.

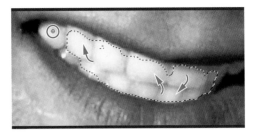 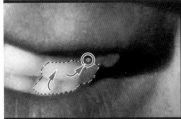

The Whiten Teeth adjustment is applied a second and third time through the new selections. The irregular selections and the softer brush setting help to create a more natural effect than re-applying the adjustment to the entire smile.

Modifying the Touch Up adjustment

Each time you applied The Whiten Teeth tool a separate adjustment layer was created in the image. Each edit remains active on its own adjustment layer—you can still alter the selection area or the way the adjustment is applied for each layer.

1 Click the Full Edit button at the top of the Task Panel to open the current photo in Full Edit mode.

2   In Full Edit mode, Expand the Layers panel if it is currently collapsed. If you don't see the layers panel, choose Window > Layers. Notice that there are three adjustment layers stacked above the original image in the Background layer. Click the eye icons to toggle each layer's visibility in turn, noticing the effect in the preview window.

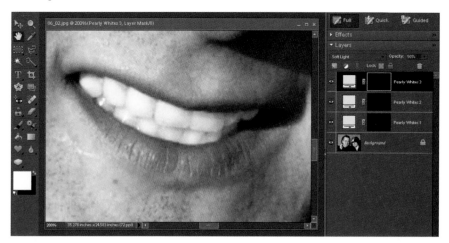

3   For the Whiten Teeth tool, Soft Light is the preset blending mode and the opacity for each layer is set to 50%. Use the controls at the top of the Layers palette to experiment with the Blending Mode and the Opacity value for each layer in turn. When you're done experimenting, choose File > Save As. Name the edited file **06_02_Dental**, select the Photoshop (*PSD, *PDD) format, and then save the file to your My CIB Work folder. Choose File > Close.

Using the Smart Brush tool

The Whiten Teeth, Blue Sky, and Black And White - High Contrast tools in the Quick Fix mode Touch Up palette are all variants on the Smart Brush tool in Full Edit mode. The Smart Brush is both a selection tool and an image adjustment tool. It creates a selection based on similarity of color and texture through which a preset edit called a Smart Paint adjustment is applied. While the selection is active, you can add to or subtract from it, without re-applying the adjustment. Each Smart Brush edit is made on a separate adjustment layer and does not affect the original image. The Smart Brush edit remains active on its adjustment layer—so you can always alter the selection area, change the way the adjustment is being applied, or even delete the adjustment layer without degrading the original image.

Applying a Smart Paint adjustment

For this exercise you'll work with a photo from the Lesson01 folder.

1 In the Organizer, use the Lesson 1 keyword tag to find the image DSC_0363.jpg.

2 Click the Editor button (▇) near the top right corner of the Organizer window and choose Full Edit from the menu.

3 Wait until the image DSC_0363.jpg opens in the Editor; then Collapse the Effects palette, expand the Layers palette and choose View > Fit On Screen.

4 Select the Smart Brush (▇) from the Tools palette; then resize the Smart Paint presets menu and drag it to a convenient position, leaving the image clear.

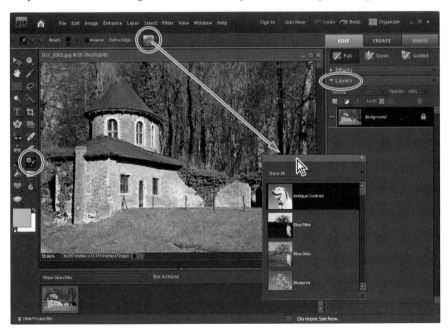

5   Click the categories menu in the moveable Smart Brush presets menu. For this exercise choose the category Nature. Scroll down through the options in the Nature category and select Greenery.

6   In the Brush Picker in the bar above the preview window, set the brush diameter to 35 pixels. Drag across about half of the lawn in front of the old building, and then release the mouse button.

Tweaking a Smart Paint adjustment

The Greenery brush has not made a very dramatic difference to the lawn. Let's try some methods for modifying the adjustment to boost the effect.

1   The Smart Paint adjustment you just applied shows a pin—a marker identifying a Smart Paint edit when the Smart Brush tool is active—at the point in the image where you began applying the Smart Brush. Right-click the pin and choose Change Adjustment Settings from the menu.

2   Experiment with using the sliders and options to in the Hue/Saturation dialog
    box to modify the Smart Paint adjustment. When you're done, click Cancel—
    you'll be looking at another way to modify the effects of the Greenery brush yet.

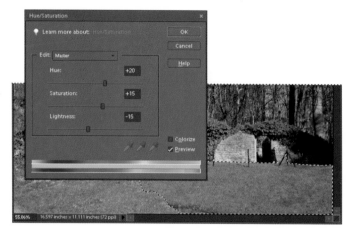

3   In the layers palette, you'll notice that the active layer is your new Greenery edit.
    Change the layer's Opacity to 75%, and the Blending Mode to Multiply.

4   This modification is much more effective. If you wish, you can go ahead and
    paint over the rest of the lawn with the new adjustment layer settings.

5   When you're done, choose File > Close without saving the changes.

Applying multiple Smart Paint adjustments

You can use the Smart Brush on the same area as many times as you wish. You can re-apply the same Smart Paint preset more and the effects are usually cumulative, though the results will vary depending on the layer blending mode for that preset. You can also apply different Smart Paint presets to the same image area.

1   Open the image DSC_0639.jpg in the Full Edit mode. Hint: this photo has the Lesson 1 keyword tag. When the image opens, choose View > Fit On Screen.

2   Select the Smart Brush tool. If the Smart Paint menu is not visible, select another tool for a moment, and then click the Smart Brush to select it again.

3   Move the Smart Paint menu to a convenient position. Choose the Nature category once more, and then select the Blue Skies brush. Drag horizontally across the sky starting from the far left, just above the horizon.

4   Choose Select > Deselect Layers to make the last edit inactive, and then use the Cloud Contrast brush, starting at the far right and dragging left. There are now two Smart Brush pins showing on the image.

5   Choose Select > Deselect Layers to make the last edit inactive, and then use the Dark Sky brush, starting at the upper left. Choose Select > Deselect Layers. You can see three pins, and there are three new layers in the Layers palette.

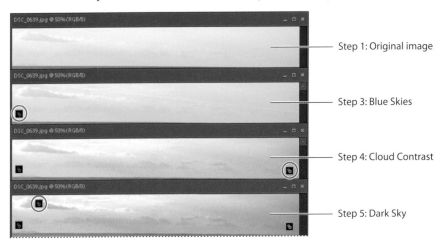

Step 1: Original image

Step 3: Blue Skies

Step 4: Cloud Contrast

Step 5: Dark Sky

6   Close the file without saving.

Before you return to the Organizer for the next lesson, open a few more files and explore more of the many options in the Smart Paint menu. Right-click the pins to try the options and experiment with the adjustment layers. For more detail on using the Smart Brush, refer to Photoshop Elements Help.

Comparing methods of fixing color

The automatic correction features in Photoshop Elements do an excellent job of bringing out the best in most photographs, but each image—and each image problem—is unique. Some photographs don't respond well to automatic fixes and require a more hands-on approach to color correction.

Photoshop Elements offers many ways to deal with color correction. The more techniques you master, the more likely you'll be able meet the challenge of fixing a difficult photograph. In this section, you'll study three different methods for correcting a color problem, and then compare the results.

Creating extra working copies of an image

In the following exercises you'll compare three different approaches to correcting the same color problem, so you'll need three copies of the same photograph.

1   In the Organizer, use the Lesson 6 keyword tag to find the file 06_03.jpg. Take care not to confuse the original file with the file 06_03_Autofix.jpg.

2   Select the file 06_03.jpg in the Photo Browser. Click the Editor button () near the top right corner of the Organizer window and choose Quick Fix from the menu. In the Quick Fix workspace, click the triangle in the lower left corner of the Editor window to show the Project bin.

3   Choose File > Duplicate. In the Duplicate Image dialog box, click OK to accept the default name 06_03 copy.jpg.

4   Repeat Step 3 to create another duplicate, 06_03 copy 2.jpg.

Leave all three copies of the image file open for the next procedures. You can tell that the files are open because their thumbnails appear in the Project Bin below the Editor preview. The image file names will appear in Tooltips when you hold the pointer over each thumbnail in the Project Bin.

Note: By now, you should have mastered the techniques of using keyword tags and text search to locate the files you need in the Organizer. From now on, the instructions for opening files will be summarized rather than stepped through in detail.

Correcting color automatically

At the beginning of this lesson, you applied all four Quick Fix options to each of the six images in the Lesson06 folder and saved the results to a separate location. In this exercise, you'll apply just one Quick Fix adjustment.

1   In the Project Bin, double-click the original image—06_02.jpg—to make it the active file.

2   In the Color palette, click Auto to correct only the color.

Compare the Before and After views of the file. Although there is a small change noticeable in the skin tones and the lighter part of the background behind the girl's head, it appears that this image is not a good candidate for an automatic color fix.

3   Choose File > Save. Save the file in your My CIB Work folder in JPEG format, changing the name to **06_02_Work**. Make sure that the Save In Version Set With Original option is disabled. Click Save, leaving all the other options unchanged in the Save dialog box and the JPEG Options dialog box.

Adjusting the results of an automatic fix

1   In the Photo Bin, double-click the image 06_02 copy to make it the active file.

2   In the Color palette, click Auto. For this image, the results are minimal.

3   Drag the Temperature slider a small amount to the left.

This makes the colors in the image cooler, reducing the predominant red and orange tones while enhancing blues and greens.

4   Examine the results, paying particular attention to the skin tones.

5 Adjust the Temperature slider until you are satisfied with the realistic balance. While removing the overly orange cast from the image, watch the right side of the girl's face, taking care to preserve a warm, natural skin tone. When you are happy with the results, click the Commit button (✔) at the top of the Color palette.

6 Choose File > Save. Save the file in your My CIB Work folder in JPEG format, changing the name to **06_02 copy_Work**. Notice that the Save In Version Set With Original option is not available, since the file 06_02 copy.jpg has not been added to the catalog. Click Save, leaving all the other options unchanged in the Save dialog box and the JPEG Options dialog box.

● **Note:** If you aren't happy with the results you're getting with the slider and wish to start over, click the Cancel button in the header of the Color palette. If click the Commit button, and then decide that you want to undo the color fix, click the Reset button above the image in the editing preview. This will revert the image to its original condition.

Tweaking results from an automatic fix

The top six commands in the Enhance menu apply the same image adjustments as the various Auto buttons in the Quick Fix palettes. These commands are available in both the Quick Fix and Full Edit modes, but not in Guided Edit.

Both the Quick Fix and Full Edit modes also offer other methods of enhancing color in images. These are found in the lower half of the Enhance menu. In this exercise, you'll use a one of these options to tweak the results produced by an automatic fix button.

1 In the Photo Bin, double-click the image 06_02 copy 2 to make it the active file.

2 In the Color palette, click Auto to apply the automatic color correction.

3 Choose Enhance > Adjust Color > Color Variations. The Color Variations dialog box appears.

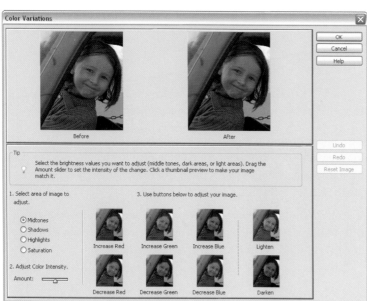

4   In the lower left area of the Color Variations dialog box, make sure that Midtones is selected, and then move the Amount slider down to about the one-third position. Click the Decrease Red thumbnail twice.

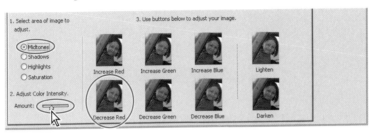

5   In the lower left area of the Color Variations dialog box. Make sure that Highlights is selected. Click the Increase Blue thumbnail twice and the Lighten thumbnail twice. Click OK.

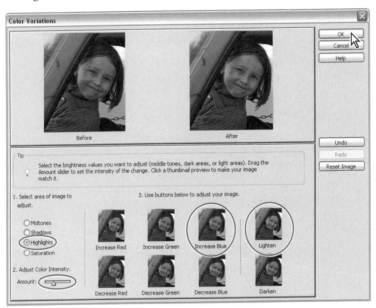

This reduces the amount of blue in the images, probably even too much. To try again, using a smaller value or a different combination of adjustments, you can undo the changes and start again. (Choose Edit > Undo Color Variations, and then try again, starting with Step 3.)

6   Choose File > Save As, and navigate to the My CIB Work folder. Rename the file **06_02 copy 2_Work**, and select the JPEG format. Click Save, leaving all other options in the Save and JPEG Options dialog boxes unchanged.

About viewing modes and image window arrangements

When you work in Quick Fix mode, only one image—the active file—appears in the work area, regardless of how many files are open. The inactive open files appear only as thumbnails in the Photo Bin.

When you work in Full Edit mode, other arrangements are possible. You can usually adjust the size and placement of image windows in the work area. If you can't arrange individual windows freely, your view is probably set to Maximize Mode. If opening or closing a file sometimes causes unexpected rearrangements of image windows, your view is probably set to Tile.

Maximize Mode (below, left) fills the work area with the active image window.

Tile (below, center) re-sizes and arranges all open images so that the image windows cover the work area. If Tile mode is active when you close an image file or open a new one, Photoshop Elements will rearrange the image windows in tile formation.

Cascade (below, right) enables you to resize, arrange, or minimize files.

There are two ways to switch from one mode to another:

- Use the Window > Images menu and choose Maximize Mode, Tile, or Cascade. If there is a check mark on the Maximize Mode command, choose Maximize Mode again disable it and switch to the mode you were using previously.

- Use the buttons on the far right end of the window title bar. The available buttons vary, depending on which viewing mode is active, and on the size of the work area on your monitor. If the work area is reduced, these buttons may not appear.

For more information, see "Working in the Editor: Viewing images in the Editor" in Adobe Photoshop Elements Help.

Comparing results

As you can tell by checking the Photo Bin, all three of your saved work files are still open in the Editor. Let's compare them to the autofix file from the batch process at the beginning of this lesson.

1   Choose File > Open. Locate and open your My CIB Work folder. Select the file 06_02_Autofix, and then click Open.

2   At the top of the Tasks pane, click the Full tab () to switch to Full Edit mode.

3   Choose Window > Images > Tile.

4   Use the Zoom tool and the Hand tool to see an area of interest in one of the images, and then choose Window > Images > Match Zoom and Windows > Images > Match Location.

5   In the toolbox, select the Zoom tool (🔍).

6   In the tool options bar above the Tools palette, activate the Zoom Out mode for the Zoom tool.

7 Click in the active image window until you can see the entire photo. Then, choose Window > Images > Match Zoom. Choose Window > Images > Match Zoom again to disable the feature.

8 In the tool options bar above the Tools palette, activate the Zoom In mode for the Zoom tool, and then click the checkbox to activate the Zoom All Windows option. Click in the active image window until you can see a detail of interest.

● **Note:** At any given time there is only one active window. Look at the text in the title bars of the open image windows; the text is dimmed in the title bars of all but the active image window.

9 In the toolbox, select the Hand tool ().

10 In the tool options bar, activate the Scroll All Windows option.

11 Click and drag within the active window to examine different areas of the image. Compare the four images and decide which looks best. Drag any corner edge of the image window to resize it so it fills the available space, and then turn off Tile mode in the Widow > Images menu.

12 Choose View > Fit On Screen to enlarge the image so it fits in the window. You can cycle through all open windows by pressing Ctrl-Tab or Ctrl-Shift-Tab.

Adjusting skin tones

Sometimes the combination of ambient light and reflection from colored objects around your subject can cause the skin tones in your image to be tinted with unwanted color. Photoshop Elements offers a unique solution that is available in both the Full Edit and Quick Fix modes.

To adjust color for skin tones do the following:

1 Choose Enhance > Adjust Color > Adjust Color For Skin Tone. The Adjust Color For Skin Tone dialog box appears.

2 In the Adjust Color For Skin Tone dialog box, make sure the Preview option is activated. As you move the pointer over the image, the cursor changes to an eyedropper tool.

Before you click, it's worth considering the peculiarities of the image at hand. Quite apart from the general orange color cast, the little girl has yellow light on one side of her face caused by light shining through colored glass. If you sample an area of the girl's skin on which this yellow light is falling, the image will be corrected too far into the blue range. Look for a relatively neutral area of skin towards the other side of the girl's face and click with the eyedropper tool.

▶ **Tip:** Even while the Adjust Color For Skin Tone dialog box is open, you can still select the Zoom or Hand tools in the Editor Tools palette to help you focus on a different area of the image. When you're ready to sample a skin tone in the image, pick up the eyedropper tool from the Tools palette.

Photoshop Elements automatically adjusts color balance for the entire photo using the color of the child's skin as reference.

3 If you're unsatisfied with the correction, click Reset and sample a different point in the image or move the Tan, Blush, and Temperature sliders to achieve the desired result.

4 When you're happy with the skin tone, click OK to close the Adjust Color For Skin Tone dialog box, and then choose File > Close All. Don't save the changes.

Working with red eye

The red eye effect occurs when a camera flash is reflected off the retina at the back of the eye so that the dark pupil looks bright red. Photoshop Elements can automatically correct red eye effects during the process of importing images into the Organizer. Simply activate the Automatically Fix Red Eyes option in the Get Photos dialog box when you're importing your photos (see the *Automatically Fixing Red Eyes* sidebar in Lesson 2). Alternatively, you can apply the red eye fix feature to images already in your catalog. In Lesson 8 you will learn how red eyes can be fixed without leaving in the Organizer, but for this exercise you'll use the tools available to you in the Editor.

Using automatic Red Eye Fix in the Editor

In Quick Fix mode, you can apply an automatic red eye correction with a single click—just as you did earlier in this lesson with the Smart Fix feature. This technique may not be suitable for some images, but for those Photoshop Elements provides other options.

In this exercise you'll be working in the Editor in Quick Fix mode, but first you'll use the Organizer to find the image for this lesson in your catalog.

1 In the Editor, click the Organizer button to load the Organizer workspace. If necessary, click the Show All button above the Photo Browser.

2 Use the Keywords Tags palette to find all images with the Lesson 6 keyword tag.

For our red eye removal exercise, you need the image 06_04.jpg—the uncorrected photo of three little girls dressed for Halloween. Take care not to confuse this file with the version that had auto red eye fix applied as part of the batch edit. If necessary, choose View > Show File Names.

3 In the Photo Browser, click the image 06_04.jpg to select it. Then, click the Editor button located near the top right corner of the Organizer window and choose Quick Fix from the menu. Wait until the Editor has finished opening the file.

4   Select Before & After - Vertical from the View menu below the preview pane. Use the Zoom and Hand tools to focus on the eyes of the girl in the centre of the photo.

5   In the Palette Bin, under General Fixes, click the Auto button next to Red Eye Fix. There is no slider available for this correction.

● **Note:** The Auto Red Eye Fix feature is also available as a command available from the Enhance menu in both the Quick Fix and Full Edit modes, together with other automatic features such as Auto Smart Fix.

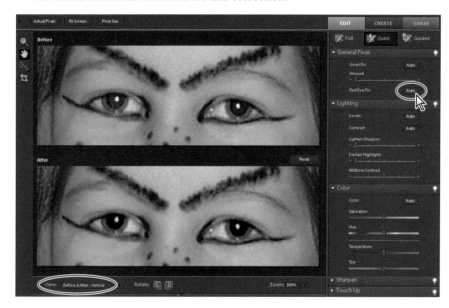

As you can see, automatic red eye correction does a great job for this little girl. Unfortunately, it hasn't worked for her sisters.

6   Use the Zoom and Hand tools to check the eyes of the other two girls.

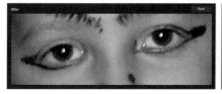 

The automatic adjustment had no discernible effect for the girls at either side of the photo. Admittedly, the red eye effect is less pronounced in both cases, but it is also more complex and difficult to remove. The pupils of the girl in the center are crisply defined against her blue irises while there is less contrast in the hazel irises of the other girls.

7   Click the Reset button above the After image to revert the photo to its state before the Auto Red Eye Fix was applied.

The Auto Red Eye Fix feature works well for most images, but when you want more control you need to use the Red Eye Removal tool.

Using the Red Eye Removal tool

For stubborn red eye problems, the Red Eye Removal tool () is a simple and efficient solution. In this exercise you'll now learn how to customize the Red Eye Removal tool to fix difficult cases.

1   If the image 06_04.jpg is not already open in Quick Fix mode—and reverted to its unedited state—from the last exercise, open it in the Editor now, in either Quick Fix or Full Edit mode.

2   Zoom and position the image so that you can focus on the eyes of the girl on the left of the photo. In Quick fix, use the Before And After - Vertical view.

3   In Full Edit mode, select the Red Eye Removal tool () from the tool palette. In Quick Fix mode, you'll find the Red Eye Removal tool in the Touch Up palette.

4   In the Red Eye Removal tool options in the bar above the Tools palette, change the Pupil Size value to 10% and the Darken Amount to 50%. You can either use the slider controls, type the new values in the text fields, or simply drag left or right over the Pupil Size and Darken Amount text.

5   With the Red Eye Removal tool selected, click once (in the After image, if you are in Quick Fix) in the reddest part of each pupil. If there is little result, Undo and click a slightly different spot.

The red is removed from both eyes. The adjustment has also darkened the less defined parts of the irises, but we'll accept that for now.

6   Use the Zoom and Hand tools to position the image so that you can focus on the eyes of the girl on the right of the photo.

7   In the Red Eye Removal tool options in the bar above the Tools palette, change the Pupil Size value to 100% and the Darken Amount to 75%.

8   With the Red Eye Removal tool still selected, drag a marquee rectangle around each eye in turn.

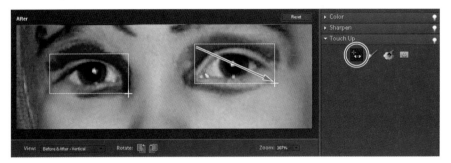

You may need to experiment with the size and positioning of the rectangle you drag around an eye to get the best results. Just Undo and try again.

9   Finally, you can re-instate the Auto Red Eye Fix for the little girl in the Middle. Zoom out to see all three faces. If you are in Quick Fix mode, click the Auto Red Eye Fix button in the General Fixes palette. If you're in Full Edit mode, choose Enhance > Auto Red Eye Fix.

10 Choose File > Save As and navigate to the My CIB Work folder. Rename the file **06_04_Work** and select the JPEG format. Disable the Save In Version Set With Original option and click Save, leaving all other options in the Save and JPEG Options dialog boxes unchanged.

11 Choose File > Close and return to the Organizer.

Making selections

By default, the entire area of an image or image layer is active: any adjustments you make are applied across the whole photo. If you want to make changes to a specific area or object within an image, you first need to make a selection. Once you have made a selection it becomes the only active area of the image—the rest of the image layer is protected or masked from the effects of your edits.

Typically, the boundaries of a selection are indicated by a selection marquee—a flashing border of dashed black and white lines. You can save a selection and re-use it at a later time. This can be a terrific time-saver when you need to use the same selection several times.

You can use several different tools to create selections; you'll get experience with most of them in the course of the lessons in this book. Selections can be geometric in shape or free form, and they can have crisp or soft edges. Selections can be created manually the mouse pointer, or calculated by Photoshop Elements based on similarities of color within the image.

Perhaps the simplest, most effective way to create a selection is to paint it on an image. This exercise focuses on the use of two selection tools in Photoshop Elements, the Selection Brush tool and the Quick Selection tool.

1   Using the Organizer, select the original image of the water lily, 06_05.psd. Click the Editor button located near the top right corner of the Organizer window and choose Full Edit from the menu or use the keyboard shortcut Ctrl+I. Wait until the Editor has finished opening the file.

Notice that this file has been saved as a Photoshop file and not as a JPEG file. The Photoshop file format can store additional information along with the image data. In this case, a portion of the flower has previously been selected and the selection has been saved in the file.

2   With the image 06_05.psd file open in the Editor, choose Select > Load Selection. In the Load Selection dialog box, choose "petals" as the Source Selection. In the Operation options, activate New Selection, and then click OK.

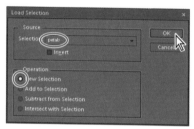

The saved selection "petals" is loaded. The flower is surrounded by a flashing selection marquee to indicate that it has become the active portion of the image.

One petal needs to be added to make the selection of the flower complete. In the following exercise, you'll add the missing petal and modify the saved selection.

3   Choose Select > Deselect to clear the current selection.

4   In the toolbox, select the Selection Brush tool, which is grouped with the Quick Selection tool.

Using the Selection Brush tool

The Selection Brush tool makes selections in either of two ways. In Selection mode, you simply paint over the area you want to select. In Mask mode you paint a semi-opaque overlay over areas you don't want selected.

1   In the tool options bar, set the Selection Brush controls to match the illustration below. Click the Add To Selection button at the far left, set the brush Size to 25 pixels wide, choose Selection from the Mode menu, and set the brush Hardness value to 100%.

2   Drag with the Selection Brush to paint over the interior of the petal at the front. Don't try to paint the edges; you'll do that in the next step.

Notice that you're actually painting a live selection onto the image, surrounded with a flashing dashed selection marquee. Release the mouse every second or two.

Now you need to reduce your brush size to paint around the edges of the petal, adding to your selection.

You could move the Size slider to change your brush size, but it's probably more convenient to press the open bracket key ([) to reduce the brush size in increments and the close bracket key (]) to enlarge it.

3   Press the left bracket key ([), to reduce the Selection Brush size to 10 pixels.

4   Drag with the Selection Brush to paint the selection to the edges of the petal. Use the bracket keys to change the brush size as needed, until the selection outline completely surrounds the petal.

Tip: Use the Zoom tool to magnify the area of interest in the photo when you need to make a detailed selection.

Tip: If you have accidentally selected an area you didn't want to select, use the buttons at the left of the tool options bar to switch the brush mode from Add To Selection to Subtract From Selection and paint back over the unwanted area.

If you found using the Selection Brush tool tedious, you'll appreciate learning about the Quick Selection tool later in this lesson. But first, you'll make use of your hard work and save the results.

Editing a saved selection

In this exercise you'll add your current selection to the "petals" selection that was saved with the file. You can modify saved selections by either replacing them, adding to them, or subtracting from them.

1   With your selection still active, choose Select > Load Selection.

2   In the Load Selection dialog box, choose the saved selection "petals" as the Source Selection. In the Operation options, activate the Add To Selection option, and then click OK. This setting will combine your current selection of the front-most petal with the saved selection of the rest of the flower.

You should now see the entire water lily outlined by the flashing selection boundary.

If you've missed a spot, simply paint it in with the Selection Brush tool. If you've selected too much, switch to Subtract From Selection mode in the options bar, set an appropriate brush size, and then paint out your mistakes.

3   Choose Select > Save Selection. In the Save Selection dialog box, choose petals as the Selection name, activate Replace Selection in the Operation options, and then click OK.

4   Choose Select > Deselect.

Using the Quick Selection tool

The Quick Selection tool enables you to select an area in the image by simply drawing, scribbling, or clicking on the area you want to select. You don't need to be precise, because while you are drawing, Photoshop Elements expands the selection border based on color and texture similarity.

In this exercise, you'll use the Quick Selection tool to select everything but the water lily, and then swap the selected and un-selected areas in the photo to establish the selection you want. This technique can be a real time-saver in situations where it proves difficult to select a comples object directly.

1 In the Tools palette, select the Quick Selection tool (🖊). Remember; the Quick Selection tool is grouped in the Tools palette with the Selection Brush you used earlier.

2 In the tool options bar just above the Tools palette, make sure the New Selection mode button on the far left is activated. Set a brush diameter in the Brush picker. For the purposes of this exercise, you can use the default brush diameter of 30 pixels.

3 Scribble over the area around the water lily, making sure to touch some of the yellow, green, and black areas as shown in the illustration on the left below. Release the pointer to see the result. As you draw, Photoshop elements automatically expands the selection based on similarity of color and texture.

▶ **Tip:** If you want to simply scribble-select an area in the image, you can use a larger brush. If you need more control to draw a more precise outline, choose a smaller brush size.

4 With an active selection already in place, the Quick Selection tool defaults to Add To Selection mode (below, right). Scribble over, or click into, un-selected areas around the water lily until everything is selected but the flower itself.

5 Finally, turn the selection inside out by choosing Select > Inverse, thereby masking the background and selecting the flower—ready for the next exercise.

Working with selections

Now that you have an active selection outline around the water lily, you can apply any adjustment you like and only the flower will be affected.

1 With the water lily still selected, click the Quick tab at the top of the Task pane to switch to Quick Fix mode.

2 To make comparison more convenient, choose Before & After - Horizontal from the View menu at the left below the editing preview pane.

3 In the Color palette on the right, click and drag the Hue slider to the left or right to change the color of the water lily.

Notice that the water lily changes color, but the background does not. Only the pixels inside a live selection are effected by edits or adjustments.

4 Click the Cancel button in the Color palette to undo your changes.

You could also invert the selection to apply changes to the background instead of the water lily.

5 Click the Full button at the top of the Edit panel to switch to Full Edit mode.

6 With the water lily still selected, choose Select > Inverse.

7 With the background around the water lily selected, choose Enhance > Convert To Black And White.

8 In the Convert To Black And White dialog box, choose Urban/Snapshots under Select A Style.

9 (Optional) Select a different style to see the effect on the image. Use the Adjustment Intensity sliders to vary the amount of change for red, green, blue, and contrast. Click Undo if you made adjustments you don't like.

10 Click OK to close the Convert To Black And White dialog box.

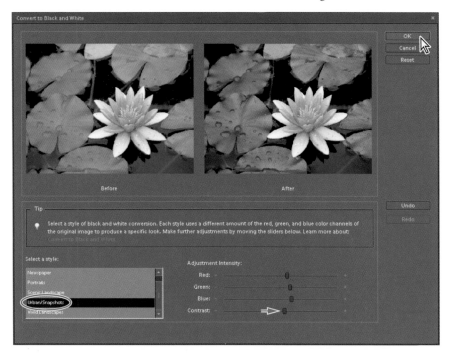

11 Choose Select > Deselect.

12 Choose File > Save As and save the file in the My CIB Work folder. In the File Name text box, type **06_05_Work**. Make sure that the Format setting is Photoshop (PSD). If the option Save Tn Version Set With Original is activated, disable it before you click Save.

13 Choose File > Close, and then switch back to the Organizer.

Congratulations, you've completed another exercise. You've learned how to use the Selection Brush tool and the Quick Selection tool to isolate areas of an image. You've also learned to mask out areas to which you don't want changes applied. You've also learned how to add a new selection to existing, saved selection. These techniques will be invaluable as you learn to use other selection tools.

Why won't Photoshop Elements do what I tell it to do?

In some situations, the changes you try to apply to an image may not seem to work. You may hear a beep, indicating that you're trying to do something that's not allowed. The following list offers explanations and solutions for common issues that might be blocking your progress.

Commit is required

Several tools, including the Type tool require you to click the Commit button before you can move on to another task. The same is true when you crop with the Crop tool or resize a layer or selection with the Move tool.

Cancel is required

The Undo command isn't available while you have uncommitted changes made with some tools—for example, the Type tool, Move tool, and Crop tool. If you want to undo these edits, click the Cancel button instead of using the Undo command or shortcut.

Edits are restricted by an active selection

When you create a selection (using a marquee tool, the Quick Selection tool, or the Selection Brush tool, for example), you limit the active area of the image. Any edits you make will apply only within the selected area. If you try to make changes to an area outside the selection, nothing happens. Edits are restricted by an active selection. If you want to deactivate a selection, choose Select > Deselect, and then you can work on any area of the image.

Move tool is required

If you drag a selection, the selection marquee moves, not the image within the selection marquee. If you want to move a selected part of the image or an entire layer, use the Move tool .

(continued on next page)

Why won't Photoshop Elements do what I tell it to do? *(continued)*

Background layer is selected

Many changes cannot be applied to the Background layer. For example, you can't erase, delete, change the opacity, or drag the Background layer to a higher level in the layer stack. If you need to apply changes to the Background layer, double-click it and rename it (or accept the default name, Layer 0).

Active layer is hidden

In most cases, the edits you make apply to only the currently selected layer—the one highlighted in the Layers palette. If an eye icon does not appear beside that layer in the Layers palette, then the layer is hidden and you cannot edit it. Or, if the image on the selected layer is not visible because it is blocked by an opaque upper layer, you will actually be changing that layer, but you won't see the changes in the image window.

The active layer is hidden, the view is blocked by an opaque upper layer, or the active layer is locked.

Active layer is locked

If you lock a layer by selecting the layer and then selecting the Lock in the Layers palette, the lock prevents the layer from changing. To unlock a layer, select the layer, and then select the Lock at the top of the Layers palette to remove the Lock.

Active layer is locked.

Wrong layer is selected (for editing text)

If you want to make changes to a text layer, be sure that layer is selected in the Layers palette before you start. If a non-text layer is selected when you click the Type tool in the image window, Photoshop Elements creates a new text layer instead of placing the cursor in the existing text layer.

Replacing the color of a pictured object

Photoshop Elements offers two methods of swapping a color in a photo: the Color Replacement tool and the Replace Color dialog box. The Color Replacement tool is grouped in the toolbox with the Brush tool, the Impressionist Brush tool, and the Pencil tool and enables you to replace specific colors in your image by painting over a targeted color with another. You can also use the Color Replacement tool for color correction.

Using the Replace Color dialog box is faster and more automatic than using the Color Replacement tool, but it doesn't work well for all types of images. This method is most effective when the color of the object you want to change is not found in other areas of the image. The photograph of a yellow car used for the following exercises is a good candidate for this approach as there is very little yellow elsewhere in the image.

Replacing a color throughout the image

In this exercise, you'll change the color of a yellow car. You'll do your work on a duplicate of the Background layer, which makes it easy to compare the finished project to the original picture.

What's great about the Replace Color feature is that you don't have to be too careful or meticulous when you apply it, yet you can still produce spectacular results. You'll do this exercise twice. First, you'll work on the entire image area, which will show you how much the color changes will affect the areas other than the car, such as the trees in the background. For the second part of the exercise you'll use an area selection to restrict the changes.

1   Using the Organizer, find the file 06_06.psd, a picture of a yellow car, and then open it in the Editor in Full Edit mode.

2   In the Editor, choose Layer > Duplicate Layer and accept the default name. Alternatively, drag the Background layer up to the New Layer button ( ) in the Layers palette. By duplicating the layer, you have an original to return to should you need it.

3 With the Background copy layer still selected in the Layers palette, choose Enhance > Adjust Color > Replace Color.

4 In the Replace Color dialog box, make sure the Eyedropper tool—the left-most of the three eyedropper buttons—is activated, and then click Image in the Selection options so that you can see the color thumbnail of the car. Click with the Eyedropper tool to sample the yellow paint of the car.

5 Below the thumbnail image in the Replace Color dialog box, change the Selection option from Image to Selection, so you see the extent of the color selection indicated as white on a black background.

6 Drag the Hue slider (and optionally the Saturation and Lightness sliders) to change the color of the selected area. For example, set the Hue value to –88 to change the yellow to pink.

7 To adjust the area of selected color—or color-application area—start by clicking the second of the three eyedropper buttons to activate the Add to Sample mode for the Eyedropper tool, and then click in the edit window in the areas where the paint on the car still appears yellow.

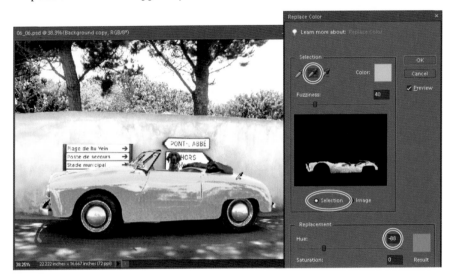

8 Drag the Fuzziness slider left or right until you find an acceptable compromise between full coverage on the car and the effect on other areas in the image. Try to avoid picking up any color in the wall.

9 When you're satisfied with the results, click OK to close the Replace Color dialog box.

Depending on what color and color characteristics you used to replace the yellow, you probably can see a shift in the color of the trees in the background. If this is a compromise you can live with, that's great—if not, you may need to try another technique. In the next exercise you'll do just that.

Replacing a color in a limited area of the image

In this exercise you'll repeat the previous procedure, but this time you'll limit the color change to a selected area of the photograph.

1 Choose Edit > Undo Replace Color, or select the step before Replace Color in the Undo History palette (Window > Undo History).

2 In the toolbox, select the Lasso tool and draw a rough selection marquee around the car. It's OK if some of the road and the wall in the background are included in the selection.

> ● **Note:** In the Tools palette, the Lasso tool is grouped with the Magnetic Lasso tool and the Polygonal Lasso tool. To switch from one lasso tool to another, click the tool in the toolbox and hold the mouse button down until a menu appears. Choose the desired tool from the menu.

3 In the tool options bar, click the Subtract From Selection button to set that
   mode for the Lasso tool.

4 Using the Lasso tool in Subtract From Selection mode, draw a shape around the
   yellow sticker on the windshield to remove it from the selection.

Note: It may be
helpful to zoom in for
this part of the process.
To avoid switching from
the Lasso to the Zoom
tool, choose Window >
Navigator and zoom in
using the slider in the
Navigator palette. You
can also zoom in using
the keyboard shortcut
Ctrl+ = (equal sign).

5 Choose Enhance > Adjust Color > Replace Color.

6 Using the same techniques and settings you used in the previous procedure,
   make adjustments in the Replace Color dialog box to change the color of the car.
   (See "Replacing a color throughout the image," steps 4-8.)

7 When you are satisfied with the results, click OK to close the Replace Color
   dialog box.

8 Choose Select > Deselect, or press Ctrl+D.

9 Choose File > Save As and save the file in the My CIB Work folder. Type **06_06_Work** for the new file name. Make sure that the Format option is set to Photoshop (PSD). If the Save In Version Set With Original option is activated, disable it before you click Save.

10 Choose File > Close, to close the file and return to the Organizer.

Take a bow—you've finished all the exercises in this lesson. In the last exercise, you learned how to make a selection with the Lasso tool and also how to edit that selection. You replaced one color with another using the Replace Color dialog box and in the process you were introduced to the Undo History palette and the Navigator.

About printing color pictures

Color problems in your photos can result from a variety of causes, such as incorrect exposure, the quality of the camera, or the conditions under which a photograph was taken. If an image is flawed, you can usually improve it by editing it with Photoshop Elements, as you did with the images in this lesson.

Sometimes, pictures that look great on your computer don't turn out so well when you print them. There are things you can do to make sure that what you get from the printer is closer to what you see on screen.

It's important that you calibrate your monitor regularly so that it's set to display the range of color in your photographs as accurately as possible.

Your prints may also look bad if your color printer interprets color information differently from your computer. You can correct that by activating the appropriate type of color management.

Working with color management

Moving a photo from your camera to your monitor and from there to a printer makes shifts the colors in the image. This shift occurs because every device has a different color gamut or color space—the range of colors that the device is capable of interpreting and producing. To achieve consistent color between digital cameras, scanners, computer monitors, and printers, you need to use color management.

Color management software acts as a color interpreter, translating the image colors so that each device can reproduce them in the same way. This software knows how each device and program understands color, and adjusts colors so that those you see on your monitor are similar to the colors in your printed image. It should be noted, however, that not all colors may match exactly.

5   The first tool you used in this lesson to make selections is the Selection Brush tool, which works like a paintbrush. The Quick Selection tool is similar to the Selection Brush tool, but is in most cases a faster, more flexible option. The Lasso tool creates free-form selections. There are more selection tools than are discussed in this lesson. The Magic Wand tool selects all the areas with the same color as the color on which you click. The Rectangular Marquee tool and the Elliptical Marquee tool make selections of fixed geometric shape. The Magnetic Lasso tool helps to draw selections along even quite irregular object edges, while the Polygonal Lasso tool restricts drawing to straight lines, making it the tool of choice to select straight-sided objects.

7 FIXING EXPOSURE PROBLEMS

Lesson Overview

You can use Photoshop Elements to fix images that are too dark or too light and to rescue photos that are dull, flat, or simply fading away. Start with Quick Fix and Guided Edit and work up to Full Edit mode.

In this lesson you'll be introduced to a variety of techniques for dealing with exposure problems:

- Brightening underexposed photographs
- Correcting parts of an image selectively
- Saving selection shapes to reuse in later sessions
- Working with adjustment layers
- Choosing layer blending modes
- Using layer opacity settings
- Enhancing overexposed and faded photographs

 You'll probably need between one and two hours to complete this lesson.

Learn how to make the most of images that were exposed incorrectly due to unusual lighting conditions such as strong backlighting. Retrieve detail from photos that are too dark and liven up images that look dull and washed-out. Find out how you can save those fading memories. Photoshop elements provides powerful, easy-to-use tools for correcting exposure problems in all three of its Edit modes.

This lesson assumes that you are already familiar with the main features of the Photoshop Elements workspace and that you recognize the two Photoshop Elements modules: the Organizer and the Editor. If you need to learn more about these subjects, see Lesson 1, "A Quick Tour of Photoshop Elements" and Photoshop Elements Help. This lesson builds on the skills and concepts covered in the earlier lessons.

Getting started

● **Note:** Before you start working on this lesson, make sure that you've installed the software on your computer from the application CD (see the Photoshop Elements 7 documentation) and that you have correctly copied the Lessons folder from the CD in the back of this book onto your computer's hard disk (see "Copying the Classroom in a Book files" on page 2).

For the exercises in this lesson you'll use the CIB Catalog you created in the "Getting Started" section at the beginning of this book. To use the CIB Catalog, follow these steps:

1   Start Photoshop Elements and click the Organize button in the Welcome Screen. The name of the currently active catalog is displayed in the lower left corner of the Organizer window. If the CIB Catalog is open, begin the first exercise, "Correcting images automatically as batch process." If the CIB Catalog is not open, complete the following steps.

2   Choose File > Catalog.

3   In the Catalog Manager dialog box, select the CIB Catalog and click Open.

If you don't see the CIB Catalog file listed, you should review the procedures in "Getting Started" at he beginning of this book. See "Copying the Lessons files from the CD" on page 2, and "Creating a catalog" on page 3.

Correcting images automatically in batches

You'll start this lesson in the same way that you began your work in Lesson 6—by batch-processing the photos in the lesson folder to apply the Photoshop Elements automatic fix adjustments. Later you can compare the automatic results with the results of the techniques you'll learn in the exercises.

▶ **Tip:** From the Welcome Screen you can go directly to the Full Edit mode by clicking the Edit button.

1   In the Organizer, click the Editor button (▨) near the top right corner of the workspace window and choose Full Edit from the menu.

If you already have the Editor open, switch to Full Edit mode by clicking the Full tab in the Task pane.

2   In the Editor, choose File > Process Multiple Files. The Process Multiple Files dialog box opens.

3   In the Process Multiple Files dialog box, set the source and destination folders as follows:

- Choose Folder from the Process Files From menu.

- Under Source, click the Browse button. Find and select the Lesson06 folder in the Lessons folder. Click OK to close the Browse For Folder dialog box.

- Under Destination, click Browse, and then find and select the My CIB Work folder that you created at the start of the book. Click OK to close the Browse For Folder dialog box.

4   Under File Naming, select Rename Files. Select Document Name from the menu on the left and type **_Autofix** in the second field. This adds the appendix "_Autofix" to the existing document name as the files are saved.

5   Under Quick Fix on the right side of the dialog box, activate all four options: Auto Levels, Auto Contrast, Auto Color, and Sharpen.

6   Review all the settings in the dialog box, comparing them to the illustration below. Make sure that the Resize Images and Convert Files options are disabled, and then, click OK.

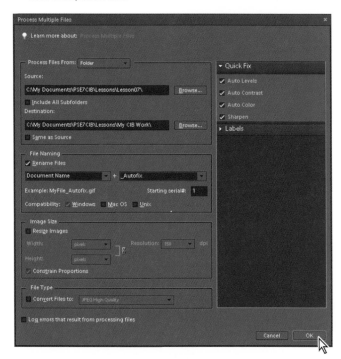

Photoshop Elements takes a few seconds to process the files. Image windows will open and close automatically as the adjustments are applied. There's nothing else you need to do. If any alerts or warnings appear, click OK.

At the end of this lesson, you can compare the results of these basic, automatic fixes with the results you achieve by applying the manual techniques as you work through the exercises. In some cases, the automatic method of fixing images may be sufficient to meet your needs.

Brightening an underexposed image

Slightly underexposed photographs tend to look dull and flat, or too dark. While the auto-fix lighting feature does a terrific job of brightening up many of these photos, in this exercise you'll learn some different methods for adjusting exposure.

Applying the Quick Fix

1 If you are still in the Editor, switch to the Organizer now.

2 In the Keyword Tags palette, click the Find box next to the Lesson 7 keyword tag.

● **Note:** To see the file names for images in the Photo Browser, choose View > Show File Names.

3 Click to select the file kat_and_kind.jpg, an underexposed image of a mother and child at the seaside.

4 Click the Editor button (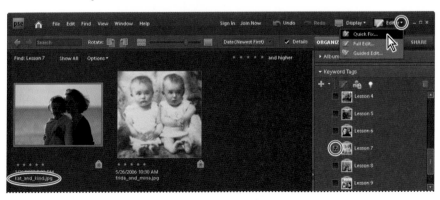) near the top right corner of the Organizer window and choose Quick Fix from the menu.

Photoshop Elements will load the Editor workspace and open the image in Quick Fix mode.

5   In the General Fixes palette, click the Smart Fix Auto button. The photo becomes a little brighter but the skin tomes are still quite dark.

6   In the Lighting palette, drag the Lighten Shadows slider to the right—just a little past the first divider bar. Drag the Midtone Contrast slider about half-way to the next divider to the right, as shown in the illustration below.

The image is substantially improved, though the skin tones are still a little cool.

7   In the Color palette, drag the Temperature and Hue sliders just fractionally to the right. Take care not to make the sky too pink or yellow.

8   When you are satisfied with the result, click the Commit button (✔) in the Color palette title bar to commit the changes.

Original image   Auto Smart Fix - Lighting sliders   Temperature & Hue tweaked

9 Choose File > Save As. In the Save As dialog box, navigate to and open the My CIB Work folder, rename the file kat_and_kind_Quick and choose the JPEG format. If the option Save In Version Set With Original is activated, disable it. Click Save. In the JPEG Options dialog box, choose High from the Quality menu, and then click OK.

10 Choose File > Close and return to the Organizer.

Without much effort the image has improved significantly. Let's try some other methods to adjust the lighting in the image and you can compare the results later.

Exploring Guided Edit

1 With the image kat_and_kind.jpg still selected in the Photo Browser, click the Editor button, and then choose Guided Edit from the menu.

The Editor workspace will load and open the original underexposed photo you used for the previous exercise—but this time in Guided Edit mode.

2 In the guided tasks menu, click the triangle beside Lighting and Exposure if necessary to see the options, and then choose Lighten Or Darken.

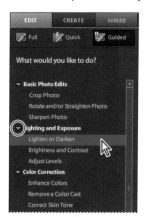

3 The Lighten Or Darken A Photo task panel opens. Click the Auto button near the top right corner of the Lighten Or Darken A Photo panel. You'll notice that in this case the result is not quite as good as you would expect. Click the Reset button at the bottom of the task panel, or choose Edit > Undo Auto Levels to revert the image to its original state.

4 Use the sliders to adjust the lighting in the image manually. Drag the Lighten Shadows slider to a value of 50 and the Midtone Contrasts to a value of 20; then, click Done.

5 Choose File > Save As. In the Save As dialog box, navigate to and open the My CIB Work folder, rename the file kat_and_kind_Guided and select the JPEG format. If the option Save In Version Set With Original is activated, disable it. Click Save. In the JPEG Options dialog box, choose High from the Quality menu, and then click OK.

6 Choose File > Close and return to the Organizer.

Again, the image now looks considerably better than its original; however, it would be ideal if the mother and child could be treated separately from the background of sea and sky.

Fixing an image in Full Edit mode

Underexposure problems are very often caused when your camera cuts down exposure to compensate for backlighting. In the case of our example image, the large area of relatively light sea and sky may contribute to the problem in this way, compounded by the fact that the lighting on our subjects is fairly low and indirect. Perhaps the camera's exposure settings were also incorrect. If your photo is a particularly difficult case, more elaborate methods than those you've used in the Quick Fix and Guided Edit modes might be necessary to achieve the best results.

In the Full Edit mode you can work with layers and blending modes and make selections to isolate different parts of an image for special treatment.

Using Blending modes

When an image file has multiple layers, each layer has its own blending mode that defines the way it will effect the layer or layers below it in the stacking order. By default, a new layer has a Normal blending mode: it will not blend with the layer below except where it contains transparency or when the opacity for the layer is set to less than 100%. The Darken and Lighten blending modes will blend a layer with the layer below it only where the result will darken or lighten the lower layer. Other blending modes produce more complex results.

If a photo is too dark, duplicating the base layer and applying the Screen blending mode to the new layer may correct the problem. If this technique produces too strong an affect, us the layer opacity setting to tone it down. Inversely, if your photo is overexposed—too light—duplicating the base layer and applying the Multiply blending mode to the new layer might be a solution.

1 With the image kat_and_kind.jpg still selected in the Photo Browser, click the Editor button, and then choose Full Edit from the menu. The Editor workspace will load and open the image in Full Edit mode.

2 In the Palette Bin, make sure that the Layers palette is open. The image has only one layer: the Background.

3 Do any one of the following to duplicate the Background layer:

   • With the Background layer selected in the Layers palette, choose Layer > Duplicate Layer, and then click OK in the Duplicate Layer dialog box, accepting the default name.

   • Right-click the Background layer in the Layers palette and choose Duplicate Layer from the context menu. Click OK in the Duplicate Layer dialog box, accepting the default name.

   • Drag and drop the Background layer onto the New Layer button ( ) in the Layers palette.

The new Background copy layer is highlighted in the Layers palette, indicating that it is the selected (active) layer.

4   With the Background copy layer selected in the Layers palette, choose Screen from the layer blending mode menu. Notice how the image becomes brighter.

● **Note:** If the layer blending mode menu is disabled, make sure that the copy layer, not the original Background layer, is selected in the Layers palette.

5   Choose File > Save As.

6   In the Save As dialog box, name the file **kat_and_kind_Screen**, choose Photoshop (PSD) from the Format menu, and make sure the Layers option is activated. Save the file to your My CIB Work folder. If the Save In Version Set With Original is activated, disable it before you click Save. If the Photoshop Elements Format Options dialog box appears, keep Maximize Compatibility selected and click OK.

7   In the Layers palette, click the eye icon to the left of the Background Copy layer to toggle its visibility so that you can compare the original with the adjusted image. When you've finished comparing, close the file without saving and return to the Organizer.

In this exercise you've seen how using a blending mode can brighten up a dull image. However, you should be careful about applying a blending mode over an entire image, as it can sometimes adversely affect parts of the photos that were OK to begin with. In this example, the sky is now overexposed and some subtle color detail has been lost. In the following exercises, you'll use other blending modes that are useful for correcting a wide range of image problems.

Adjusting color curves

Using the Adjust Color Curves command is a great way to fix common exposure problems, from photos that are too dark as a result of backlighting to images that appear washed-out due to overly harsh lighting. You can choose one of the preset adjustment styles as a solution or as a useful starting point—or improve color tones by adjusting the highlights, mid-tones, and shadows separately.

In the Adjust Color Curves dialog box, you can quickly see the results of each preset in the before and after preview. To fine-tune the adjustment, simply use the sliders. To preserve your original image, experiment with color curve adjustments on a duplicate layer.

To open the Adjust Color Curves dialog box, choose Enhance > Adjust Color > Adjust Color Curves. To adjust only a specific area of the image, select it with one of the selection tools before you open the Color Curves dialog box.

For of our sample image, the Lighten Shadows style preset made a good starting-point for some manual fine-tuning, mainly to the shadows and mid-tones.

Adding adjustment layers

Sometimes you need to go back and tweak an adjustment after you have had time to assess your first efforts. You may even want to alter your settings during a much later work session—perhaps to fit the image to a particular purpose for a project or presentation. This is when you will appreciate the power and versatility of adjustment layers and fill layers.

An adjustment layer is like a overlay or lens over the underlying layers, perhaps darkening the image, perhaps making it appear pale and faded, or intensifying its hues—but remaining separate. Any effects applied on an adjustment layer can be easily revised, because the pixels of the image are not permanently modified. This is an appreciable advantage, especially when you wish to apply the same changes to several images. You can either copy the adjustment layer and place it on top of the layers in another photo, or use the Process Multiple files command (for more information please refer to Photoshop Elements Help).

Creating adjustment layers for lighting

In this next exercise, we'll continue to use the same underexposed photograph to explore the possibility of improving the image by using an adjustment layer.

1   With the image kat_and_kind.jpg still selected in the Photo Browser, click the Editor button, and then choose Full Edit from the menu.

2   With the Background layer selected in the Layers palette, click the Create Adjustment Layer button (⬤) and choose Brightness/Contrast from the menu.

3   In the Brightness/Contrast dialog box, make sure that the Preview box is checked. Drag the dialog box aside, if necessary, so that you can see most of the image in the preview window. Drag the Brightness and Contrast sliders to set values of +80 and +25 respectively, and then click OK.

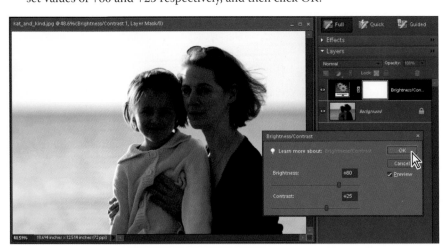

4   Click the Create Adjustment Layer button again, but this time choose Levels (instead of Brightness/Contrast) from the menu. Levels is an effective tonal and color adjustment tool. Notice the additional layer created in the Layers palette.

5   In the Levels dialog box, drag the black, gray, and white arrows (assigned to shadows, mid-tones and highlights respectively) under the graph to the left or right until the balance of dark and light areas looks right to you. We used values of 11, 1.2, and 250.

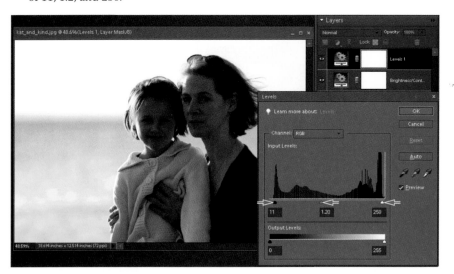

6   Click OK to close the Levels dialog box.

7   Choose File > Save As. In the Save As dialog box, name the file **kat_and_kind_ Adjustment**, choose the Photoshop (PSD) format, make sure the Layers option is activated. If the option Save In Version Set With Original is activated, disable it before saving the file to your My CIB Work folder. If the Photoshop Elements Format Options dialog box appears, keep Maximize Compatibility selected and click OK.

8   Close the file and return to the Organizer.

The beauty of adjustment layers is that you can always return to adjust your settings, even in future work sessions—as long as you have saved the file in the Photoshop (PSD) format, preserving the layers (the default). If you reopen the file you just closed and double-click the adjustment controls icon in the Brightness/Contrast layer, your original settings (+80 and +25) will still appear in the Brightness/ Contrast dialog box—the adjustment is still live and can be refined. If necessary, you could even revert to the original, uncorrected image by either hiding or deleting the adjustment layers.

Correcting parts of an image

Although the adjustment layers do a lot to help bring out the color and image detail from our dark original image, the background is now overexposed. So far in this lesson, all the corrections you've made to the image have been applied to the entire photo. In the next exercise you'll apply adjustments selectively to just part of the image.

Creating a selection

In this exercise you'll divide the image into two parts: our subjects in the foreground, and the sea and sky in the background. You'll start by selecting the silhouette of the mother and child and saving the selection.

There are different ways of making a selection—you've already explored some of them in Lesson 6. The choice of selection tool depends largely on the picture. For this exercise, we'll start with the Quick Selection tool, which makes a selection based on similarity in color and texture. All you need to do is scribble inside a pictured object and the Quick Selection tool automatically determines the selection borders for you.

1   With the image kat_and_kind.jpg still selected in the Photo Browser, click the Editor button, and then choose Full Edit from the menu.

2   In the toolbox, select the Quick Selection tool (<img>), which is grouped with the Selection Brush tool.

3   Make sure the New Selection mode is selected for the Quick Selection tool in the tool options bar.

4   Place the cursor at the lower right corner of the woman and slowly drag a line to the top of her head and then down across the child's face and body. Notice that the active selection automatically expands to create a border around the silhouette of our subjects. Not bad at all for a quick first pass.

Next you need to refine the border a little to capture the silhouette as closely as possible. You'll need to deselect the small area of background between the child's shoulder and her mother's chin and pay attention to hair and highlight areas. To refine your selection, you'll alternate between the Quick Selection tool's Add To Selection () and Subtract From Selection () modes. Buttons for these modes are located next to the New Selection mode button in the tool options bar.

5   Choose the Subtract From Selection () mode for the Quick Selection tool from the tool options bar.

6   With the Subtract From Selection tool, click in the space between the girl's shoulder and her mother's chin. The selection contracts to exclude this background area.

7   Keeping the Quick Selection tool active, press Ctrl+= (equal sign) to zoom in to the image, and hold the spacebar for the Hand Tool to move the image as required. Press the left bracket key '[' on your keyboard repeatedly to reduce the brush size for the Quick Selection tool. Alternate between the Add To Selection () and Subtract From Selection () modes and use a combination of clicks and very short strokes to modify the selection border around the area you deselected in step 6, paying attention to the hair and the small spaces in-between.

8   Without being overly fussy, continue to refine the selection around the subjects' heads using the same technique. Your work will be much simpler if you use

the keyboard shortcuts to navigate in the image and for the tool settings. Press Ctrl+= (equal) and Ctrl+- (minus) to zoom in and out. Hold the spacebar for the hand tool to move the image in the preview window. Increase and decrease the brush size by pressing the right and left bracket keys: ']' and '['. With the Quick Selection tool in New Selection mode, you can switch temporarily to Add To Selection mode by holding the Shift key, and to Subtract From Selection mode by holding the Alt key.

9   Finally, pay attention to the brightly highlighted area that runs from the little girl's right cheek down her arm and includes a portion of her mother's fingers. You should end up with a tight flashing selection outline around the silhouettes of both of the subjects.

10 To soften the hard edges of the selection, you can smooth and feather the outline. Click Refine Edge in the tool options bar.

11 In the Refine Edge dialog box, enter a value of 2 for Smooth and 1 pixel for Feather. These settings are quite low, but should be appropriate for our lesson image, which has a relatively low resolution. Notice that the Refine Edge dialog box has its own Zoom and Hand tools to help you get a better view of the details of your selection. Click OK.

12 Choose Select > Save Selection. In the Save Selection dialog box, choose New from the Selection menu, type **Mother and Child** to name the selection, and then click OK. Saving a selection is always a good idea, because you may find you wish to re-use it later—after assessing your adjustments you can always reload the selection and modify them.

Using layers to isolate parts of an image

Now that you've created a selection that includes only the figures in the foreground of the photo, you can adjust the exposure and color for the subjects and the background independently. You can bring out the shaded detail in the faces without overexposing the sky, and bring out the blue in the background without making the skin tones too cold.

The approach is to divide and conquer—to apply different solutions to different areas of the image. The next step in this process is to use your selection to isolate the foreground and background areas on separate layers. To make the job easier, let's make sure that the layer thumbnails are of a satisfactory size.

1 Choose Palette Options from the Layers palette Options menu.

2 In the Layers Palette Options dialog box, select either the large or medium thumbnail option. Any thumbnail size will work, just as long as you don't choose None—seeing the layer thumbnails can help you visualize the layers you're working with. Click OK.

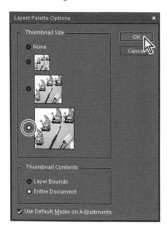

3 Choose View > Fit On Screen or, if the Zoom tool is active, click the Fit Screen button in the tool options bar so that you can see the entire image.

4 Do one of the following:

- If the selection you made in the previous exercise is still active, choose Select > Inverse, and then go on to Step 5.

- If the selection you made in the previous exercise is not still active, choose Select > Load Selection. Under Source, select Mother and Child from the

Selection menu and click the check box to activate the Invert option. Make sure New Selection is selected under Operation, and then click OK.

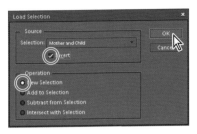

5   Choose Edit > Copy to copy the selected area.

6   Choose Edit > Paste. The copied area is pasted onto a new layer, named *Layer 1* by default.

You can see the new layer in the Layers palette, already selected. In the image window the selection is no longer active.

7   In the Layers palette, select the Background layer. Choose Select > Load Selection. Under Source, choose Mother And Child from the Selection menu, but this time do not activate the Invert option. Click OK.

8   Choose Edit > Copy.

9   With the Background layer still selected in the Layers palette, choose Edit > Paste.

Now you have three layers: Layer 1 with the sea and sky, Layer 2 with the figures in the foreground, and the Background layer with the entire image.

A new layer, whether it's created by pasting into the image or by clicking the new layer button or using the menu command—always appears immediately above the selected layer. The checker-board pattern in layers 1 and 2 indicates transparent areas.

10 You'll find it easier to work with the Layers palette if you name your layers descriptively—especially when you're working with images with a lot of layers. Double-click the name of Layer 2. The pointer changes to the text cursor and the name text is selected. Type **Figures** as the new name for the layer. Change the name of Layer 1 to **Sea & Sky**.

Now you're ready to work on each layer independently to improve the photo as a whole.

Correcting underexposed areas

We can now apply the most effective technique from the earlier exercises to the subjects of our photo selectively, and then fine-tune the result.

1 In the Layers palette, select the Figures layer and choose Screen from the blending menu. The figures are brighter and clearer, while the Sea & Sky layer remains unchanged.

2 Choose Enhance > Adjust Color > Adjust Color For Skin Tone. The pointer becomes an eyedropper. Sample a neutral skin area such as the center of the child's forehead, and then click OK.

Adding more intensity

Now that the figures in the foreground looks so much better, the sea and sky in the background need to be adjusted to appear less dull and murky.

1   In the Layers palette, select the Sea & Sky layer.

2   Choose Enhance > Auto Levels. Not only do the sea and sky look blue again —and far more vibrant—but we have also recovered a lot of textural detail in the background. However, the effect is too strong to sit well with the subdued late-afternoon light in the foreground.

3   Change the opacity of the Sea & Sky layer to 60% by dragging the Opacity slider or typing the new value into the text box.

With these few adjustments to the separate layers, the photograph now looks much more lively. There are still a lot of possibilities to continue playing around with for improving different areas of the image; for example you could separate the sky onto a new layer and intensify the cloud contrast. There is also more you could do with blending modes and layer opacity—you'll learn more about those techniques later in this lesson and as you work further through this book.

4   Choose File > Save As.

5   In the Save As dialog box, name the file kat_and_kind_Layers and save it to your My CIB Work folder, in Photoshop (PSD) format with the Layers option activated. The option Save In Version Set With Original should be disabled.

If the Photoshop Elements Format Options dialog box appears, keep Maximize Compatibility selected and click OK.

6 Close the file and return to the Organizer.

In Lesson 6 you learned how you can tile image windows to best compare the results of your different methods for adjusting an image. It's a good idea to use that technique now to compare the six adjusted and saved versions of this photo before moving on to the next exercise.

Improving faded or overexposed images

In this exercise, you'll work with the scan of an old photograph that has faded badly and is in danger of being lost forever—a photo of a beloved grandmother and her twin sister when they were babies. Like our example, such a photo may not be an award-winning shot, but it could represent a valuable and treasured aspect of personal history, which you might want to preserve for future generations.

The automatic fixes you applied to a copy of this image at the beginning of this lesson (see "Correcting images automatically in batches") improved the photograph markedly. In this project, you'll try to do even better using other techniques.

Creating a set of duplicate files

You'll compare a variety of techniques during the course of this project. You can begin by creating a separate file to test each method. You'll name each file for the technique it demonstrates.

1   If the Organizer is not currently active, switch to it now. In the Keyword Tags palette, click the Find box next to the Lesson 7 keyword tag.

2   In the Photo Browser, click to select the image frida_and_mina.jpg, a faded photo of twin babies.

3   Click the Editor button (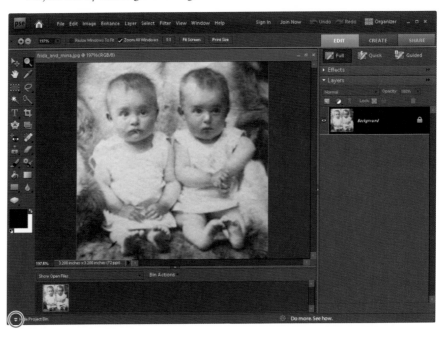) near the top right corner of the Organizer window and choose Full Edit from the menu. In the Full Edit workspace, open the Project Bin by clicking the triangle in the lower left corner of the window.

4   In the Editor, choose File > Duplicate. In the Duplicate Image dialog box, type frida_and_mina_Shad_High, and then click OK.

5   Repeat Step 5 twice more, naming the duplicate files frida_and_mina_Bright_ Con and frida_and_mina_Levels.

6   In the Project Bin, double-click the frida_and_mina.jpg thumbnail to make that image active. You can see the name of a file in the Project Bin displayed in a Tooltip window when you hold the pointer over the thumbnail image.

7   Choose File > Save As. In the Save As dialog box, type **frida_and_mina_Blend_ Mode** as the new file name and select Photoshop (PSD) from the Format menu. Select your My CIB Work folder as the Save In location. If Save In Version Set With Original is activated, disable it before you click Save.

8   Click OK to accept the default settings in any dialog boxes or messages that appear. Leave all four images open for the rest of the project.

While you're working in the Editor, you can always tell which images you have open—even when a single active photo fills the edit window—by looking in the project bin. When you can see more than one photo in the edit window, you can identify the active image by the un-dimmed text in its title bar.

9   Choose Window > Images > Tile.

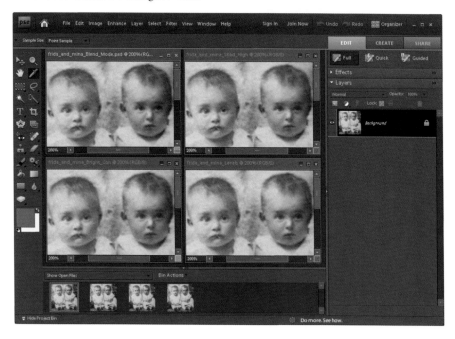

Using blending modes to fix a faded image

Blending modes make layers interact with the layers beneath them in a variety of ways. The Multiply mode intensifies or darkens pixels in an image. The Overlay mode tends to brighten an image while preserving its tonal range. For this project, you'll use the Overlay mode to add clarity and brilliance without canceling out the effect of the Multiply blending mode you'll use on the underlying layers.

1 Make sure that the image frida_and_mina_Blend_Mode.psd is the active window. If necessary, double-click its thumbnail in the Project Bin to make it active.

2 Duplicate the Background layer by choosing Layer > Duplicate Layer. Click OK in the Duplicate Layer dialog box, accepting the default name, Background copy.

Leave the Background copy layer selected in the Layers palette for the next step.

3 In the Layers palette, choose Multiply from the layer blending mode menu.

4 Drag the Background copy layer with its Multiply blend mode onto the New Layer button ( ) in the Layers palette to create a copy of the Background copy layer. Accept the default name, Background copy 2.

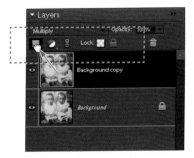

5 In the Layers palette, change the blending mode for the Background copy 2 layer from Multiply to Overlay. Set the layer's Opacity value to 50%, either by dragging the Opacity slider or by typing the new value in the text field.

The stacking order of the layers makes a difference to how blending modes affect an image In our example, if you drag the layer with the Multiply blending mode to a position above the layer with the Overlay mode, you'll see slightly different results.

6 (Optional) Fine-tune the results by adjusting the Opacity settings for the two background copy layers until you achieve a pleasing balance.

● **Note:** You cannot change the Opacity or the layer Blending mode of the locked Background layer.

The Multiply blending mode made the image bolder and the Overlay blending mode brightens it considerably, but the contrast is still unimpressive.

7 Choose File > Save to save the file in the My CIB Work folder. Leave the file open.

8 If a message appears about maximizing compatibility, click OK to close it, or follow the instructions in the message to prevent it from appearing again.

Adjusting shadows and highlights manually

Although both Auto-fix and the technique using blending modes do a good job of correcting fading images, some of your own photos may be more challenging. You'll try three new techniques in the next exercises.

The first method involves making manual adjustments to the Shadows, Highlights, and Midtone Contrast of the image.

1 In the Project Bin, double-click the thumbnail for the image frida_and_mina_ Shad_High to make it the active window.

2 Choose Enhance > Adjust Lighting > Shadows/Highlights.

3 Activate the Preview option in the Shadows/Highlights dialog box if it is not already active. If necessary, move the dialog box so that you can also see most of the frida_and_mina_Shad_High image window.

By default, the Lighten Shadows setting is 25%. You can see difference in the image by toggling the Preview option on and off in the Shadows/Highlights dialog box.

4   In the Shadows/Highlights dialog box, set the Lighten Shadows value to 30%, the Darken Highlights value to 15%, and the Midtone Contrast slider to +20%.

▶ **Tip:** The controls you are using to make the adjustments for this technique are also available in the Lighting palette in Quick Fix mode.

5   Adjust the three settings as needed until you think the image is as good as it can be. When you're done, click OK to close the Shadows/Highlights dialog box.

6   Choose File > Save As and save the file as frida_and_mina_Shad_High to your My CIB Work folder, in JPEG format. Click OK to accept the default settings in the JPEG Options dialog box and leave the file open in the Editor.

Adjusting brightness and contrast manually

The next approach you'll take to fixing an exposure problem uses another command that is available from the Enhance > Adjust Lighting menu.

1   In the Project Bin, double-click the image frida_and_mina_Bright_Con to make it active.

2   Choose Enhance > Adjust Lighting > Brightness/Contrast.

If necessary, drag the Brightness/Contrast dialog box aside so that you can see most of the frida_and_mina_Bright_Con image window.

3   In the Brightness/Contrast dialog box, click the checkbox to activate Preview, if it is not already active.

4   Drag the Brightness slider to -20, or type -20 in the text field, being careful to include the minus sign when you type. Set the Contrast to +40.

5   Adjust the Brightness and Contrast settings until you are happy with the quality of the image. Click OK to close the Brightness/Contrast dialog box.

6   Choose File > Save As and save the file as frida_and_mina_Bright_Con to your My CIB Work folder, in JPEG format. Click OK to accept the default settings in the JPEG Options dialog box and leave the file open in the Editor.

Adjusting levels

The Levels controls (again, available from the Enhance > Adjust Lighting menu) affect the range of tonal values in an image—the degree of darkness or lightness, regardless of color. In this exercise, you'll enhance the photograph by shifting the reference points that define the spread of those tonal values.

1   In the Project Bin, double-click the image frida_and_mina_Levels to make it active.

2   Choose Enhance > Adjust Lighting > Levels.

3   Activate the Preview option in the Levels dialog box, if it is not already active.

The Levels graph represents the distribution of pixel values in the image. As you can see, in this image there are no truly white pixels or truly black pixels. By dragging the end sliders inward to where the pixels start to appear in the graph, you redefine which levels are calculated as black or white. This will enhance the contrast between the lightest pixels in the image and the darkest ones.

If necessary, drag the Levels dialog box aside so that you can also see most of the image window.

4   In the Levels dialog box, drag the black triangle below the left end of the graph to the right and position it under the point where the graphed curve begins to climb. The value in the first Input Levels box should be approximately 42.

5   Drag the white triangle from the right side of the graph until it reaches the end of the steepest part of the graphed curve. The value in the third Input Levels box should be approximately 225.

6   Drag the gray triangle below the center of the graph toward the right to set the mid-tone value to approximately 0.90. Click OK to close the Levels dialog box.

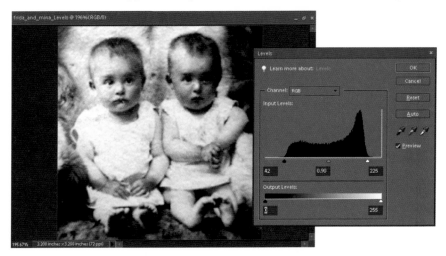

7   Choose File > Save As and save the file to your My CIB Work folder as frida_and_mina_Levels, in the JPEG format. Click OK to accept the default settings in the JPEG Options dialog box and leave the file open in the Editor.

Comparing results

You can now compare the six versions of the image: the original file, the four files you saved showing the results of the preceding exercises, and image that was fixed automatically as part of a batch process at the beginning of this lesson.

1   In the Editor, choose File > Open. Locate and open the file frida_and_mina_Autofix.jpg in the My CIB Work folder. If you don't see the file in the Open dialog box, make sure All Formats is selected in the Files Of Type menu.

2   Repeat the same process to open the file frida_and_mina.jpg in the Lesson 7 folder. Again, if you don't see the file in the Open dialog box, make sure All Formats is selected in the Files Of Type menu.

3   Check the Project Bin to make sure that only the six files for this project are open: the original image, frida_and_mina.jpg, and five others with the appendixes _Blend_Mode.psd, _Shad_High.jpg, _Bright_Con.jpg, _Levels.jpg,

and _Autofix.jpg. To see the file names displayed under the thumbnails in the Project Bin, right-click an empty area in the Project Bin and choose Show Filenames from the context menu.

4   Choose Window > Images > Tile.

5   Now you'll set the zoom level for all active windows. Select the Zoom tool. In the tool options bar, click the Zoom Out button and activate Zoom All Windows. Click in any of the image windows so that you can see a large enough area of the photo to be able to compare the different results. Zoom in to focus on details. Select an area of interest in one window, and then choose Window > Images > Match Zoom and Windows > Images > Match Location.

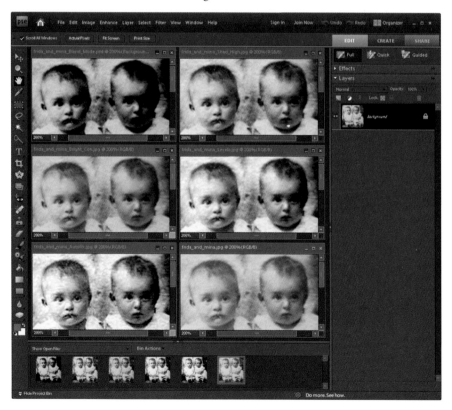

6 Compare the results and pick your favorite. The best method for fixing a file depends on the type of problem being addressed, the areas of the image that are affected, and how you intend to use the adjusted image.

7 Choose Window > Images > Cascade or Window > Images > Maximize to disable image tiling.

8 Choose File > Close All. Save your changes to your CIB Work folder if you're prompted to do so and return to the Organizer.

Congratulations! You've finished another lesson. In the exercises in this lesson you used a variety of both automatic and manual techniques for correcting exposure problems. You've tried auto-fixes, layer blending modes, and lighting adjustment controls. You've learned how to apply these different methods either to layers, in selections, separately, and in combination to get the most from a problem image.

Review questions

1 Describe two ways to create an exact copy of an existing layer.

2 Where can you find the controls for adjusting the lighting in a photograph?

3 How do you change the arrangement of image windows in the work area?

4 What is an adjustment layer and what are its unique benefits?

Review answers

1 Photoshop Elements must be in Full Edit mode to copy a layer. You can select the layer you want to duplicate in the Layers palette, and then choose Layer > Duplicate Layer. Alternatively, drag the layer to the New Layer button in the Layers palette. In either case, you get two layers, identical in all but their names, stacked one above the other.

2 You can adjust the lighting for a photo in either Full Edit, Guided Edit, or Quick Fix mode. In Full Edit, you can use the Enhance > Adjust Lighting menu to open various dialog boxes that contain the controls. Or, you can choose Enhance > Auto Levels, Enhance > Auto Contrast, or Enhance > Adjust Color > Adjust Color Curves. In the Guided Edit mode, choose Lighting and Exposure. In Quick Fix mode, you can use the Lighting palette in the Palette Bin.

3 You cannot rearrange image windows in Quick Fix and Guided Edit modes, which display only one photograph at a time. In the Full Edit workspace, there are several ways you can arrange them. One is to choose Window > Images, and select one of the choices listed there. Another method is to use the maximize or tile windows buttons in the upper right corner of each edit window. A third way is to drag the image window title bar to move an image window, and drag a corner to resize it (provided Maximize mode is not currently active).

4 An adjustment layer does not contain an image. Instead, it modifies some quality of all the layers below it in the Layer palette. For example, a Brightness/Contrast layer can alter the brightness and contrast of any underlying layers. One advantage of using an adjustment layer instead of adjusting an existing layer directly is that adjustment layers are easily reversible. You can click the eye icon for the adjustment layer to remove the effects instantly, and then restore the eye icon to apply the adjustments again. You can change a setting in an adjustment layer at any time—even in a later editing session when the file has already been saved.

8 REPAIRING AND RETOUCHING IMAGES

Lesson Overview

Sometimes you may need to deal with image flaws other than color or exposure problems. You may have an antique photograph that is damaged or a scanned image with dust and scratches. Your photo may be tilted or spoilt by red eye effect or spots and blemishes on a person's skin.

In this lesson, you'll learn some techniques for repairing and retouching flawed images:

- Using the Straighten tool
- Removing red eyes in the Organizer
- Retouching skin with the Healing Brush tool
- Repairing creases with the Clone Stamp tool
- Using the Selection Brush tool
- Masking parts of an image

 You'll probably need between one and two hours to complete this lesson.

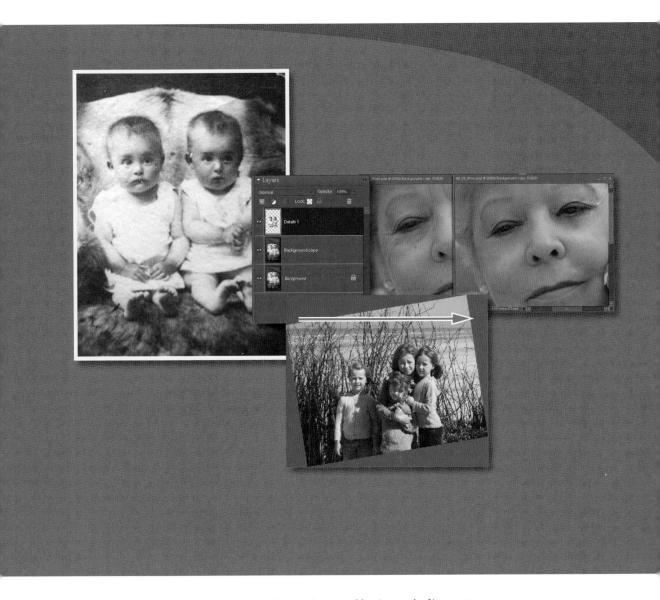

Not every image problem is a result of incorrect exposure or color imbalance. Learn how to improve an image by straightening it or by retouching blemishes on your subject's skin. The same techniques and tools used to remove spots or repair creases and tears when restoring a treasured keepsake can be used creatively to remove an object that's spoiling an image, or even to add one that would enhance it.

259

Getting started

Note: Before you start working on this lesson, make sure that you've installed the software on your computer from the application CD (see the Photoshop Elements 7 documentation) and that you have correctly copied the Lessons folder from the CD in the back of this book onto your computer's hard disk (see "Copying the Classroom in a Book files" on page 2).

The lesson includes four independent exercises—you can do them all at once or in separate work sessions. The first three projects vary only slightly in length and complexity, while the fourth is a little more involved. For the exercises in this lesson you'll use photos from the CIB Catalog you created in the "Getting Started" section at the beginning of this book.

1 Start Photoshop Elements and click the Organize button in the Welcome Screen.

The name of the currently active catalog is displayed in the lower left corner of the Organizer window.

If the CIB Catalog is already open, you can skip ahead to step 3. If the CIB Catalog is not already open, complete step 2 first.

2 Choose File > Catalog. In the Catalog Manager dialog box, select the CIB Catalog and click Open.

If you don't see the CIB Catalog file listed, you should review the procedures in "Getting Started" at he beginning of this book. See "Copying the Lessons files from the CD" on page 2, and "Creating a catalog" on page 3.

3   In the Keyword Tags palette, click the Find box next to the Lesson 8 keyword tag. Click to select the file 08_01.jpg in the Photo Browser. If you don't see the filenames below the thumbnails in the Photo Browser, choose View > Show File Names.

4   In the Organizer, click the Editor button () near the top right corner of the workspace window and choose Full Edit from the menu. The photo 08_01.jpg opens in the Editor.

As you can see, the picture is not exactly horizontal. When you're taking a photo it's easy to be distracted or rushed by awkward shooting conditions or the need to focus your attention on live subjects and the result is often an image that would be just fine—if only it were straight!

Using the Straighten tool

With the Straighten tool you can manually specify a line in a tilted image that should be horizontal or vertical and Photoshop will straighten the image accordingly.

1   In the toolbox, select the Straighten tool ().

2   For this image, the horizon is visible and can be used as a natural reference. With the Straighten tool, drag a line along the horizon from the top left to the right border.

▶ **Tip:** If you wish to straighten a photo relative to an element in the image that should be vertical— such as an architectural detail or perhaps a signpost—hold down the Ctrl key on your keyboard as you drag with the Straighten tool. The image will be rotated so that your line is vertical.

3   When you release the mouse button, Photoshop Elements straightens the image relative to the line you've just drawn.

4   In the toolbox, select the Crop tool (⯐). Drag a cropping rectangle inside the image, which is now displayed at an angle, being careful not to include any of the gray area around the photo. When you're satisfied with the crop, click the green Commit button in the lower right corner of the cropping rectangle.

▶ **Tip:** For some images, you may want to consider using the commands Image > Rotate > Straighten Image or Image > Rotate > Straighten and Crop Image, which perform straightening functions automatically.

5   The straightened and cropped image is much more comfortable to look at than the tilted original. Choose File > Save As. In the Save As dialog box, navigate to your My CIB Work folder. Disable the Save in Version Set with Original option, choose JPEG from the Format menu, name the file **08_01_Straight.jpg**, and then click Save.

6   Click OK in the JPEG Options dialog box to accept the default settings.

7   Choose File > Close to close the file.

Removing red eye in the Organizer

The red eye effect is caused by the reflection of the camera's flash from the subject's retinas. You'll see it more often when taking pictures in a darkened room, because the subject's pupils are then wide open.

You can have Photoshop Elements automatically fix red eyes as part of the import process (see the sidebar "Automatically Fixing Red Eyes" in Lesson 2). Lesson 6 discusses the tools available in the Editor for fixing red eye effects (see "Using automatic Red Eye Fix in the Editor" and "Using the Red Eye Removal tool" in Lesson 6).

For this exercise you'll fix the problem without even leaving the Organizer. You can use a menu command to remove the red eye effect from one or more selected photos while viewing them in the Photo Browser.

1   In the Organizer, click the Find box next to the Lesson 8 keyword tag.

2   In the Photo Browser, click to select the file 08_02.jpg, a picture of a startled child staring straight into the camera. If you don't see the filenames below the thumbnails in the Photo Browser, choose View > Show File Names.

3   In the Fix panel of the Task pane, click the Auto Red Eye Fix button. If you prefer to use a menu command, choose Edit > Auto Red Eye Fix. Both commands trigger the same process.

A progress window will appear displaying the progress of the red eye fix.

When the fix is complete, the Auto Fix Red Eye dialog box may appear informing you that a version set was created. Version sets are identified by the version set icon in the upper right corner of the thumbnail. *(See the illustration on the next page.)*

4   Click OK, to close the Auto Red Eye Fix Complete dialog box.

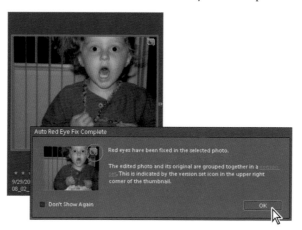

5   If it's not still selected, click to select the image 08_02.jpg in the Photo Browser. To view the results in the Editor, click the Editor button located near the top right corner of the Organizer window and choose Full Edit from the menu. Alternatively, click the Full Edit button in the Fix panel of the Task pane.

6   In the Editor, click the Zoom tool (🔍) in the toolbox. Select the Zoom In mode for the tool in the tool options bar, and then click the photo to view the results of the Auto Fix Red Eye fix. The red has been removed from the child's eyes.

7   Choose File > Close to close the file and return to the Organizer.

Fixing Blemishes

There are three main tools in Photoshop Elements for fixing flaws in your photos:

The Spot Healing Brush tool

The Spot Healing Brush is the easiest way to remove wrinkles in skin and other small imperfections in your photos. Either click once on a blemish or click and drag to smooth it away. By blending the information of the surrounding area into the problem spot, imperfections are made indistinguishable.

The Healing Brush tool

The Healing Brush can fix larger imperfections with ease. You can define one part of your photo as a source to be sampled and blended into another area. The Healing Brush is so flexible you can even remove large objects from a uniform background—such as a person in a wheat field.

The Clone Stamp tool

Rather than blending the source and target areas, the Clone Stamp tool paints directly with a sample of an image. You can use the Clone Stamp tool to remove or duplicate objects in your photo. This tool is great for getting rid of garbage, power lines, or a signpost that may be spoiling a view.

Removing wrinkles and spots

In this exercise, you'll explore several techniques for retouching skin flaws and blemishes to improve a portrait photograph. Retouching skin can be a real art, but luckily Photoshop Elements provides several tools that make it easy to smooth out lines and wrinkles, remove blemishes, and blend skin tones.

1   In the Organizer, find and select the file 08_03.jpg, which is tagged with the Lesson 8 keyword tag. If you don't see the filenames below the thumbnails in the Photo Browser, choose View > Show File Names.

2   Click the Editor button located near the upper right corner of the Organizer workspace window and choose Full Edit from the menu.

3   The Editor opens in Full Edit mode. If the Palette Bin and Project Bin are not already open, you can open them now by choosing Window > Palette Bin and Window > Project Bin. You should see a check mark beside both menu options.

4   If the Layers palette is not visible in the Palette Bin, choose Windows > Layers to open it now.

● **Note:** For help working with palettes and the Palette Bin, see "Using the Palette Bin" in Lesson 1, "A Quick Tour of Photoshop Elements."

Preparing the file for editing

Before you actually start retouching, you'll set up the layers that you'll need and save the file with a new name to make it easy to identify as your work file.

1 In the Layers palette of the Editor, drag the Background layer to the New Layer button ( ) in the Layers palette to create another layer, which will be called Background copy. Drag the Background copy layer to the New Layer button to create a third layer, which will be called Background copy 2.

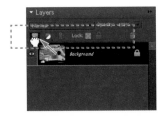  

2 Choose File > Save As and save the file in Photoshop (PSD) format as **08_03_Work** in your My CIB Work folder. If the option Save In Version Set With Original is activated, disable it before you click Save. Make sure the Layers checkbox is selected.

Using the Healing Brush tool

Now you're ready to retouch the subject's skin using the Healing Brush tool.

1 Make sure the layer Background copy 2 is still active. Zoom in on the upper half of the photo, as you'll be retouching the skin around the woman's eyes first.

2 Select the Healing Brush tool ( ), which is grouped with the Spot Healing Brush tool in the toolbox.

3   In the tool options bar, click the small arrow to open the Brush Picker and set the Diameter to 15 px. Set the brush Mode to Normal and the Source to Sampled. Disable the Aligned and All Layers options, if they are active.

4   With the Healing Brush tool, Alt-click a smooth area of skin on the woman's right cheek to sample that area as the reference texture. The Healing Brush tool won't work until you establish the sample area. If you switch to another tool and then back to the Healing Brush, you'll need to repeat this step.

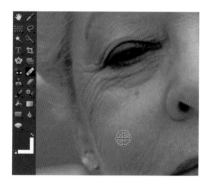

5   Draw a short horizontal stroke under the left eye. As you drag, it looks as if you're creating a strange effect, but when you release the mouse button, the color is blended and natural skin tones fill in the area.

▶ **Tip** Be very careful to keep your brush strokes short. You can also try just clicking rather than dragging. Longer strokes may produce unacceptable results. If that happens, choose Edit > Undo Healing Brush, or use the Undo History palette to backtrack. Also, make sure that Aligned is not selected in the tool options bar.

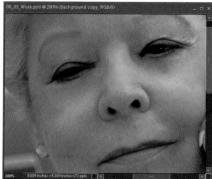

6   Continue to smooth the skin on the face, hands, and neck with the Healing Brush. Avoid the areas very close to the eyes or near the edges of the face. As you work, reestablish the reference texture occasionally by Alt+clicking in other parts of the face to sample different skin tones.

7   Use the Undo History palette (Window > Undo History) to quickly undo a series of steps. Every action you perform is recorded in chronological order from top to bottom of the palette. To restore the file to an earlier state, simply select an earlier action in the Undo History palette. If you change your mind before making any further changes to the file, you can still restore the image to a later state by selecting a step lower in the list.

The Healing Brush tool copies texture from the source area, not color. It samples the colors in the target area—the area it brushes—and arranges those colors according to the texture of the reference area. Consequently, the Healing Brush tool appears to be smoothing the skin. So far, the results are not convincingly realistic, but you'll work on that in the next exercise.

▶ **Tip:** To remove spots and small imperfections in your photo, try the Spot Healing Brush as an alternative to the Healing Brush. You can either click or drag with the brush to smooth away imperfections.

Refining the healing brush results

In this next exercise, you'll use layer opacity and another texture tool to finish your work on this image.

1   Use the Navigator palette (Window > Navigator) to zoom in to the area of the woman's face around the eyes and mouth.

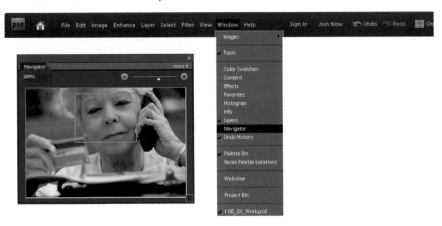

Extensive retouching can leave skin looking artificially smooth, like molded plastic. Reducing the opacity of the retouched layer gives the skin a more realistic look by allowing some of the wrinkles on the original Background layer to show through.

2   In the Layers palette, change the Opacity of the layer Background copy 2 to about 60%, using your own judgment to set the exact percentage.

3   Select the layer Background copy to make it the active layer.

4   In the toolbox, select the Blur tool (). In the tool options bar, set the brush diameter to approximately 13 px and set the Blur tool's Strength to 50%.

5   With the layer Background copy selected and active, drag the Blur tool over some of the deeper lines around the eyes, mouth, and brow. Use the Navigator palette to change the zoom level and shift the focus as needed. Reduce the Blur tool brush diameter to 7 px, and then smooth the lips a little, avoiding the edges.

Compare your results to the original, the version retouched with the Healing Brush, and final refined version below. Toggle the visibility of the retouched layers to compare the original image with your edited results.

Original

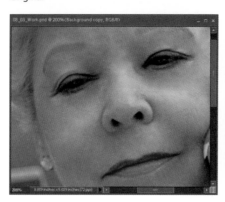

Healing Brush 100% Opacity

Healing Brush 60% Opacity with Blur tool

6   Choose File > Save to save your changes, and then close the file and return to the Organizer.

In this exercise, you've learned how to set an appropriate source for the Healing Brush tool, and then sample the texture of the source area to repair flaws in another part of the photograph. You also used the Blur tool to smooth textures, and an opacity change to create a more realistic look.

Restoring a damaged photograph

All sorts of nasty things can happen to precious old photographs—or precious new photographs, for that matter—and it is often impossible to locate the negative. For this exercise you'll work with an uncropped version of one of the photos you adjusted in the previous chapter.

The scanned image of an antique photograph that you'll use in this project is a challenging restoration job, because of large creases in the original print, among other flaws.

Unfortunately, there's no way to fix such significant damage in just one or two keystrokes but to rescue an important heirloom photograph like this one, a little effort is worthwhile and the results can be dramatic.

Photoshop Elements provides the tools you'll need to restore this picture to a convincing simulation of its original condition. You'll repair creases and replace parts of the image that are actually missing, fix frayed edges, and remove dust and scratches. You may be surprised to discover how easy it is to achieve impressive results.

Preparing a working copy of the image file

The first thing you need to do is to set up a work file with a duplicate layer.

1   In the Organizer, find and select the file 08_04.psd, a scanned antique photo of twin babies, tagged with the Lesson 8 keyword tag. Click the Editor button in the upper right of the Organizer window and choose Full Edit from the menu.

2   In the Editor, choose File > Save As. In the Save As dialog box, name the file **08_04_Work** and choose Photoshop (PSD) from the Format menu. If the option Save In Version Set With Original is active, be sure to disable it before you save the file to your My CIB Work folder.

3   Choose Layer > Duplicate Layer and in the Duplicate Layer dialog box, click OK to accept the default name: Background copy.

Using the Clone Stamp tool to fill in missing areas

The first thing you'll do is to eliminate the creases using the Clone Stamp tool. The Clone Stamp tool paints with information sampled from an image, which is perfect for both covering unwanted objects and replacing detail that is missing, as is the case for the worn areas along the creases.

1 With the help of the Navigator palette or the Zoom tool, zoom in on the crease in the lower right corner.

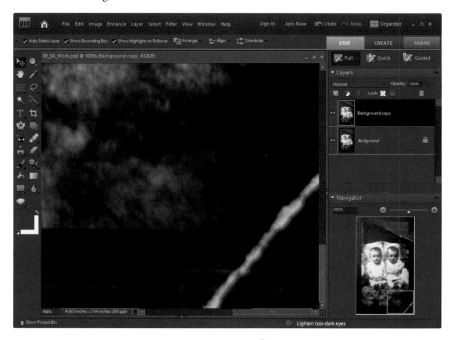

2 In the toolbox, select the Clone Stamp tool (📑), which is grouped with the Pattern Stamp tool.

3 On the left end of the tool options bar, click the triangle and choose Reset Tool from the menu.

The Reset Tool command reinstates the default values for the Clone Stamp tool: Size: 21 px, Mode: Normal, Opacity: 100%, and the Aligned option is activated.

4   In the tool options bar, open the Brush Picker. Choose Basic Brushes from the Brushes menu, and then select a hard mechanical brush with the size of 48 pixels. Set the Mode to Normal, the Opacity to 100%, and select Aligned.

5   Move the Clone Stamp tool to the left of the crease at the bottom of the picture. Hold down the Alt key and click to set the source position—the area to be sampled. Centering the source on a horizontal line makes it easier to align the brush for cloning. The tool duplicates the pixels at this point in your image as you paint.

6   Position the brush over the damaged area so that it is aligned horizontally with the source reference point. Click and drag to the right over the crease to copy the source image onto the damaged area. As you drag, cross-hairs appear, indicating the source—that is, the area that the Clone Stamp tool is sampling.

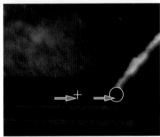

Note: If necessary, you can reset the source by at any time by Alt-clicking in a different location.

7   To repair the upper part of the crease, set the source position in the area above the crease and drag downwards. This will help you blend the repair with the vertical edges of the photograph's mount.

8   Continue to drag the brush over the creased, damaged area, resetting the source position as necessary, until the repair is complete.

The cross-hairs follow the movement of the brush. With the Aligned option acti-vated in the tool options bar, the cross-hairs maintain the same position relative to the brush that was set when you made the first brush stroke. When the Aligned option is disabled, the cross-hairs return to their original position at the beginning of each new stroke, regardless of where it is made.

9   Now, smooth out the crease across the upper right corner. For this operation the Healing Brush tool () is the best choice, because the crease is quite severe and has caused significant variations in the background color. The Healing brush set to a small brush size is also the right tool to restore large white speck on the ear of the baby on the right.

10 Choose File > Save to save your changes.

Using the Selection Brush tool

The next step in restoring this photo is to use the Dust & Scratches filter to remove the stray spots and frayed edges from the scanned image. This filter smooths out the pixels by blurring the image just slightly. This is fine for the background, but the subjects—the children—should be kept as detailed and sharp as possible. To do that, you'll need to create a selection that includes only the areas you want to blur.

▶ **Tip:** In the same way that the Spot Healing Brush tool can provide a quicker alternative to the Healing Brush, the Quick Selection tool is a faster alternative to the Selection Brush. However, the Quick Selection Brush tool automatically makes a selection based on similarities in color and texture, so it's more effective in some situations than others.

1   In the toolbox, select the Selection Brush tool (), which is grouped with the Quick Selection tool. Be careful to not select a painting brush tool by mistake.

2   In the tool options bar, select a round brush shape and set the brush size to about 60 pixels. Leave the other options at the default values: Mode should be set to Selection and Hardness should be set to 100%.

3   Drag the brush around the edges of the photograph and move inwards. Increase or decrease the brush size as needed as you paint the selection to include everything but the children. There's no need to be too precise around the outlines of the babies. It's no problem if some of your strokes overlap on the children; you'll be refining the selection in the next exercise.

4   Choose Select > Save Selection.

5   Name the new selection **Backdrop** and click OK to close the Save Selection dialog box.

Painting a selection with the Selection Brush tool is an intuitive way to create a complex selection. In images like this one, where there are no distinct color blocks, few sharp boundaries between pictured items, and few crisp geometric shapes, the Selection Brush tool is especially useful.

Another advantage of the Selection Brush tool is that it is very forgiving. You can hold down the Alt key while dragging to remove an area from a selection. Alternatively, you can use the Selection Brush in Mask mode, which is another intuitive way of refining the selection, which you'll be doing in the next exercise.

What is a mask?

A mask is simply the opposite of a selection. A selection is an area that you can modify; everything outside the selection is unaffected by the changes you make. A mask protects an area from changes, just like the solid areas of a stencil or the masking tape you'd put on window glass at home before you paint the frame.

Another difference between a mask and a selection is the way Photoshop Elements presents them visually. You're familiar with the flashing black and white dashed outline that indicates a selection marquee. A mask appears as a colored, semi-transparent overlay on the image. You can change the color and opacity of the mask overlay using the overlay color and opacity settings that become available in the tool options bar when the Selection Brush tool is set to operate in Mask mode.

Refining a saved selection

As you progress through this book, you're gathering lots of experience with saving selections. In this procedure, you'll amend a saved selection and replace it with your improved version.

1   In the work area, make sure that your Backdrop selection is still active in the image window. If it's not still active, choose Selection > Load Selection, choose the saved selection, and then click OK.

2   Make sure the Selection Brush tool ( ) is still selected in the toolbox.

3   In the tool options bar, select Mask from the brush Mode menu. You can see the mask as a semi-transparent colored overlay on the unselected—or protected—areas of the image. In this mode, the Selection Brush tool paints a mask rather than a selection.

4   Examine the image, looking for unmasked areas with details that should be protected (places where the Selection Brush strokes overlapped onto the children) and parts of the backdrop that are masked and should not be.

Use the Navigator palette slider or the Zoom tool ( ) to adjust your view of the image, as necessary.

5 Reduce the brush size for the Selection Brush to about 30 pixels, and then paint in any areas you want to mask. Press the Alt key while painting to remove an area from the mask.

6 Switch back and forth between Selection and Mask modes, making corrections until you are satisfied with the selection (or the mask, if you like). Your goal is to make sure that fine details you want to preserve are masked.

7 Choose Select > Save Selection. In the Save Selection dialog box, choose Backdrop from the Selection menu. Under Operation, activate the Replace Selection option and click OK.

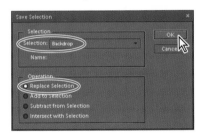

8 While the Selection Brush tool is still active, make sure that the Selection mode—not the Mask mode—is selected in the Mode menu in the tool options bar. Keep the selection active for the next procedure.

Filtering flaws out of the backdrop area

Now that you've made your selection, you're ready to apply the filter that will soften the selected areas, reducing the tiny scratches and dust specks in the background of the image.

1 If the Backdrop selection is no longer active, choose Select > Load Selection and choose Backdrop before you click OK to close the dialog box.

2 Choose Filter > Noise > Dust & Scratches.

3 In the Dust & Scratches dialog box, make sure that Preview is selected, and then drag the Radius slider to 6 pixels and the Threshold slider to 10 levels. Move the dialog box so that you can see most of the image window, but don't close it yet.

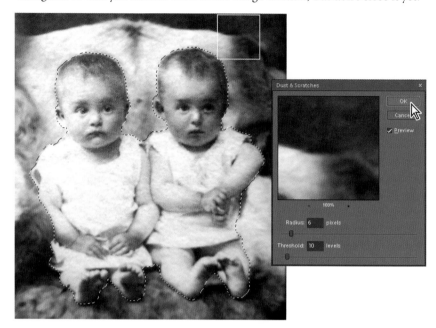

4 Examine the results in the image window. The frayed edges of the image should be softened and the stray dust and tiny scratches eliminated. Move the cursor inside the magnified preview in the Dust & Scratches dialog box and drag with the hand tool to change the area of the image that is displayed.

5 Make adjustments to the Radius and Threshold values until you are satisfied with the results, and then click OK to close the Dust & Scratches dialog box.

6 Choose Select > Deselect, and then choose File > Save to save your work.

The Dust & Scratches filter does a good job of clearing away spots created by flaws on the negative, without affecting the unselected—or masked—areas.

Adding definition with the Smart Brush

The Smart Brush provides a quick and easy way to apply an adjustment to just part of a photo. Unfortunately, like the Quick Selection tool, the Smart Brush makes its selection based on similarities of color and texture in an image, which makes it a little difficult to use on an image such as our example. However, you have already spent time with the Selection Brush to create a selection that will isolate the subjects of the photo from the background; for this exercise you can use that saved selection to quickly tidy up any effect from the Smart brush that extends outside the area you intend to adjust.

1   In the Layers palette, select the layer Background copy and choose Layer > Duplicate Layer. In the Duplicate Layer dialog box, click OK to accept the default name for the new layer: Background copy 2.

2   Select the Smart Brush tool (🖌) in the toolbox. The floating Smart Paint palette appears. If the palette does not appear, you can open it by clicking the colored thumbnail in the tool options bar. Drag the Smart Paint palette aside so that you can see the two babies in the Edit window.

3   From the categories menu at the top of the Smart Paint palette, choose Lighting, and then select Darker from the list of Smart Paint adjustments.

4   In the tool options bar, open the Brush Picker and set the brush Diameter to 30 px and the Hardness to 75%.

5   Make sure the layer Background copy 2 is selected. With the Smart Brush, paint over the face of the baby on the left and over the arms and legs of both babies. You can hold down the Alt key as you paint to remove areas from the selection. Don't worry about the selection spilling over onto the background, but try to exclude the babies' clothes.

6 Choose Select > Deselect Layers to make the adjustment inactive.

7 From the categories menu at the top of the Smart Paint palette, choose Portrait, and then select Details from the list of Smart Paint adjustments.

8 With the Smart Brush, paint completely over both babies and their clothes. This time you can be even more casual with your brushwork; don't worry at all if the effect spills over onto the background—you'll tidy it up in a moment.

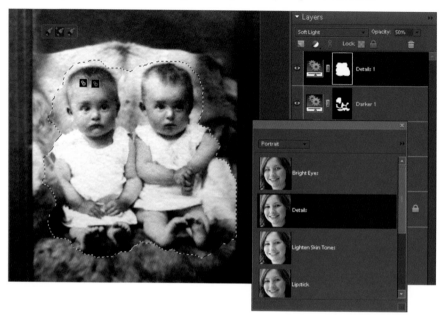

9 Choose Select > Deselect Layers to make the adjustment inactive and close the floating Smart Paint adjustments palette.

Merging layers

You'll now merge the two Smart Brush adjustment layers with the Background copy 2 layer beneath them.

1 In the Layers palette, Ctrl-click to select the top three layers: Background copy 2, Darker 1, and Details 1.

2 Choose Layer > Merge Layers. The three selected layers are merged into one. The new merged layer takes its name from the layer that was on top in the stacking order: Details 1. The Smart Brush adjustments are no longer active or able to be edited.

3 Make sure the new merged layer is still active in the Layers palette and choose Select > Load Selection.

4 In the Load Selection dialog box, choose the saved selection Backdrop from the Selection menu, and then click OK.

5 Choose Edit > Delete, and then Select > Deselect. The background is removed from around the two babies in the merged layer Details 1.

6 To see the effects of your Smart Brush adjustments, toggle the visibility of the layer Details 1 by clicking the eye icon beside its name in the Layers palette.

 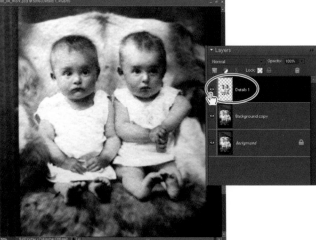

7 In the Layers palette, Ctrl-click to select the top two layers: Background copy and Details 1.

8 Choose Layer > Merge Layers. The two selected layers are merged into one. The new merged layer takes its name from the layer that was on top in the stacking order: Details 1.

Finishing up the project

Compared to the original condition of the photograph, the image is already vastly improved, but if you're in a perfectionist mood you can fix just a few more areas before saving your work.

1 Use the Zoom and Hand tools—or the Navigator palette—to examine the entire image, looking for dark or light flecks created by dust on the negative or the ravages of time, especially in the dark areas of the photograph.

2 In the toolbox, select the Blur tool ( ) and type **40 px** as the brush Size in the tool options bar.

3 Click or drag the tool over any dust spots you find, to blend them into the surrounding area.

4 Use the Clone Stamp tool to remove the pink smudge from the dress of the baby on the right and the Healing Brush to remove the black mark on the calf of the child on the left.

5 Choose File > Save, and then close the file.

Original   Retouched

Congratulations, you've finished this lesson on repairing and retouching images. You've explored a variety of techniques for fixing visual flaws in your photos, from straightening an image to smoothing wrinkles from skin. You sampled one area of an image to repair another with both the Clone Stamp and the Healing Brush and worked with selections and masks. You learned how to reset a tool to its default settings and worked more with layers and the Smart Brush. Take a moment to review the lesson by reading through the review on the next page before you move on to chapter 9, "Working with Text."

Review questions

1 What tools can you use to fix the red eye effect sometimes caused by a flash?

2 How can you quickly undo a whole series of edit steps at once?

3 What are the similarities and differences between the Healing Brush tool and the Spot Healing Brush tool for retouching photos?

4 Why was it necessary to make a selection before applying the Dust & Scratches filter to restore our damaged photograph?

5 What is the difference between a selection and a mask?

Review answers

1 You can choose to have red eye effects corrected automatically during the import process—simply activate the Automatically Fix Red Eye option in the Import dialog box. To fix red eye after the photos have been imported, choose Edit > Auto Red Eye Fix in the Organizer. In either the Full Edit or Quick Fix mode of the Editor, choose Enhance > Auto Red Eye Fix. Alternatively, you can fine-tune the Red Eye Removal tool from the toolbox if you need more control.

2 Use the Undo History palette to quickly undo a series of steps at once. Every action performed on the file is recorded in chronological order in the Undo History palette. To restore the file to an earlier state, simply select an earlier action—higher in the list—in the Undo History palette. If you change your mind before making any further changes to the file, you can still restore the image to a later state by selecting a step lower in the list.

3 Both the Healing Brush tool and the Spot Healing Brush tool blend pixels from one part of an image into another. The Spot Healing Brush tool, especially with the Proximity Match option selected, enables you to remove blemishes more quickly than does the Healing Brush, because it only involves clicking and/or dragging on an imperfection to smooth it. The Healing Brush can be customized, and requires that you Alt-click to establish a source reference area.

4 The Dust & Scratches filter smooths out pixels in an image by blurring them slightly, effectively putting detail slightly out of focus. It was necessary to create a selection so that only the background was blurred, preserving sharpness and detail in the subjects.

5   A mask is simply the opposite of a selection. A selection is an active area to which adjustments can be applied; everything outside the selection is unaffected by any changes that are made. A mask protects an area from changes. Another difference between a mask and a selection is the way Photoshop Elements presents them visually. A selection marquee is indicated by a flashing border of black and white dashes, whereas a mask appears as a colored, semi-transparent overlay on the image. You can change the color and opacity of the mask overlay using the Overlay Color options that appear in the tool options bar when the Selection Brush tool is set to operate in Mask mode.

9 WORKING WITH TEXT

Lesson Overview

Adding text messages to your photos is another way to make your images and compositions even more memorable and personal.

In this lesson you'll learn the skills and techniques you need to work with text in Photoshop Elements:

- Adding a border to an image

- Formatting and editing text

- Overlaying text on an image

- Copying a text layer from one image to another

- Applying effects and Layer Styles

- Warping text

- Hiding, revealing, and deleting layers

- Creating a type mask

 You'll probably need between one and two hours to complete this lesson.

Photoshop Elements provides you with the tools you'll need to add crisp, flexible, and editable type to your pictures. Whether you want classic typography or wild effects and wacky colors, it's all possible in Photoshop Elements. Apply effects and layer styles to make your text really stand out or blend it into your image using transparency. Create a type mask and fill your text with any image you can imagine.

For the exercises in this lesson, you'll use images from the CIB Catalog you created earlier in the book. If necessary, open this catalog in the Organizer by choosing File > Catalog and selecting the CIB Catalog in the Catalog Manager dialog box.

Getting started

This lesson assumes that you are already familiar with the Photoshop Elements interface, and that you recognize the Organizer and Editor workspaces. If you find that you need more background information as you go along, review "Getting Started" and "A Quick Tour of Photoshop Elements" at the start of this book, or refer to Photoshop Elements Help.

This lesson includes several projects, each of which builds on the skills learned in the previous exercises.

Placing text on an image

The first project involves creating a text layer, and then formatting and arranging text on a photograph. You'll add a border and a greeting to a photo so it can be printed as a card or even mounted in a picture frame.

The original photograph and the completed project file.

● **Note:** Before you start working on this lesson, make sure that you've installed the software on your computer from the application CD (see the Photoshop Elements 7 documentation) and that you have correctly copied the Lessons folder from the CD in the back of this book onto your computer's hard disk (see "Copying the Classroom in a Book files" on page 2).

Using Text Search in the Organizer to find a file

If you've worked through previous chapters you're already very familiar with locating the files for a lesson by their keyword tags. Although the image files for this lesson are tagged "Lesson 9," all of them also have descriptive names, which will make it easy to find just the file or files required for each exercise, rather than all the files in the Lesson09 folder.

1 Open Adobe Photoshop Elements, and click the Organize button in the Welcome screen.

2 Once the Organizer has opened, type the word **happy** in the Text Search box, at the left of the bar above the Photo Browser pane.

3 The Photo Browser displays a single photo—happy_holidays.jpg—an image of four young girls in the snow. Select the image in the Photo Browser, click the Editor button (▨) at the top right of the Organizer window, and choose Full Edit from the menu. The photo happy_holidays.jpg opens in the Editor.

Adding an asymmetrical border

In this exercise you'll enlarge the canvas without increasing the size of the image. By default, the canvas—which is the equivalent of the paper on which a photo is printed—is the same size as the image.

By increasing the size of the canvas without enlarging the image you can effectively add a border. By default, the extended canvas, and therefore the border, takes on the Background color as set in the color swatches at the bottom of the Toolbox.

You'll create the border in two stages in order to make it asymmetrical.

1 Choose Image > Resize > Canvas Size.

2 Set up the Canvas Size dialog box as shown in the illustration:

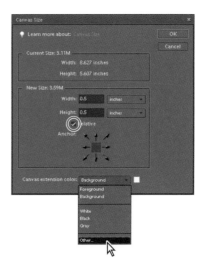

- Activate the Relative option.

- Choose Inches from the units menus and type **0.5** for both the Width and Height of the border.

- Leave the default centered setting for the Anchor control.

- From the Canvas Extension Color menu, choose Other. The Select Canvas Extension Color dialog box appears, with a color picker.

3 The pointer becomes an eye-dropper cursor when you move it over the image. Sample a purple-blue from the glove of the girl on the left.

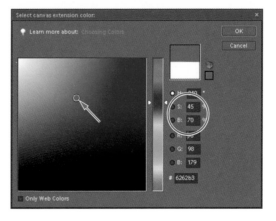

4 This color could make a good choice for the new border, as it's reflected at several points throughout the image; however, it is a little dark. Lighten the color by dragging the circular indicator upwards and to the left in the color field, or type new values of 45% for Saturation (S) and 70% for Brightness (B), and then Click OK.

5 Click OK to close the Canvas Size dialog box. The new colored border appears around the photo in the edit window.

6 Now let's extend the border above the image to create a space for the text greeting. Choose Image > Resize > Canvas Size. In the Canvas Size dialog box, confirm that the Relative check box is still activated.

7 Set the Width value to **0** and the Height to **1**. In the Anchor control diagram, click the center square in the bottom row. Leave the Canvas Extension Color setting unchanged and click OK.

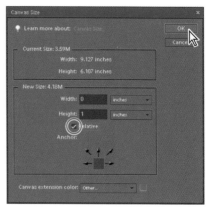

Now the border around the image is deeper at the top, providing a perfect stage for the text you'll add in the next exercise.

Adding a quick border

When precision isn't important, you can quickly add a border to an image by using the Crop tool, rather than increasing the size of the canvas.

1   Zoom out far enough so that you can see some of the gray art-board surrounding the image in the edit window.

2   Use the crop tool to drag a cropping rectangle right around the image.

3   Drag the corner handles of the crop marquee outside the image area onto the art-board to define the size and shape of border that you wish to create.

4   When you're satisfied, click the Commit button in the lower right corner of the image. The canvas expands to fill the cropping rectangle, taking on the background color set in the color swatch at the bottom of the toolbox.

Adding a text layer

With the Horizontal Type and Vertical Type tools you can place type anywhere on your image. When you use the Type tool, Photoshop Elements automatically creates a new text layer in your image. The type you enter remains active on the text layer—you can edit it, resize it, reposition it, or change the text color at any time.

● **Note:** Photoshop Elements includes several variants of the Type tool. Throughout the remainder of this lesson, the term Type tool will always refer to the Horizontal Type tool, which is the default variant.

1   In the toolbox, select the Horizontal Type tool (**T**).

2   Set up the tool options bar as shown in the illustration below. Choose Myriad Pro from the Font Family menu, Bold from the Font Style menu, and type **44 pt** in the Font Size box. Choose Center Text (▤) from the paragraph alignment options and set the Leading value to 30 pt. Click the triangle beside the color swatch—not the swatch itself—and select white as the text color.

3   Click in the colored border area above the photo to set the cursor, and then type
    HAPPY HOLIDAYS! in uppercase.

4   Click the Commit button (✔) in the tool options bar to accept the text. Don't
    worry about the positioning of the text or any typing errors—you'll get a chance
    to correct those later.

● **Note:** Don't press
the Enter or Return keys
on the main part of your
keyboard to accept
text changes. When
the Type tool is active,
these keys add a line
break in the text. Click
the Commit button in
the tool options bar to
accept the text or press
the Enter key in the
numeric keypad potion
of your keyboard.

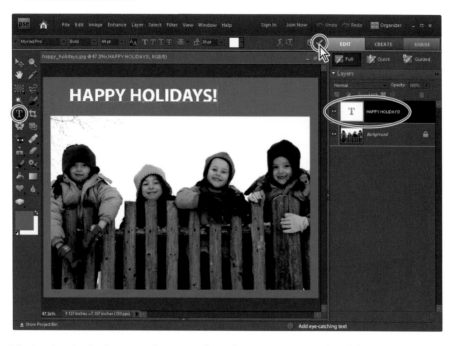

Notice that in the Layers palette—in the Palette Bin at the right of the workspace—
the image now has two layers: a locked Background layer containing the image and
a text layer containing your holiday greeting. Most of the text layer is transparent, so
only the text itself blocks your view of the Background layer.

5   Make sure the text layer is still selected in the Layers palette, and then select the
    Move tool (▶⊕) in the toolbox.

6   Place the cursor inside the text and drag so that the message is centered
    horizontally in the border above the image.

Editing a text layer

Adding vector-based text is a nondestructive process; your original image is not overwritten by the text. If you save your file in native Photoshop (PSD) format, you can reopen it and move, edit, or delete the text layer without affecting the image.

Using the Type tool is much like typing in a word processing application. If you want to edit the message, select the text and type over it. To change the font style or text color, select the characters you want to change, and then adjust the settings.

1   If necessary, choose View > Zoom In to enlarge the image until you can comfortably read the text you added in the previous exercise.

2   Confirm that the text layer HAPPY HOLIDAYS! is still selected in the Layers palette and the Type tool is still active.

3   Click to the right of "HOLIDAYS!," and then press Enter to add a line break in the text. Type **Season's Greetings from The Evans Family,** (this time in upper and lowercase) so that the text reads:
    "HAPPY HOLIDAYS!
    Season's Greetings from The Evans Family".

Now we want to change the font style, size, and color for the second line of text.

4   Zoom out far enough so that you can select all of the text in the second line. Don't worry that the text seems to disappear outside the image—you can still drag to select it. In the tool options bar, leave MyriadPro selected as the Font Family, choose Regular from the Font Style menu, and set the Font Size to 30 pt.

5   This time, click the color swatch to open the Color Picker. When you move the pointer over the image it becomes an eye-dropper cursor. Use the eye-dropper to sample the purple color from the border you created.

6 In the Color Picker, set the Saturation (S) value to 10% and the Brightness value to 90% so that the text will stand out against the background color.

You should keep this in mind when you're choosing color for text—always choose light colors against a dark or bold background and vice versa. Click OK.

▶ **Tip:** If you need to correct any typing errors you may have made, remember that using the Type tool is like working in a word processing application. Click once to place the insertion point within the text. Use the arrow keys to move the text cursor forward or back. Drag to select multiple characters. Type to add text or to overwrite selected characters. Press Backspace or Delete to erase characters. Click the Commit button in the tool options bar to accept your editing changes.

7 If you need to adjust the position of the text, make sure the text layer is selected, and then select the Move tool in the toolbox. The text is surrounded by a bounding box. You can now either drag the text with the Move tool or use the arrow keys on your keyboard to nudge it in small increments.

Saving a work file with layers

You can save your work file complete with layers so you can return to it later. As long as you save in the right format, text and adjustment layers remain editable.

1 Choose File > Save. The Save As dialog box opens. Navigate to your My CIB Work folder, name the file **happy_holidays_Work,** and choose Photoshop (PSD) from the Format menu.

2 Under Save Options, confirm that the options Include In The Organizer and Layers are activated, and that the option Save In Version Set With Original is disabled.

3 Review your settings and click the Save button. If the Photoshop Elements Format Options dialog box appears, keep Maximize Compatibility selected and click OK.

4 Choose File > Close.

Bravo, you've finished your first text project. In this section, you've formatted and edited text, and worked with a text layer. You've also created a photo border by increasing the canvas size without enlarging the image itself.

Distinguishing between Pixel-based and Vector Graphics

Computer graphics can be divided into two types: pixel-based images (otherwise called bit-mapped, or raster images), which are primarily created by cameras and scanners, and vector images—graphics constructed with drawing programs.

Pixel-based images such as photos are made up of pixels that you can detect when you zoom in. To produce a medium quality print of a photo, you need to make sure that the file is at least 250 ppi (pixels per inch). For viewing on screen, 72 ppi is fine.

Vector images consist of artwork formed from paths, like a technical line drawing. Vectors may form the outlines of an illustration, a logo, or type. The big advantage of vector images over pixel-based images is that they can be enlarged or reduced by any factor without losing detail. Live type on a text layer has this advantage.

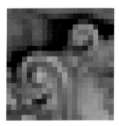
Pixel-based image

Vector type

Rasterized type

About Type

A font is a collection of characters—letters, numerals, punctuation marks, and symbols—in a particular typeface, which share design characteristics such as size, weight, and style. A typeface family is a collection of similar fonts designed to be used together. One example is the Myriad typeface family, which is a collection of fonts in a number of styles including Regular, Bold, Italic, Condensed and other variations. Other typeface families might consist of different font style variations.

Font family
Myriad Pro
Font style
Regular, **Bold**, *Italic*, Condensed

Times New Roman
Regular, **Bold**, *Italic*

Traditionally, font sizes are measured in points, but can also be specified in millimeters or inches, as with large lettering on signs, for example. The most common formats for computer fonts are Type 1 PostScript, TrueType, and OpenType.

Each font conveys a feeling or mood. Some are playful or amusing, some are serious and businesslike, while others might convey an impression of elegance and sophistication. To get a feel for which typeface best suits your project, it's a good idea to try out several fonts. One way to find out more about type is to go to www.adobe.com/type. Adobe Type offers more than 2,200 fonts from the world's leading type designers, which you can browse by categories such as style, use, theme, classification, and designer. This will make it easy to find the perfect font for any assignment. You can even type in your sample copy and compare different fonts.

Overlaying text on an image

In the last exercise, you preserved the layering of your work file by saving in a file format that supports layers. This gives you the flexibility to make changes to the images, text, and effects even after the file has been saved, without needing to rebuild the image from the beginning or modify the original. Your layers have kept the text and effects separate from the image itself.

In this project, you'll do what professional photographic studios sometimes do to protect proprietary images—stamp a copyright notice over the photo. You'll apply a style to a text layer so that it appears as if the type is set in clear glass overlaid on the images.

Creating a new document for the text

You'll start by preparing the text in its own file. In this procedure, you'll see a gray-and-white checkerboard pattern. This pattern indicates 100% transparency, where an area or complete layer acts like a pane of clear glass onto which you can place text or graphics.

1   If you're not already in the Editor, switch to it now. Make sure the Editor is in Full Edit mode. In the Editor, choose File > New > Blank File.

2   In the New dialog box, name the file **Overlay**. Type **600** for both the Width and Height values and choose Pixels from both units menus.

3   Set the file Resolution to **72** pixels/inch, the Color Mode to RGB Color, and the Background Contents to Transparent. Click OK.

The edit window should show only a checkerboard pattern. If it does not, choose Edit > Undo and repeat the first three steps, being careful to select Transparent from the Background Contents menu. If you still don't see a checkerboard pattern, check your preferences:. Choose Edit > Preferences > Transparency. The checkerboard pattern represents the transparent background that you specified when you created the file.

4   Select the Type tool (**T**), and then set up the tool options bar as shown in the illustration below. Choose Arial from the Font Family menu, choose Bold from the Font Style menu, and type **120** pt in the Font Size box. Choose Centered for the paragraph alignment. Click the triangle beside the color swatch—not the swatch itself—and choose black as the text color.

5   Click near the left side of the image window and type **copyright 2009**. Click the green Commit button (✔) in the tool options bar to accept the text you've typed.

6   Select the Move tool (▶⊹) in the toolbox and drag the text to center it in the image window. Position the Move tool outside a corner of the text bounding box so that the pointer changes to a rotate cursor—a curved, double-ended arrow. Drag the text counter-clockwise around its center so it appears at an angle.

7   Click the Commit button near the lower left corner of the bounding box.

● **Note:** You can scale or reshape the text by dragging the corners of the bounding box with the Move tool. Because Photoshop Elements treats text as vector shapes, the letter shapes remain smooth even if you enlarge the text. If you tried this with bit-mapped text, you'd see jagged, stair-step edges in the enlarged text.

Applying a Layer Style to a text layer

Next, you'll apply an effect to your text by adding a Layer Style. Layer Styles are combinations of adjustments that can be applied to your text layer in one easy action. Photoshop Elements gives you a wide variety of choices, from bevels and drop shadows to imaginative chrome and neon effects.

Note: For help working with palettes and the Palette Bin, see "Using the Palette Bin" in Lesson 1, "A Quick Tour of Photoshop Elements."

1   In the Palette Bin, click the triangle in the upper left corner of the Effects palette to expand it. If you don't see the Effects palette in the Palette Bin, choose Window > Effects.

2   At the top of the Effects palette, Click the Layer Styles button (▤), and then choose the second last category in the effects categories menu, Wow Plastic.

3   In the top row of the Effects palette, select the Wow Plastic Clear effect and click Apply. You could also apply the effect to the selected text layer by double-clicking the swatch, or even by dragging the effect swatch directly onto your text.

When you apply a Layer Style to a Text layer, both the text and the effect remain editable. You could go back and change the year of the copyright in the text layer without affecting the layer style, or double-click the *fx* icon on the text layer and edit, replace, or remove the effect without affecting your ability to edit the text.

4   Choose File > Save and save the file to your My CIB Work folder in Photoshop
    (PSD) format. Make sure you activate the Layers option. You don't want to create
    a version set. Click Save. If the Photoshop Elements Format Options dialog box
    appears, keep Maximize Compatibility selected, and then click OK.

Adding text to multiple images

Now that you've prepared the copyright text, you'll place it onto a series of images.

1   Click the Organizer button at the top right of the Editor window to switch to the
    Organizer.

2   In the Organizer, type **x file** in the Text Search box at the left of the bar above the
    Photo Browser pane to find the images you'll use for this exercise.

3   Control-click to select the four images of paintings named **x_file_01.jpg** to
    x_file_04.jpg. Click the Editor button () and choose Full Edit from the menu.

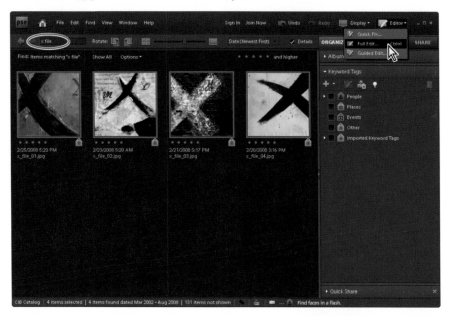

4   To see all the images that are open in the Editor,
    choose Window > Images > Tile.

    To view the same corner of all the open images,
    choose Window > Images > Match Location.
    The view in all of the windows will shift to
    match the active image. To see each image at the
    same magnification as the active image, choose
    Window > Images > Match Zoom.

5   Now choose Window > Images > Cascade. Press Ctrl+= (equal sign) or Ctrl+- (minus sign) to zoom in or out for the foremost image until the image window is small enough to see the entire image and arrange it in the edit window with the others at the same size as in the illustration below. Make sure you have the Photo Bin open at the bottom of the edit window.

6   In the Photo Bin (the row of thumbnails across the bottom of the workspace), click the file Overlay.psd to make it the active file. The title bars of all the other files are dimmed. The Layers palette shows the text layer copyright 2009.

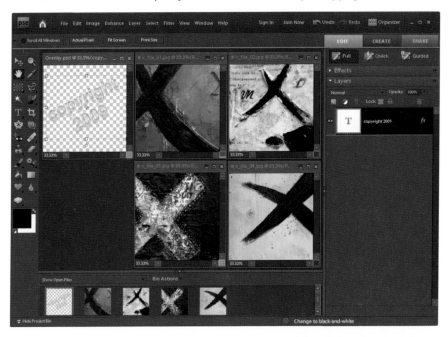

7   Hold down the Shift key and drag the text layer copyright 2009 from the Layers palette onto the image of the red painting, x_file_01.jpg.

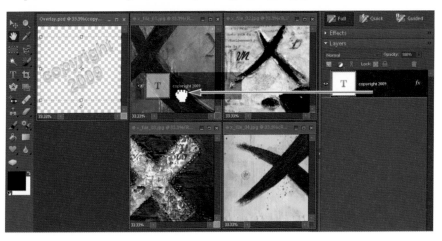

8 To make the overlay more transparent, reduce the opacity to 50% either by typing **50** into the box, or by dragging the Opacity slider to the left.

9 Make sure that the image of the red painting, x_file_01.jpg, is still the active file. In the Layers palette, double-click the *fx* icon on the copyright 2009 layer. The Style Settings dialog box appears.

10 In the Style Settings dialog box, you need to change only one setting. In the Glow options, change the size of the Outer Glow from 22 pixels to 10 pixels. Click OK to close the Style Settings dialog box.

11 Hold down the Shift key and drag the copyright 2009 text layer with its refined layer style from the image x_file_01.jpg onto the other three images. Zoom in to each image and use the Move tool to position the copyright message as you wish for each image independently. The copyright message looks less visible against some of the images than it does against the red painting. Tweak the Opacity value for the text layer on each of the other three images accordingly.

12 Choose File > Close All. If you wish, you can save your efforts to your My CIB Work folder. If you do save the files, be sure to activate the Layers option for the Photoshop (PSD) format so that the layers in the files are preserved.

Done! In this project, you've created a new Photoshop (PSD) format document without an image and added text to that document. You've used the Effects palette to apply a Layer Style to the text layer, copied the text layer to other image files, and edited the layer style and opacity.

Using Layer Styles and distortions

In this next exercise you'll have more fun with text. You'll distort text and apply effects, all the while keeping the text layer live and editable.

Adding a layer style

You can start by finding the image file that you'll use for this project.

1   If you're still in the Editor, click the Organizer button located at the top right of the Editor workspace to switch to the Organizer.

2   In the Organizer, type the word **sky** in the Text Search box at the left of the bar above the Photo Browser pane. The Photo Browser displays only one image named **big_sky.jpg**.

3   Select the image in the Photo Browser, click the Editor button, and then choose Full Edit from the menu.

4   Select the Type tool (**T**) from the toolbox, and then set up the tool options bar as shown in the illustration below. From the Font Family menu, choose a bold sans-serif style such as Impact (as an alternative, you could choose Arial Black). Type **200** pt in the Font Size box, and choose Centered from the paragraph alignment options. Click the triangle beside the color swatch (not the swatch itself) to open the color palette. For the text color, choose Pastel Cyan Blue.

5 Using the Type tool, click near the center of the image and type **MAYBE**—all in upper case.

6 Click the Commit button (✔) in the tool options bar to accept the text.

7 Choose the Move tool (▶⊕) in the toolbox and drag the text to center it as shown in the illustration below.

8 Expand the Effects palette and click the Layer Styles button (▦). Choose the category Bevels from the effects categories menu and double-click the last effect in the second row: Simple Sharp Outer.

9 In the Layers palette, change the opacity of the text layer to 75%, either by typing the new value directly into the text box or by dragging the Opacity slider.

10 Save the file in your My CIB Work folder. Name the file big_sky_Work, choose the Photoshop (PSD) format and make sure the Layers option is activated.

Warping text

It's easy to stretch and skew text into unusual shapes using the Photoshop Elements Warp Text effects; the difficulty is in avoiding overusing the effects!

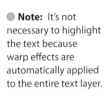

Note: It's not necessary to highlight the text because warp effects are automatically applied to the entire text layer.

1   Make sure the Type tool is active, and then click anywhere on the text "MAYBE" in the image window.

2   In the tool options bar, click the Create Warped Text button ( ) to open the Warp Text dialog box. Choose the Fisheye effect from the Style menu.

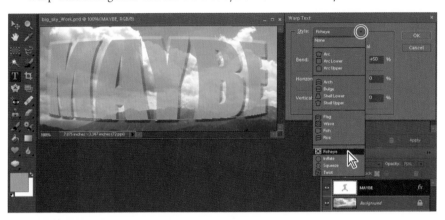

3   The Horizontal and Vertical orientation options are unavailable because the fisheye effect is applied on both axes by default. Set the Bend value to +75% and click OK to close the Warp Text dialog box.

4   The text layer is still editable. You can check this out by dragging to select the word MAYBE with the Type tool, and then typing over it.

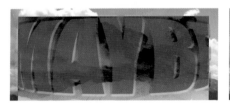

5   Choose Edit > Undo Edit Type Layer, and then File Save.

Creating an un-stylized copy of the text layer

In the next exercise, you'll experiment with an effect that requires your type layer to be simplified, meaning that the vector text will be converted to a bitmap image and will therefore no longer be editable. For this purpose you'll create a separate copy of the text layer.

1 In the Layers palette, select the text layer. Click the double triangle in the upper right corner of the palette to open the Layers palette Options menu. From the palette Options menu, choose Duplicate Layer. Click OK to accept the default layer name: MAYBE copy.

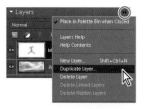

▶ **Tip:** You can also duplicate a layer by dragging it onto the New Layer button at the top left of the Layers palette, or by selecting the layer and choosing Layer > Duplicate Layer.

2 Click the eye icon to the left of the original text layer: MAYBE. The layer becomes invisible in the image window.

3 In the Layers palette, change the opacity of the layer MAYBE copy to 100%. The warped text once more appears as solid blue.

4 Right-click / Ctrl-click on the text layer Maybe copy and choose Clear Layer Style from the context menu.

The warped text now appears without the bevel effect, as it did before you applied the Layer Style.

Simplifying text and applying a pattern

You can now add a different look to the copy of the text layer. In preparation, you'll lock the transparent pixels on the text layer, which will enable you to paint on the shapes in the layer without needing to be careful about the edges.

1 In the toolbox, select the Pattern Stamp tool, which is grouped with the Clone Stamp tool. Set up the tool options bar as shown in the illustration below: set the brush Size to **50** px, the brush Mode to Normal, and the Opacity to 100%. Click on the triangle next to the Pattern swatch to open the Pattern menu. Choose the Pink Fur pattern.

2   Make sure that the text layer MAYBE copy is selected in the Layers palette, and then click once on the text in the image window with the Pattern Stamp tool. A message appears, asking if you want to simplify the layer. Click OK.

3   In the Layers palette, click the Lock Transparent Pixels button to prevent changes being made to the transparent areas of the simplified MAYBE copy layer. Notice that there is now a lock icon displayed on the MAYBE copy layer.

4   Make sure the Pattern Stamp tool is still selected in the toolbox and paint over the text in the image window, applying the pattern as solidly or as unevenly as you like. The pattern is applied only to the simplified text; the locked transparent pixels remain unaffected.

Of course, the pattern is painted only onto the selected layer (the simplified text) and does not affect the Background layer or the text layer that is currently hidden.

Remember that once you simplify a text layer, the text is no longer live—it can no longer be edited with the Type tool. However, you can still change the appearance of the simplified text by painting it as you've done in this exercise, by changing the layer's blending mode and opacity, or by adding a Layer Style such as a Bevel or Drop Shadow using the Effects palette.

Hiding and revealing layers

Toggling the visibility of layers by clicking the eye icons in the Layers palette makes a great way to assess different design solutions within one file.

1   In the Layers palette, click the eye icon beside the top text layer, MAYBE copy, to hide it. The eye icon is hidden also, leaving an empty box to indicate that the layer is not visible.

Note that although the layer is selected, the Blending Mode and Opacity options are dimmed and unavailable. You cannot edit a hidden layer.

2 In the Layers palette, click the empty box to the left of the text layer MAYBE. The eye icon reappears and the warped blue text with the bevelled effect is once more visible in the document window.

Deleting layers and layer styles

You can now delete the layer with the pink fur pattern, leaving just the Background layer with the original image, and the text layer MAYBE just above it. Deleting layers that you no longer need reduces the size of your image file.

1 To delete the layer MAYBE copy, first make sure the layer is visible—you should be able to see the eye icon to the left of the layer's name in the Palette menu. Right-click / Ctrl-click the layer and choose Delete Layer from the context menu.

You can use this method to delete more than one layer at the same time—just make sure all the layers are visible and selected, and then right-click / Ctrl-click any of them. You can also delete selected layers by choosing Layer > Delete Layer from the main menu bar, or by clicking the double triangles at the right of the Layers palette's title bar and choosing Delete Layer from the Layers palette Options menu.

2 In the Layers palette, select the remaining text layer, MAYBE. Right-click / Ctrl-click the layer and choose Clear Layer Style from the context menu. Alternatively, choose Layer > Layer Style > Clear Layer Style or choose Clear Layer Style from the Layers palette Options menu.

The type in text layer MAYBE no longer has a bevelled effect, but it is still warped.

3 In the toolbox select the Type tool, and then click the Create Warped Text button in the tool option bar to open the Warp Text dialog box. Choose None from the Style menu, and then click OK to close the Warp Text dialog box.

4   Now you're back to where you began, before applying the bevelled Layer Style and before you added the fisheye text warp effect. Choose File > Save. Save the file to your My CIB Work folder as big_sky_Work, in Photoshop (*.PSD, *.PDD) file format with the Layer option activated. If the option Save In Version Set With Original is activated, disable it before you click Save. If the Photoshop Elements Format Options dialog box appears, keep Maximize Compatibility selected and click OK.

5   Choose File > Close.

In this section, you've applied a Layer Style to live text, warped it, and painted it with pink fur. You should be ashamed of yourself! You learned about locking transparent pixels on a layer and how to edit or clear layer styles and text effects. You also learned how to hide, reveal or delete a layer.

Working with Paragraph type

With point type, or headline type, each line of type is independent—the line expands or shrinks as you edit it, but it doesn't wrap to the next line. Point type (the name derives from the fact that it is preceded by a single anchor point) is perfect for small blocks of text like headlines, logos, and headings for Web pages. Probably most of the text you add to your images will be of this type.

If you work with larger blocks of type and you want your text to reflow and wrap automatically, it's best to use the paragraph type mode. By clicking and dragging with the type tool you'll create a text bounding box on your image. The bounding box can be easily resized to fit your paragraph text perfectly.

Creating a type mask

You can have a lot of fun with the Type Mask tool. The Type Mask tool has two variants—one for horizontal type and the other for vertical type. The Type Mask tool turns text outlines into a mask through which an underlying image is visible.

1. If you are still in the Editor, switch to the Organizer now.

2. In the Organizer, type the word **stripes** in the Text Search box at the left of the bar above the Photo Browser pane. The Photo Browser displays only one image named **stripes.jpg**.

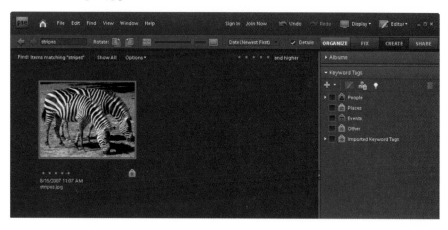

3. Click the Editor button at the top right of the Organizer window and choose Full Edit from the menu.

Working with the Type Mask tool

The Type Mask tool (⊞) enables you to fill letter shapes with parts of an image. This can create a much more interesting effect than using plain text filled with a solid color.

1   In the tool box, select the Horizontal Type Mask tool (🆃).

2   Set up the tool options bar as shown in the illustration below: choose Stencil from the Font Family menu, Bold from the Font Style menu, and set the font Size to 100 pt. Choose Left Align Text from the text alignment options. You don't need to worry about the color attributes as the type will be filled with detail from an image.

3   Click near the point where the front zebra's hind leg meets its belly and type the word **ZOO**.

4   The background pattern of zebra stripes shows through the shapes of the letters you just typed, while the rest of the picture is masked, as indicated by the red, semi-transparent overlay. Click the green Commit button in the tool options bar. The outline of the text becomes an active selection. If you are not satisfied with the placement of the text, you can use the arrow keys on your keyboard to nudge it into place.

5 Select Edit > Copy, and then Edit > Paste. you'll notice that the new type image has been placed onto a new layer.

6 In the Layers palette, hide the layer Background by clicking the eye icon to the left of the layer's name.

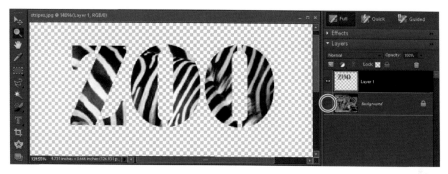

The text is no longer live—it was converted to a selection outline and can no longer be edited; however, you can still apply a layer style or an effect to enhance it or make it more prominent.

7 Select Layer 1 in the Layers palette to make it the active layer.

8 Expand the Effects palette and click the Layer Styles button (⬛). Select the effects category Drop Shadows from the menu.

9 In the Drop Shadows palette, double-click the shadow effect called Noisy: the second drop-shadow effect in the second row.

You can tweak the drop shadow effect by double-clicking the *fx* icon on Layer 1 in the Layers palette. The Style Settings dialog box appears, where you can change the angle, distance, color, and opacity of the drop shadow as you wish.

10 Since you no longer need the background layer with the photo of the zebras, delete it by choosing Flatten Image from the Layers palette Options menu. Click OK in the dialog box that appears to ask whether you want to discard the hidden layer.

11 Choose File > Save As. In the Save As dialog box, name the file **stripes_Work**, choose Photoshop (PSD) as the file format, and save the file to your My CIB Work folder.

Congratulations! You've completed another lesson. You've learned how to format and edit text, and how to work with a text layer. You've created a photo border by working with the document canvas, used the Effects palette to apply Layer Styles, warped and painted your text, and created a text mask. You learned about locking transparent pixels on a layer and how to edit or clear layer styles and text effects. You also learned how to hide, reveal and delete a layer. Take a moment to work through the lesson review on the next page before you move on.

Review questions

1 What is the advantage of having text on a separate layer?

2 How do you hide a layer without removing it?

3 In the Layers palette, what do the lock buttons do and how do they work?

4 What's the difference between point type and paragraph type?

Review answers

1 Because the text remains separate from the image, Photoshop Elements text layers remain "live"—text can be edited in later work sessions, just as it can be in a word processing application.

2 You can hide a layer by clicking the eye icon to the left of the layer's name in the Layers palette. To make the layer visible again, click the empty box where the eye icon should be to restore it.

3 Lock buttons prevent changes to a layer. The Lock All button, which looks like a padlock, locks all the pixels on the selected layer so that the layer is protected from changes. Blending and Opacity options become unavailable. The Lock Transparent Pixels button, which looks like a checkerboard, locks only the transparent pixels on a layer. To remove a lock, select the locked layer and click the active lock icon to toggle it off. (This does not work for the Background layer, which can be unlocked only by renaming and converting it into an ordinary layer.)

4 Point type is ideal for headlines, logos and other small blocks of text where each line is independent and does not wrap to the next line. Paragraph text is used where you want larger amounts of text to wrap automatically to the next line. The size of the paragraph text bounding box can be easily changed to fit the text perfectly to your design.

10 COMBINING MULTIPLE IMAGES

Lesson Overview

You can do a lot to improve a photo with tonal adjustments and color corrections, but at times the best way to produce the perfect image is to fake it!

In this lesson you'll learn some of the tricks you'll need for combining multiple photos to create that great shot that you didn't actually get:

- Merging multiple photos into a panorama

- Assembling the perfect group shot

- Removing unwanted elements

- Combining images using layers

- Resizing and repositioning selections

- Creating a gradient clipping mask

- Defringing a selection

 You'll probably need between one and two hours to complete this lesson.

If you're ready to go beyond fixing pictures in conventional ways, this lesson is for you. Why settle for that scenic photo that just doesn't capture the way it looked when you were there? Or that group portrait where someone's eyes are closed? Combine images to produce the perfect shot. Merge photos to make a stunning panorama, remove obstructions from the view, and even get little Jimmy to stop making faces.

Getting started

Note: Before you start working on this lesson, make sure that you've installed the software on your computer from the application CD (see the Photoshop Elements 7 documentation) and that you have correctly copied the Lessons folder from the CD in the back of this book onto your computer's hard disk (see "Copying the Classroom in a Book files" on page 2).

For this lesson you'll be using images from the CIB Catalog you created at the start of the book. To open your CIB Catalog, follow these steps:

1 Start Photoshop Elements. In the Welcome Screen, click the Organize button. The name of the currently active catalog is displayed in the lower left corner of the Organizer window. If the CIB Catalog is open, skip to the first exercise: "Merging photos into a panorama." If the CIB Catalog is not open, complete the following steps.

2 Choose File > Catalog.

3 In the Catalog Manager dialog box, select the CIB Catalog from the list, and then click Open.

If you don't see the CIB Catalog listed, you should review the procedures in "Getting Started" at he beginning of this book. See "Copying the Lessons files from the CD" on page 2, and "Creating a catalog" on page 3.

Merging photos into a panorama

The images you'll use for this first exercise are two slightly overlapping photos taken at Mont Saint Michel in France. The camera lens used for these shots did not have a wide enough angle to capture the entire scene. These pictures provide an ideal opportunity for learning how to create a panorama, having Photoshop Elements do most of the work for you.

1 If you're not already in the Organizer, switch to it now.

2 In the Keyword Tags palette, click the Find box next to the Lesson 10 keyword tag.

3 Ctrl-click to select the two pictures of Mont Saint Michel, named 10_01_a.jpg and 10_01_b.jpg in the Photo Browser.

Note: If you don't see the file names displayed below the thumbnails in the Photo Browser, choose View > Show File Names.

4   Choose File > New > Photomerge Panorama.

Photoshop Elements will load the Editor workspace in Full Edit mode and open the Photomerge dialog box.

5   Under Source Files in the Photomerge dialog box, select Files from the Use menu, and then click the Add Open Files button.

6   Under Layout, select Auto, and then click OK.

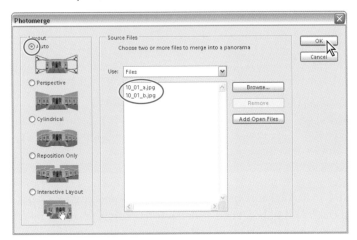

● **Note:** You can use more than two files to create a Photomerge Panorama composition.

▶ **Tip:** Select Folder from the Use menu, and then click Browse to add all the photos from a specific folder on your hard disk. To remove photos from the selection, select them in the source file list, and then click Remove.

Choosing a Photomerge layout option

Auto Photoshop analyzes the source images and applies either a Perspective or Cylindrical layout, depending on which produces a better photomerge.

Perspective Creates a consistent composition by designating one of the source images (by default, the middle image) as the reference image. The other images are then transformed (repositioned, stretched or skewed as necessary) so that overlapping content across layers is matched.

Cylindrical Reduces the "bow-tie" distortion that can occur with the Perspective layout by displaying individual images as on an unfolded cylinder. Overlapping content across layers is still matched. The reference image is placed at the center. Best suited for creating wide panoramas.

Reposition Only Aligns the layers and matches overlapping content, but does not transform (stretch or skew) any of the source layers.

Interactive Layout Choose this option to open the source images in a dialog and position them manually for the best result (see "Creating a Photomerge Panorama interactively").

—From Photoshop Elements Help

7 Wait while Photoshop Elements creates the panorama and opens it in a new image window.

That's really all there is to it! All that remains to crop the image and save your work. But first, let's have a closer look at how good a job Photoshop Elements did of merging the two images. Depending on your source files, you might sometimes spot little problem areas, in which case you'd then need to try a different layout option to merge your photos.

8 In the Layers panel, click the eye icon (👁) beside the top layer to hide it.

In the edit window, you can now see which part of the image in the lower layer was used to create the panorama. The unused portion is hidden by a layer mask. You can see a black and white thumbnail of the layer mask in the Layers palette; black represents the masked area of the image and white represents the part of the image that has contributed to the panorama.

9 Choose View > Actual Pixels, or zoom in even closer if you wish, and then use the Hand tool to move the image in the edit window so that you can inspect the edge of the layer mask. Click the eye icon (👁) for the top layer repeatedly to hide and reveal that layer while you look for irregularities along the edge between the two images. Look for pixels along the masked edge of one image that appear misaligned with pixels in the other. Use the Hand tool to inspect the entire edge of the mask.

Hide the top layer to reveal the edge of the image mask.

Show the top layer and check for irregularities along the edge between the two source images.

10 If your inspection does not reveal any problem areas, make the top layer visible and you're ready to crop the picture and save it. If you do find problems in a merged panorama, close the file without saving it and repeat the procedure trying a different Photomerge layout option when you get to step 6. Later in this lesson, the section "Creating a Photomerge Panorama interactively" explains the interactive layout option, which gives you the most control over the way the panorama is put together.

Cropping the merged image

As the merged image has an irregular outline, you'll use the Crop tool to create a uniform edge. The Crop tool removes those parts of an image that fall outside an adjustable cropping rectangle. Cropping can also be very useful for changing the visual focus of a photo. When you crop an image, the resolution remains unchanged.

1   Choose View > Fit On Screen.

2   Choose Image > Crop. A cropping rectangle appears on the image. Drag the handles of the cropping rectangle to make it as large as possible, being careful not to include any of the checkerboard areas where the image is transparent. When you're happy with the result, click the Commit button in the lower right corner of the cropping rectangle.

▶ **Tip:** You could also select the Crop tool directly from the toolbox. In Quick Fix mode you can choose between the Image > Crop command or the Crop tool in the toolbox. In Guided Edit mode you'll find a Crop Photo procedure in the Basic Photo Edits palette. In the Organizer, you can use the Crop button in the Fix pane.

3   Choose File > Save and save the merged image to your My CIB Work folder as **10_01_Work**, in Photoshop (*.PSD,*PDD) format, making sure that the Layers option is activated. Saving your file in Photoshop format preserves the layers, so that you can always return to adjust them if necessary. If you save in JPEG format the layer information will be lost.

Cropping ratio options

Though you won't need to do so for this exercise, you can set options for the Crop tool in the tool options bar.

In the Aspect Ratio menu you can choose between several options. The option No Restriction lets you crop the image to any proportions. The option Use Photo Ratio retains the aspect ratio of the original photo. The menu also offers a range of preset sizes for your cropped photo, should you want your final output to fit a particular layout or a favorite picture frame.

The Width and Height fields enable you to specify custom dimensions that are not available from the Aspect Ratio menu.

4　Choose File > Close to close the file 10_01_Work.psd, but keep the two source files, 10_01_a.jpg and 10_02_b.jpg, open in the Editor.

Creating a Photomerge Panorama interactively

The automatic layout options in the Photomerge dialog box usually do a good job, but if you need manual control over the way source images are combined to create a panorama, choose the Interactive Layout option in the Photomerge dialog box.

1　With the files 10_01_a.jpg and 10_02_b.jpg still open in the Editor, choose File > New > Photomerge Panorama.

2　Under Source Files in the Photomerge dialog box, select Files from the Use menu, and then click the Add Open Files button. Under Layout, select Interactive Layout, and then click OK.

3　Wait while Photoshop Elements opens the interactive Photomerge dialog box.

● **Note:** If the composition can't be assembled automatically, a message will appear on screen. You can assemble the panorama manually in the Photomerge dialog box by dragging photos from the photo bin into the work area, and arranging them as you wish.

4　Explore the tools and controls in the Photomerge dialog box:

- Use the Zoom tool (🔍) or the Navigator controls to zoom in or out of the image. Drag the red rectangle in the Navigator to shift the view in the zoomed image.

- Use the Select Image tool (🔪) to select any of the photos in the work area. Drag with the pointer or use the arrow keys on the keyboard to reposition a selected image. To remove a photo from the composition, drag it from the work area into the light box strip above. To add an image to the composition, drag it from the light box into the work area.

- Use the Rotate Image tool (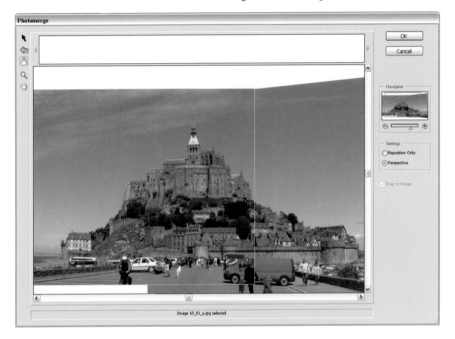) to rotate a selected photo.

- Choose between the Reposition Only and Perspective settings.

- With the Perspective option activated, you can click in the selected image with the Set Vanishing Point tool ( ) to set a new vanishing point—the reference around which the other images will be composed.

5 When you're satisfied with the result, click OK. The Photomerge dialog box closes, and Photoshop Elements goes to work. You'll see windows open and close as you wait for Photoshop Elements to create the panorama.

6 If you like your new composition better than the one you created in the previous exercise, crop the image and save your work in the My CIB Work folder.

7 Choose File > Close All to close all open windows. When asked whether you want to save your changes, click No.

8 Switch back to the Organizer.

Vanishing Point

A vanishing point is the point at which receding parallel lines seem to meet when seen in perspective. For example, as a road stretches out ahead of you, it appears to grow narrower with distance, until it has almost no width at the horizon. This is the vanishing point.

You can change the perspective of the Photomerge Panorama composition by specifying the location of the vanishing point. Select Perspective under Settings in the Photomerge dialog box, and then click in the image with the Vanishing Point tool to reset the location of the vanishing point in reference to which the Photomerge Panorama will be composed.

Creating a composite group shot

Shooting the perfect group photo is a difficult task, especially if you have a large family of squirmy kids. Fortunately, Photoshop Elements offers a solution: a powerful photo blending tool called Photomerge Group Shot. The next exercise will show you how multiple photos can be blended together into one with amazing precision. Gone are those family photos where someone has their eyes closed, someone else has looked away at the wrong moment, and you-know-who has just made an even odder facial expression than usual. Photomerge Group Shot lets you merge the best parts of several images into the perfect group photo.

1   If the Organizer is not currently active, switch to it now.

2   In the Keyword Tags palette, click the Find box for the Lesson 10 keyword tag.

3 In the Photo Browser, Ctrl-click to select the three pictures of a girl sitting on a wall: 10_02_a.psd, 10_02_b.psd, and 10_02_c.psd.

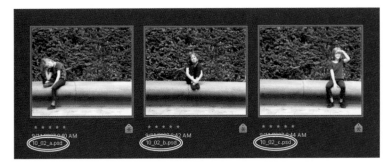

For the purposes of this exercise, we'll use these three distinctly different source images to make it easier for you to learn the technique but you would usually use the Photomerge Group Shot feature to create a merged image from a series of very similar source images such as you might capture with your camera's burst mode.

▶ **Tip:** The Photomerge Faces tool works similarly to the Photomerge Group Shot tool, except that it's specialized for working with faces. You can have a lot of fun merging different faces into one. Try merging parts of a picture of your own face with one of your spouse to predict the possible appearance of future offspring. Choose File > New > Photomerge Faces, or click the Faces button in the Photomerge palette In Guided Edit mode to create your own Frankenface.

4 Choose File > New > Photomerge Group Shot.

Photoshop Elements will load the Editor workspace and start the Photomerge Group Shot process.

5 (Optional) If you want to work with photos not currently in the Organizer (or you want to avoid switching to the Organizer first), you can also open the photos directly in the Editor. Select the image thumbnails in the Project Bin, switch to Guided Edit mode, and select Group Shot under Photomerge.

6 Photoshop Elements has automatically placed the first image (10_02_a.psd) as the source image. Drag the yellow framed image (10_02_b.psd) from the Project Bin and drop it into the Final image area on the right.

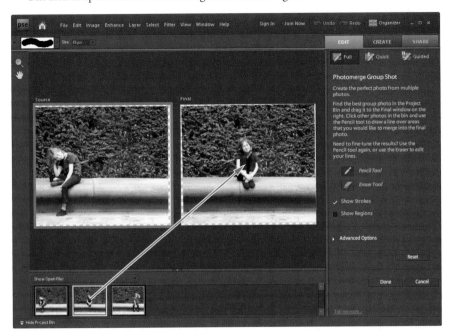

7 Use the Zoom tool to zoom in on the image so you can see all of the girl in the Source image and at least part of the girl in the Final image. Use the Hand tool to reposition the view if necessary.

8 In the Photomerge Group Shot panel, select the Pencil Tool.

9 With the Pencil tool(✏), draw one stroke from head to toe of the girl in the source image, as shown in the illustration below. When you release the pointer, Photoshop Elements will merge the girl from the Source image into the Final image—including her shadow on the stone! Seeing the magic of this tool in action will probably cause you some healthy mistrust whenever you come across an unlikely photo in the future. If necessary, use the Pencil tool to add additional image areas from the source. You can use the Eraser tool (✏) to delete a stroke—or parts of a stroke—drawn with the Pencil tool. The image copied to the Final image will be adjusted accordingly.

● **Note:** Sometimes it can be a little tricky to make the perfect selection—especially when you're working with a more complex source image than our example. You may find you are copying more of the source image than you want. If you've switched several times between the Pencil and Eraser tools but you still can't get the selection right, it's better to undo the operation and start again. Try modifying the shape that you're drawing with the Pencil tool and making shorter strokes.

10 Double-click the green framed image (10_02_c.psd) in the Project Bin to make it the Source image. Use the Hand tool to move the Source image in its frame so you can see the girl, and then use the Pencil tool to add her to the Final image.

11 To see which part of each of the three source images was used for the merged composition, first click the Fit Screen button above the edit pane so that you can see the entire image, and then activate the Show Regions option in the Photomerge Group Shot panel. The regions in the Final image are color coded.

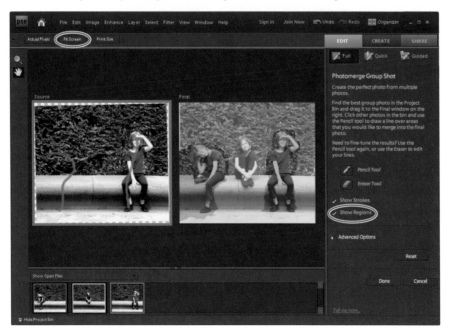

12 Click the Actual Pixels button above the edit pane, or zoom in even closer, and then use the Hand tool to position the image at a region boundary in the Final image. Toggle Show Regions off and on while you look for imperfections along the region boundaries in the merged image. If necessary, you can use the Pencil and Eraser tools to add to or subtract from the portions of the source images that are being merged to the Final image. When you are satisfied with the result, click Done in the Photomerge Group Shot panel.

13 The merged image needs to be cropped slightly. In Full Edit mode, choose Image > Crop to place a cropping rectangle on the image. In Guided Edit mode, click Crop Photo in the Basic Photo Edits palette. In Full Edit mode, hold the Shift key as you drag the handles of the cropping rectangle to constrain the aspect ratio to that of the original photo. In Guided Edit mode, choose Use Photo Ratio from the Crop Box Size menu to maintain the original proportions. Click the Commit button at the bottom right of the cropping rectangle.

14 Choose File > Save and save the merged image to your My CIB Work folder as **10_02_Work**, in Photoshop (*.PSD,*PDD) format, making sure that the Layers option is activated. If you are not in Full Edit mode, switch to it now, and then choose File > Close All and return to the Organizer.

Removing unwanted intruders

The Photomerge Scene Cleaner helps you improve a photo by removing passing cars, tourists, and other unwanted elements. This feature works best when you have several shots of the same scene, and when the objects that you wish to remove were moving. In fact, when you're sightseeing you should deliberately take a few extra shots of any busy scene so that later you can use the Photomerge Scene Cleaner to put together an unobstructed view.

Using the Scene Cleaner tool

In this first exercise, you'll politely remove a tourist who walked into shot at just the wrong moment.

1   In the Organizer, click the Find box next to the Lesson 10 keyword tag in the Keyword Tags palette. In the Photo Browser, Ctrl-click to select the images 10_03_a.jpg and 10_03_b.jpg. Click the Editor button at the top right corner of the Organizer window and choose Full Edit from the menu.

2   In the Editor, Ctrl-click to select both photos in the Photo Bin, and then choose File > New > Photomerge Scene Cleaner. Wait while Photoshop Elements auto-aligns the photos.

3   The first image in the Photo Bin, 10_03_b.jpg (framed in blue), has been loaded as the Source image. Drag the image framed in yellow, 10_03_a.jpg, into the Final pane. This is the image we will clean: the base image for your composite.

Note: You can use up to ten images in a single Scene Cleaner operation; the more images you use, the more chance that you'll produce a perfect result.

4   Zoom in and use the Hand tool to position the images so that you can see the lower right corner. Scroll down in the Photomerge Scene Cleaner Guided Edit panel so that you can see the tools at the bottom.

5   Select the Pencil tool () in the Photomerge Scene Cleaner panel and drag a line through the man's head in the foreground of the Final image.

6   Move the pointer away from the image window and wait a moment while information is copied from the source photo to cover the unwanted area in the Final image.

7   Click the Fit Screen button above the edit window. You can see that the Source image has some information across the top and down the right hand side of the photo that is missing from the Final image. Make sure the Pencil tool is selected, and then drag a line through those areas in either image. *(See the illustration on the next page.)*

▶ **Tip:** You can hold down the Shift key as you drag with the Pencil tool to constrain the movement to a straight line.

8 Working with only two images, there's not a lot more we can do. Click Done in the Photomerge Scene Cleaner panel, and then click the Fit Screen button above the edit window.

9 You can see that there are small empty patches in both the top left corner and the bottom right corner of the photo. You can crop the image to remedy that. Choose Image > Crop and drag the corner handles of the cropping rectangle to maximize the image while avoiding the empty areas. When you're satisfied, click the Commit button in the corner of the bounding box.

10 Choose File > Save. Name the file **10_03_Work** and save it to your My CIB Work folder, in Photoshop (PSD) format with the Layers option activated. Choose File > Close All and return to the Organizer.

8 Release the mouse button, and then click the Commit button in the corner of the bounding box to accept the changes.

Creating a gradient clipping mask

A clipping mask allows part of an image to show while hiding the rest by making it transparent.

In the next steps you'll create a gradient that fades from fully opaque to fully transparent, and then use this gradient as a clipping mask to blend the castle and aircraft layers together.

1 In the Layers palette, click the New Layer button ( ) to create a new blank layer, named Layer 2.

2 In the toolbox, select the Gradient tool ( ) and click the Default Foreground And Background Colors button beside the foreground and background color swatches, or press the D key on your keyboard.

3 In the tool options bar, click the arrow to open the gradient selection menu. Locate the Foreground to Transparent thumbnail (the name of the swatch appears in a tooltip when you roll the cursor over it). Double-click the Foreground To Transparent gradient swatch.

4 Make sure that the other settings in the tool options bar are as set up as you see in the illustration. Click the Radial Gradient ( ) button. Set the Mode to Normal, the Opacity to 100%, disable Reverse, and activate Transparency.

5 Make sure that Layer 2 is still selected in the Layers palette. Drag a short line downwards from the center of the airplane with the Gradient tool, and then release the mouse button.

The circular gradient appears on layer 2, fading from opaque black in the center and gradually becoming transparent towards the edges. You'll use this gradient as a clipping mask for the image of the airplane in Layer 1, making the airplane visible while the sky that surrounds it blends smoothly into the sky of the background image.

Applying the clipping mask to a layer

Now that you have your gradient layer, it's time to put it to work.

1 In the Layers palette, drag Layer 2—the layer with the new gradient—into the position below Layer 1.

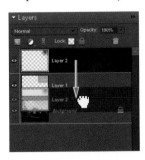

2 Select Layer 1, now the top layer, and then choose Layer > Group With Previous.

This action defines Layer 2 as the clipping mask for Layer 1. In the Layers palette, Layer 1 is now indented and shows a tiny arrow beside its thumbnail, pointing down to Layer 2. In the image window, the image of the airplane image now blends nicely with the castle photo.

3   Choose File > Save As. In the Save As dialog box, name the file **10_04_Work** and save it to your My CIB Work folder, in Photoshop (PSD) format with the Layers option activated. If Save in Version Set with Original is selected, disable it before you click Save. If the Photoshop Elements Format Options dialog box appears, keep Maximize Compatibility selected and click OK.

Creating a clean edge with defringing

Defringing removes the annoying halo of color that often surrounds a selection pasted into another image. In this exercise you'll composite an image of a family so that they appear to be standing in front of the fence in the castle picture by selecting and deleting the background and using the Defringe feature to blend the selection halo into the background.

1   Switch to the Organizer, select the file 10_04_c.jpg, the picture of the family, and open it in Full Edit mode.

2 With the image 10_04_c.jpg selected as the active window in the edit pane, choose Select > All. Choose Edit > Copy, and then File > Close. Select the Background layer of the image 10_04_Work.psd, and then choose Edit > Paste. The image of the family is placed on a new layer, named Layer 3, just above the background layer.

3 With Layer 3 still selected in the Layers palette, choose Image > Resize > Scale.

4 In the tool options bar, make sure Constrain Proportions is selected, and then type **80%** in the W (width) field. Click the Commit button near the lower right corner of the bounding box to accept the changes.

5 If necessary, scroll to see the lower left corner of the image in the document window. Select the Move tool and drag the image in Layer 3 to position it flush with the lower left corner of the castle image.

6 Select the Magic Wand tool (✨). In the tool options bar, set the Tolerance to **25**, activate Anti-alias, and disable Contiguous and All Layers. Click on the pink-colored background of the family image with the Magic Wand tool. If necessary, hold down the Shift key and click to select any unselected pink areas in the background.

7   Press the Delete key to delete the pink background. Press Ctrl+D, or choose Select > Deselect to clear the selection.

8   Zoom in to the area between the man's right hand and his sweater in the lower left corner of the image. A pinkish fringe or halo is clearly visible here.

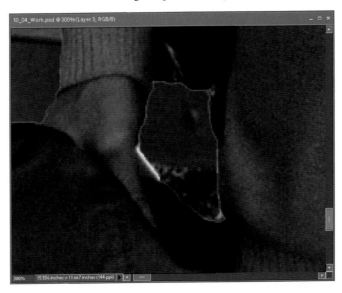

9   Choose Enhance > Adjust Color > Defringe Layer. In the Defringe dialog box, enter **1** pixel for the width and click OK. The fringe is eliminated.

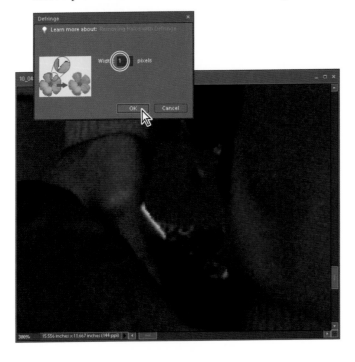

10 Double-click the Hand tool in the toolbox, or click the Fit Screen button in the tool options bar, to fit the whole image in the edit window.

11 Make sure that Layer 3 is still selected in the Layers palette. Select the Move tool in the toolbox and drag the top right handle of the selection rectangle to enlarge the image of the family so that they become more the focus of the composition. Click the Commit button near the lower right corner of the selection rectangle to accept the changes.

12 Choose File > Save, and then close the document and return to the Organizer.

Congratulations, you've completed the last exercise in this lesson. You've learned how to create a stunning composite panorama, how to merge multiple photos into the perfect group shot, how to remove obstructions from a view, and how to compose several photos into a single image by arranging layers and using a gradient layer as a clipping mask. Take a moment to work through the lesson review on the next page before you move on to the next chapter, "Advanced Editing Techniques."

Review questions

1   In the Photomerge dialog box, which tools can be used to fine-tune a panorama created from multiple images, and how do they work?

2   What does the Photomerge Group Shot tool do?

3   Why is it that sometimes when you think you're finished with a transformation in Photoshop Elements you cannot select another tool or perform other actions?

4   What is a fringe and how can you remove it?

Review answers

1   The Select Image tool is used to select a specific image from within the merged panorama. This tool can also be used to drag an image so that it lines up more closely with the other images in the panorama. The Rotate Image tool is used to rotate merged images so that their content aligns seamlessly. The Set Vanishing Point tool is used to specify the vanishing point for the perspective in the panorama. Setting the vanishing point in a different photo changes the point around which the other photos will be stretched and skewed to match the perspective.

2   With the Photomerge Group Shot tool you can pick and choose the best parts of several pictures taken successively, and merge them together to form one perfect picture.

3   Photoshop Elements is waiting for you to confirm the transformation by clicking the Commit button, or by double-clicking inside the transformation boundary.

4   A fringe is the annoying halo of color that often surrounds a selection pasted into another image. When the copied area is pasted onto another background color, or the selected background is deleted, you can see pixels of the original background color around the edges of your selection. The Defringe Layer command (Enhance > Adjust Color > Defringe Layer) blends the halo away so you won't see an artificial-looking line.

11 ADVANCED EDITING TECHNIQUES

Lesson Overview

In this final chapter you'll learn some advanced editing techniques and try some of the innovative tools that Adobe Photoshop Elements provides to help you improve the quality and clarity of your images.

This lesson will introduce some essential concepts and skills for making the most of your photos:

- Working with raw images

- Save conversions in the DNG format

- Using a histograms to assess a photo

- Improving the quality of highlights and shadows

- Resizing and sharpening an image

- Creating custom effects in the filter gallery

- Using the Cookie Cutter tool

 You'll probably need between one and two hours to complete this lesson.

Discover the advantages of working with raw images in the Camera Raw window, where the easy-to-use controls make it simple to correct and adjust your photos like a professional. Learn how to use the Histogram palette to help you understand what a less-than-perfect picture needs and to give you visual feedback on the solutions you apply. Finally, have some fun putting together your own filter effects.

Getting started

Note: Before you start working on this lesson, make sure that you've installed the software on your computer from the application CD (see the Photoshop Elements 7 documentation) and that you have correctly copied the Lessons folder from the CD in the back of this book onto your computer's hard disk (see "Copying the Classroom in a Book files" on page 2).

The exercises in this chapter build on the skills and concepts covered in earlier lessons. This lesson assumes that you are already familiar with the Photoshop Elements interface, and that you recognize the Organizer and Editor workspaces. If you find that you need more background information as you go along, review "Getting Started" and "A Quick Tour of Photoshop Elements" at the start of this book, or refer to Photoshop Elements Help.

1 Start Adobe Photoshop Elements, and choose Organize in the Welcome screen.

2 For the exercises in this lesson, you'll use images from the CIB Catalog you created earlier in the book. The name of the currently active catalog is displayed in the lower-left corner of the Organizer window. If necessary, choose File > Catalog and select the CIB Catalog in the Catalog Manager dialog box.

   If you don't see the CIB Catalog, you should review the procedures in "Copying the Lessons files from the CD" on page 2, and "Creating a catalog" on page 3.

3 In the Organizer, type the word **coast** into the Text Search box at the left of the bar above the Photo Browser. The Photo Browser shows only the file 11_01_coastline.ORF, a raw image from an Olympus digital camera. Select the file in the Photo Browser, click the Editor button at the upper right of the Organizer window and choose Full Edit from the menu.

4 The Camera Raw dialog box appears. Make sure that Preview is activated.

What is a raw image?

Raw files are referred to as such because, unlike many of the more common image file formats that you may recognize, such as JPEG or GIF, they are unprocessed by the digital camera or image scanner. In other words, a raw file contains all the image data captured for every pixel by the camera's sensors, without any software instructions about how that data is to be interpreted and displayed as an image on any particular device.

A limited but basically effective analogy or model for understanding the distinction is the difference between sending a film off for automatic processing by a commercial machine and using your own darkroom where you can control everything from the development of the negative to the way the image is exposed and printed onto paper.

The benefits of a raw image

Raw images are high-quality image files that contain the maximum amount of original image data in a relatively small file size. Though larger than a compressed image such as a JPEG file, a raw image contains more data than a TIFF image and uses less space.

Many types of image processing result in loss of data, effectively degrading the quality of the image. If a camera produces compressed files for instance, some data deemed superfluous is discarded. If a camera maps the whole range of captured image data to a defined color space, the spread of the image data can be narrowed. Processes such as sharpening and white balance correction will also alter the original captured data.

Whether you are an amateur photographer or a professional, it can be difficult to understand all the process settings on your digital camera and just what they mean in terms of data loss and image degradation. One solution is to use the camera's raw setting. Raw images are derived directly from the camera's sensors, prior to any camera processing. Not all digital cameras have the capability to capture raw images, but many of the newer and more advanced cameras do offer this option.

Capturing your photos in a raw format means you have more flexibility when it comes to producing the image you want. Many of the camera settings such as sharpening, white balance, levels, and color adjustments can be undone when you're working with your image in Photoshop Elements. For instance, automatic adjustments to exposure can be undone and recalculated based on the raw data.

Another advantage is that, because a raw image has 12 bits of data per pixel, you are able to extract shadow and highlight detail that would have been lost in the 8 bits/channel JPEG or TIFF formats.

Raw files provide an archival image format, much like a digital negative. In much the same way that you could produce a range of vastly different prints from the same film negative in a darkroom, you can reprocess a raw file repeatedly to achieve whatever results you want. Photoshop Elements doesn't save your changes to the original raw file; rather, it saves the settings you used to process it.

Note: Raw filenames have different extensions, depending on the camera used to capture the image. Examples are Canon's .CRW and .CR2, Epson's .ERF, Fuji's .RAF, Kodak's .KDE and .DER, Minolta's .MRW, Olympus'.ORF, Pentax's .PTX and .PEF, Panasonic's .RAW, and the various flavors of Nikon's .NEF.

Workflow overview for raw images

To use raw files, you need to set your camera to save files in its own raw file format. Photoshop Elements can open raw files only from supported cameras. For an up-to-date list of supported cameras and raw file formats, please visit: www.adobe.com/products/photoshop/cameraraw.html.

After processing the raw image file in the Camera Raw window, you can then open the image in Photoshop Elements, where you can work with it in the same way as you would with any other photo. You can save the results in any format supported by Photoshop Elements.

Note: The RAW plug-in, which is used to open files from a digital camera, is updated over time as new cameras are added to the list of those supported. It may be necessary to replace your plug-in with the latest version from the www.adobe.com website.

Improving a camera raw image

> **Note:** Any adjustment you make to an image results in a loss of data. Because you are working with much more information in a RAW file, any changes you make to settings such as exposure and white balance will have less impact in this way than if you made the same changes in a .PSD, TIFF, or JPEG file.

On the right side of the Camera Raw window is a control panel with three tabs: Basic, Detail and Camera Calibration. The Basic tab contains controls for image correction that allow you to make adjustments that are not possible with the standard editing tools in Photoshop Elements. The Detail tab contains controls for applying sharpening and reducing noise. For this exercise you'll use the controls in the Basic tab.

When you open a camera raw file, Photoshop Elements reads information in the file to ascertain which model of camera created it and applies the appropriate camera settings to the image data. In the control panel Options menu you can save the current settings as the default for the camera that created the image by choosing Save New Camera Raw Defaults, or have Photoshop Elements use the default settings for your camera by choosing Reset Camera Raw Defaults.

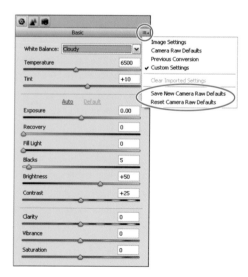

Adjusting the white balance

White balance presets can be helpful when you need to compensate for color casts in a photo caused by poor lighting conditions when the image was captured or incorrect camera settings. For example, if your camera was not set up correctly to deal with sunny conditions, you could correct the image by choosing the Daylight preset from the White Balance menu.

1   Experiment with some of the presets available in the White Balance menu. Compare the As Shot, Auto, Daylight, and Cloudy settings. Notice the effects on the preview image as you change the white balance preset. In the following pages you'll discover why setting the correct white balance is so important to the overall look of the image.

2   For now, choose As Shot from the White Balance presets menu.

3   Zoom into the image by choosing 100% from the Zoom Level menu in the lower left corner of the preview window.

4   Select the Hand tool (🖐) from the toolbar above the preview window, and drag the image in the preview window so that you can see parts of the blue sky as well as some of the green grass on top of the cliffs.

5   Select the White Balance tool (🖉), right beside the Hand tool in the toolbar.

6   Sample a neutral color in the image—a good choice is a medium-light gray that is neither too warm or too cool—by clicking it with the White balance tool.

The White Balance is now set to Custom and the image has lost its blue cast.

Camera Raw white balance settings

A digital camera records the white balance at the time of exposure as metadata, which you can see when you open the file in the Camera Raw dialog box. This setting usually yields the correct color temperature. You can adjust it if the white balance is not quite right. The Basic tab in the Photoshop Camera Raw dialog box includes three controls for correcting a color cast in your image:

White Balance Sets the color balance of the image to reflect the lighting conditions under which the photo was taken. A white balance preset may produce satisfactory results or you may want to customize the Temperature and Tint settings.

Temperature Fine-tunes the white balance to a custom color temperature. Move the slider to the left to correct a photo taken in light of a lower color temperature; the plug-in makes the image colors bluer to compensate for the lower color temperature of yellowish ambient light. Move the slider to the right to correct a photo taken in light of higher color temperature; the plug-in makes the image colors warmer to compensate for the higher color temperature of bluish ambient light.

Tint Fine-tunes the white balance to compensate for a green or magenta tint. Move the slider to the left to add green to the photo; move it to the right to add magenta.

To adjust the white balance quickly, click an area in the preview image that should be a neutral gray or white with the White Balance tool. The Temperature and Tint sliders automatically adjust to make the selected color as close to neutral as possible. If you're using a white area to set the white balance, choose a highlight area that contains significant white detail rather than a specular highlight.

—From Photoshop Elements Help

Working with the Temperature and Tint settings

The White Balance tool accurately removes any color cast or tint from an image but you may still want to tweak the Temperature and Tint settings. Depending upon the subject matter and the effect you wish to achieve, you might actually want a slight, controlled color tint. In this instance, the color temperature seems fine, but you can fine-tune the green/magenta balance of the image using the Tint control.

1   Zoom out to view the entire picture either by double-clicking the Hand tool or by choosing Fit In View from the Zoom Level menu in the lower left corner of the preview window.

2   Test the Temperature slider in the Basic tab by dragging it from one end of its range to the other. You'll see that the colors of the image become cooler or warmer as you move the slider. In this case, the corrected temperature of the image seemed fine but this slider could help you on other occasions—for toning down the overly warm tones resulting from tungsten lighting, for example.

3   Reset the Temperature control to the corrected value of 6050 either by dragging the slider or typing the value 6050 into the Temperature text box.

4   Experiment with the extremes of the Tint slider. The corrected value was +6. Change the setting to +10 with the slider or type **+10** into the Tint text box.

Using the tone controls on a raw image

The settings for tonal adjustments are located below the White Balance controls in the Basic tab. In this exercise, you'll use these controls to correct exposure, check highlights and shadows, and adjust brightness, contrast, and saturation. Before you adjust any of the settings, you should understand what each of the controls does:

Exposure adjusts the lightness or darkness of an image. Underexposed images are too dark and look dull and murky; overexposed images are too light and look washed out. Use the Exposure control to lighten an underexposed image or correct the faded look of an overexposed image.

Recovery attempts to recover details from burned-out highlights. The Recovery control can reconstruct some details in areas where one or two color channels are clipped to white. Clipping occurs when a pixel's color values are higher or lower than the range of values that can be represented in the image; over-bright values are clipped to output white, and over-dark values are clipped to output black.

Fill Light recovers details from shadows, without brightening blacks. The Fill Light control does something close to the inverse of the Recovery control, reconstructing detail in areas where one or two color channels are clipped to black.

Blacks specifies which input levels are mapped to black in the final image. Raising the Blacks value expands the areas that are mapped to black.

Brightness adjusts the brightness of the image, much as the Exposure slider does. However, instead of clipping the image in the highlights (areas that are completely white, with no detail) or shadows (areas that are completely black, with no detail), Brightness compresses the highlights and expands the shadows when you move the slider to the right. In general, use the Brightness slider to adjust the overall brightness after you have set the white and black clipping points with the Exposure and Blacks sliders.

Contrast is the amount of difference in brightness between light and dark areas of an image. The Contrast control determines the number of shades in the image, and has the most effect in the midtones. An image without enough contrast can appear flat or washed out. Use the Contrast slider to adjust the midtone contrast after setting the Exposure, Blacks, and Brightness values.

Clarity sharpens the definition of edges in the image. This process helps restore detail and sharpness that tonal adjustments may reduce.

Vibrance adjusts the saturation so that clipping is minimized as colors approach full saturation, acting on all lower saturated colors but having less impact on higher saturated colors. Vibrance also prevents skin tones from becoming oversaturated.

Saturation is the purity, or strength, of a color. A fully saturated color contains no gray. The Saturation control makes colors more vivid (less black or white added) or more muted (more black or white added).

First you'll adjust the Exposure setting, checking for clipping in the brighter areas.

1   Hold down the Alt key as you drag the Exposure slider to see where clipping occurs in the highlights—which parts of the image will be forced towards white. Set the Exposure to +0.25. You can also see the clipping in the histogram.

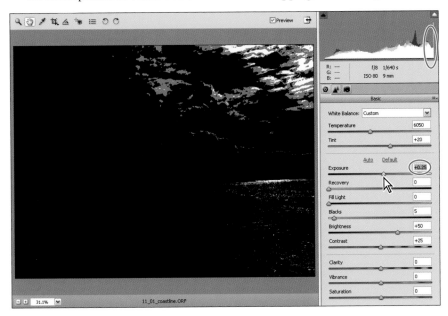

2   Hold down the Alt key as you drag the Recovery slider to 60. Most of the clipping is corrected, as you can see in both the preview and the histogram.

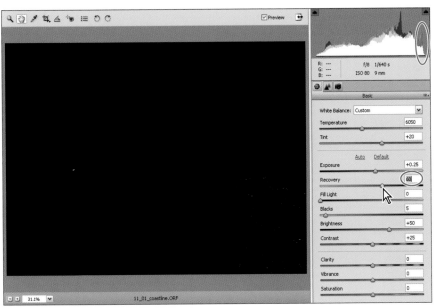

3 Hold down the Alt key and drag the Black slider. Any areas that appear in the clipping preview will be forced to a solid black. Release the mouse button when only the deepest areas of shadow in the image register as black. We moved the slider to 10.

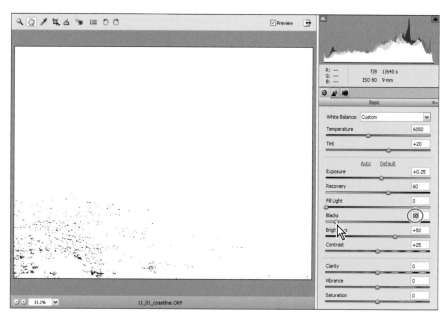

▶ **Tip:** For an interesting effect, drag the Saturation slider all the way to the left, essentially creating a three-color gray-scale.

4 Click the Brightness slider and press the up arrow on the keyboard to increase the value to 64. Click the Contrast slider and press the up arrow key on the keyboard to increase the value to +50. Drag the Clarity slider to 28.

The image, which was shot on a cloudy day and looked a little dull, now shows a larger range of detail and is more vivid and warmer in color.

Saving the image

You can reprocess this raw file repeatedly to achieve the results you want by saving it in the DNG format. Photoshop Elements doesn't save your changes to the original raw file—it saves only the settings you used to process it.

About the DNG format

Raw file formats are becoming common in digital photography. However, each camera manufacturer has its own proprietary raw format. This means that not every raw file can be read by software other than that provided with the camera. This may make it difficult to use these images in the future, as the camera manufacturers might not support these file formats indefinitely. Proprietary formats are also a problem if you want to use software other than that supplied by the camera manufacturers.

To help alleviate these problems, you can save raw images from Photoshop Elements in the DNG format, a publicly available archival format for raw files generated by digital cameras. The DNG format provides an open standard for files created by different camera models, and helps to ensure that you will be able to access your files in the future.

1 To convert and save the image, click the Save Image button at the lower left of the Camera Raw dialog box. The Save Options dialog box appears.

2 Under Destination, click the Select Folder button. In the Select Destination Folder dialog box, click your My CIB Work folder, and then click Select.

3 Under File Naming, leave Document Name selected in the menu on the left. Click the menu on the right and select 1 Digit Serial Number. This adds the number 1 following the name.

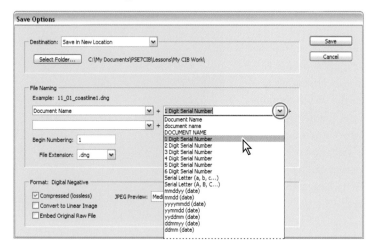

4　Click Save. The file, along with the present settings, will be saved in DNG format, which you can reprocess repeatedly.

5　Click the Open Image button in the right lower corner of the Camera Raw dialog box. Your image will open in the Editor window of Photoshop Elements.

6　In the Editor, choose File > Save. Navigate to your My CIB Work folder, name the file 11_01_coastline_Work.psd, choose the Photoshop format, and then click Save.

7　Choose File > Close.

You've now experienced some of the advantages of using a camera raw format. Even though this format gives you more control and allows you to edit your image in a non-destructive way, a lot of professionals choose not to use raw format. Raw files are usually considerably bigger than high-quality JPEGs and take much longer to be saved in your camera—quite a disadvantage for action shots or when you're taking a lot of pictures.

About histograms

For your images in JPEG, TIFF, and PSD formats, you'll do most of your serious editing in Full Edit mode. In this part of the lesson, you will learn how to use the histogram to understand what changes can be made to your images to improve their quality.

In the next exercises, you'll work on an image that was shot in poor lighting and also has a slight magenta cast. This is quite a common problem—many digital cameras introduce a slight color cast into images.

Using the histogram

A histogram is a graph representing the spread of tonal ranges present in an image. The Histogram palette in the Editor (Window > Histogram), indicates whether the image contains enough detail in the shadows (at the left end of the curve), midtones, and highlights (at the right end of the curve). The histogram can help you recognize where changes need to be made in the image.

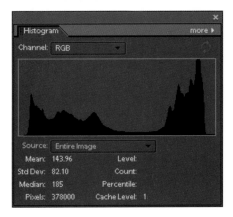

In the histogram below it's very apparent that there is not a good spread of tonal information in this image. You can see clearly that the image is deficient in the mid-tones, which is why it has a flat appearance, lacking in midtone contrast.

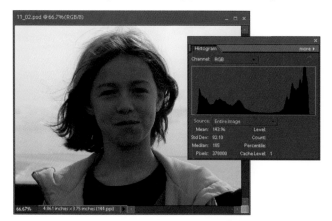

Tonal corrections such as lightening an image remove information. Excessive correction causes posterization, or color-banding in the image. The histogram in the illustration below reveals that this image is already lacking detail. You can see gaps, bands, and anomalous spikes in the curve. Any further modifications made to the image will degrade it even more.

Understanding highlights and shadows

In the next part of this lesson, you'll adjust the highlights and shadows and make additional tonal corrections to a photo while keeping an eye on the Histogram.

1   In the Editor, make sure you are in Full Edit mode. Choose File > Open, navigate to your Lesson11 folder, select the file 11_02.psd, and click Open.

2   Choose File > Save As. Name the image **11_02_Work** and save it to your My CIB Work folder in Photoshop (PSD) format.

3   If the Histogram palette is not already visible, choose Window > Histogram.

4   In order to see the effects of your adjustments more directly, you can drag the Histogram palette and position it beside the face of the girl. You'll notice that the face is a little dark.

According to the histogram, there is a lack of data in the midtone range for this image—it needs more information in the midtones and less in the shadows and highlights. You'll adjust the tonal range of this image using the Levels controls.

Adjusting levels

1   Choose Enhance > Adjust Lighting > Levels. The Levels dialog box appears. Make sure that Preview is activated.

In this exercise you'll use the shadows (left), midtone (middle), and highlights (right) sliders below the histogram graph in the Levels palette as well as the Set Black Point (left), Set Gray Point (middle), and Set White Point (right) eyedroppers.

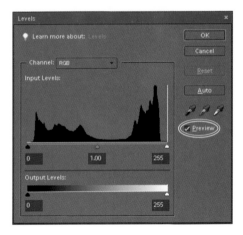

Although the midtones range is the most problematic area of this image, it is important to first adjust the highlights and shadows correctly.

We'll look at two slightly different methods for setting the white and black points in the image using the Levels controls.

2   In the Levels dialog box, hold down the Alt key as you drag the highlights slider to the left to a value of 242—just inside the right-hand end of the tonal curve. The clipping preview shows you where the brightest parts of the image are: a few highlights in the girl's hair and a portion of the sky near the upper right corner of the image.

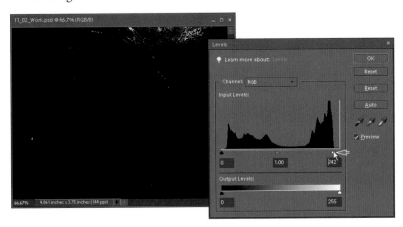

3   Watch the histogram as you release first the Alt key and the mouse button. The curve in the histogram shifts—possibly a bit far—to the right. You can see that the right-hand end of the curve is truncated. Move the highlights slider in the Levels controls to a value of 245. The histogram is adjusted accordingly.

4   In the Levels dialog box, click Reset and we'll try another method for adjusting the highlights. Select the Set White Point Eyedropper tool and watch the histogram as you click in the brightest part of the sky.

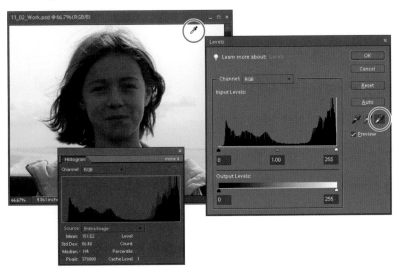

Tip: If your image has an easily identified neutral tone, you can remove a color cast quickly using the Set White Point Eyedropper tool. Neutrals are areas in the image that contain only a gray tone mixed with as little color as possible.

The result is very similar to the previous method, but it won't be as easy to fine-tune the clipping at the right end of the curve. Now you'll correct the shadows.

5 Hold down the Alt key and drag the shadow slider to the right to a value of 16, where the area below the girl's right ear shows as a dark spot in the clipping preview. Watch the histogram as you release the mouse button and the Alt key.

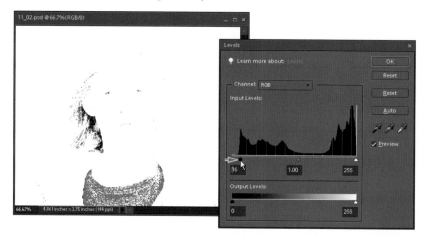

6 In the Levels controls, drag the midtone slider (the gray triangle below the center of the graph) to the left to set the midtone value to 1.50.

7 Notice the change in the Histogram. Compare the original data (displayed in gray) to the data for the corrections that you have made (displayed in black). Some gaps have been created. You want to avoid creating large gaps—even if the image still looks fine on screen, large gaps may cause a loss of data that will be visible as color banding when printed.

8 Click OK to close the Levels dialog box. If an Adobe Photoshop Elements alert dialog box appears, click Yes.

9 Select Edit > Undo Levels, or press Ctrl+Z to see how the image looked prior to redistributing the tonal values. Choose Edit > Redo Levels, or Press Ctrl+Y to reinstate your corrections. Leave this image open for the next part of this lesson.

About Unsharp Mask

Now you can add some crispness to the image, which will make it look much better when printed. Using the sharpening tools correctly can improve an image significantly.

In this exercise you'll use the Unsharp Mask feature in Photoshop Elements. How can something be *un*sharp and yet sharpen an image? The term unsharp mask has it roots in the print production industry: the technique was implemented by making an out-of-focus negative film—the unsharp mask—and then printing the original in a sandwich with this unsharp mask. This produced a halo around the edges of objects—optically giving them more definition.

If you are planning to resize an image, do it before you apply the Unsharp mask filter. The halo effect mentioned above can appear as an obvious artefact if it is scaled with the image.

1 With the file 11_02_Work.psd still open in the Editor, choose Image > Resize > Image Size.

This image needs to be made smaller, but with a higher resolution (pixels per inch).

2 If necessary, disable the Resample Image check box at the bottom of the dialog box, and then type **300** in the Resolution text field. Notice that the width and height values adjust. This method increases the resolution in the image without losing information.

Resolution refers to the fineness of detail you can see in an image, measured in pixels per inch (ppi): the more pixels per inch, the greater the resolution. Generally, the higher the resolution of your image, the better the printed result.

3 Now select Resample Image, to reduce the height and width of the image without affecting the resolution. Click OK.

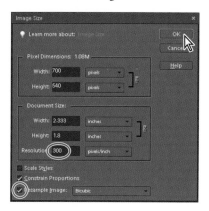

4 Choose File > Save. Keep the file open for the next part of this lesson.

Applying the Unsharp Mask filter

Before you apply any filter in Adobe Photoshop Elements, it is best to set the zoom level to 100%.

1 With the file 11_02_Work.psd still open in the Editor, choose View > Actual Pixels.

2 Choose Enhance > Unsharp Mask. The Unsharp Mask dialog box appears.

The amount of unsharp masking that you apply is determined by the subject matter. A portrait, such as this image, should be softer than an image of an object such as an automobile. The adjustments range from 1 to 500, with 500 being the sharpest.

3 Drag the Amount slider or type **125** in the Amount text field. Leave the Radius at 1 pixel.

4 Increase the Threshold only slightly to 2 pixels. Threshold is a key control in this dialog box, as it tells the filter what not to sharpen. In this case the value 2 means that a pixel will not be sharpened if it is within 2 shades of the pixel beside it (on a scale of 255).

▶ **Tip:** Disable the preview in the Unsharp Mask window by clicking on the preview pane and holding down the mouse button. When you release the mouse button, the preview is enabled again. To see another part of the image, drag the image in the preview pane.

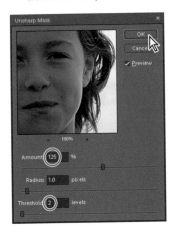

5 Click OK to close the Unsharp Mask dialog box.

6 Choose File > Save, and then File > Close.

Without sharpening.

Unsharp mask applied.

As you've seen, the Unsharp Mask filter can't mysteriously correct the focus of your image. It only gives the impression of crispness by increasing the contrast between adjacent pixels. As a rule of thumb, the Unsharp Mask filter should be applied to an image only once, as a final step in your processing. If you use Unsharp Mask too much, you'll run the risk of over sharpening your image producing artefacts that will give it a flaky, grainy look.

● **Note:** There are other ways to adjust the sharpness of your photos: Choose Enhance > Auto Sharpen or, if you want more control over the sharpening process, choose Enhance > Adjust Sharpness.

Creating effects using the filter gallery

► **Top:** Not all filters are available from the Filter Gallery—some are available only individually as Filter menu commands. The Filter Gallery does not offer effects and layer styles as does the Effects palette.

You can have a lot of fun experimenting with filter effects using the Filter Gallery, where you can apply multiple filters to your image and tweak the way they work together, effectively creating new custom effects. Each filter has its own slider controls, giving you a great deal of control over the effect on your photo. The possibilities are endless—it's up to you to make the most of these filters and to apply them with discretion. Have a look at "About Filters" in Photoshop Elements Help to find out more about the different filters.

1 In the Organizer, use the Lesson 11 keyword tag to find the file 11_03.jpg in your Lesson 11 folder, Select the image in the Photo Browser, click the Editor button, and choose Full Edit from the menu.

2 Choose File > Save As. Navigate to your My CIB Work folder, name the file 11_03_Work, choose the Photoshop (*.PSD,*.PDD) format, and then click Save.

Many filters use the foreground and background colors currently active in the toolbar to create effects, so you should take a moment to set them now.

3 Click the Default Foreground And Background Color button beside the color swatches at the bottom of the toolbar. This resets the default colors: black in the foreground and white for the background.

4 Choose Filter > Filter Gallery. The Filter Gallery dialog box appears.

5 If necessary, use the menu in the lower left corner of the dialog box to set the magnification level at 100%. This view brings the image much closer so that the effects of the filters you apply are more obvious.

6   When you move the pointer over the image in the preview pane, the pointer changes into the hand tool (). Drag the image in the preview pane so that you can see the two kids on the right of the photo.

The center pane in the Filter Gallery window lists the available filters by category.

7   Expand the Brush Strokes category by clicking the arrow to the left of the category name, and then choose the Crosshatch filter.

8   Experiment with the control sliders. You can see the effect of the filter in the preview pane. Set the sliders as shown in the illustration below.

9 Click the New Effect layer button () at the lower right of the Filter Gallery dialog box, expand the Artistic filters category, and choose the Sponge filter. The Crosshatch and Sponge filters are applied simultaneously.

10 Set the Brush Size to 0, Definition to 2, and Smoothness to 8.

11 Click the New Effect Layer button again. If necessary, scroll down in the list of filters to see the Texture category. Expand the Texture category and select the Patchwork filter. Set both sliders to 0. Once again, the image has changed totally.

Experimenting with filters in the gallery

The possibilities are endless for the effects that you might create in your image by combining different filters at varied settings.

Tip: It's a good idea to apply filters to a duplicate layer in your image, as it is not possible to undo filters after you've saved your file. Press Ctrl+J to duplicate a layer.

1 Click the button at the top right of the filters pane to hide the filters menu. Choose Fit In View from the zoom menu at the bottom left of the Preview pane.

2 Experiment with the three filters that you've applied, turning them off or on by clicking the eye icon to the left of each filter name.

3 Re-arrange the order of the filters by dragging them to new positions in the list. This will alter the way the filters interact.

4 There is no need to apply the changes to the image. Click Cancel to close the Filter Gallery dialog box, keeping the file open for the next exercise.

Using the Cookie Cutter tool

The Cookie Cutter tool enables you to crop an image with one of a library of Cookie Cutter shapes. In this exercise, you'll crop the image with a heart-shaped cutter.

1 Select the Cookie Cutter tool from the toolbox.

Tip: There are many more cutout shapes available. Click the double arrow in the upper right corner of the shapes palette to see a menu of 22 different categories.

2 Click the Shapes menu in the tool options bar to view the default selection of shapes.

3 Double-click to select the shape named Heart Card (the shape of a heart). The name of each shape appears as a tool tip when you move the pointer over its swatch.

4 From the Set Shape Options menu in the tool options bar, choose From Center.

Set Shape Options

Unconstrained Draws the shape to any size or dimension you'd like.

Defined Proportions Keeps the height and width of the cropped shape in proportion.

Defined Size Crops the photo to the exact size of the shape you choose.

Fixed Size Specifies exact measurements for the finished shape.

From Center Draws the shape from the center.

Enter a value for **Feather** to soften the edges of the finished shape.

Note: Feathering softens the edges of the cropped image so that the edges fade out and blend in with the background.

—From Adobe Photoshop Elements Help

5 Drag in the image to create the cutter shape. Press the Shift key as you drag to maintain the original aspect ratio of the shape, or press the Space key to reposition the shape. After releasing the pointer, you can use the handles on the bounding box to scale the shape. Click inside the bounding box and drag the shape to reposition it.

6 Click the Commit button at the lower right corner of the bounding box, or press Enter to crop the image. To cancel the cropping operation, click the Cancel button or press the Esc key.

7 Choose File > Save, and then File > Close.

Congratulations, you have finished the lesson on advanced editing techniques in Adobe Photoshop Elements. You discovered how to take advantage of the Camera Raw plug-in and learned how to correct images using the Histogram palette as both a diagnostic tool and a feedback reference. You also found out how to create custom effects using the Filter Gallery had a little fun with the Cookie Cutter tool.

Learning more

We hope you've gained confidence in using Photoshop Elements to bring out the best in your photographs. You've picked up some great tricks and techniques, but this book is just the start. You can learn even more by using the Photoshop Elements Help system, which is built into the application. Also, don't forget to look for tutorials, tips, and expert advice on the Adobe website, www.adobe.com.

Review questions

1 What is a camera raw image, and what are some of its advantages?

2 What are the different methods for adjusting the white balance in the Camera Raw window?

3 How do you use the Levels controls to correct highlights and shadows?

4 What is the Cookie Cutter tool used for?

Review answers

1 A raw file is one that is unprocessed by a digital camera. Not all cameras create raw files. One of the advantages of raw images is the flexibility of having detailed control over settings that are usually pre-applied by the camera. Image quality is another plus—because raw formats have 12 bits of available data, it's possible to extract shadow and highlight detail that would have been lost in an 8 bits/channel JPEG or TIFF file. Finally, raw files provide an archival image format, much like a digital negative: you can reprocess the file repeatedly to achieve the results you want, while your raw data remains unchanged.

2 In the Camera Raw window you can set the white balance in an image automatically by using the White Balance eyedropper. Clicking on a neutral color with the White Balance eyedropper automatically adjusts the Temperature and Tint sliders. Alternatively, you can choose a preset from the White Balance menu. The options include corrections based on a range of common lighting conditions. It's also possible to correct the white balance manually with the Temperature and Tint sliders.

3 In the Levels dialog box, you can adjust the shadows and highlights in your image by using either the slider controls below the Levels histogram, or the Set Black Point and Set White Point eyedroppers. You can hold down the Alt key as you drag a slider to see a clipping preview, which gives you visual feedback on the location of the darkest and lightest areas of your image. With the Set Black Point and Set White Point eyedroppers you can click directly in the image to define the white and black points, or double-click the eyedroppers to call up the color picker where you can define the values precisely.

4 The Cookie Cutter tool is used to crop an image into a variety of shapes. Use the default shapes set, or select a shape from an extensive library.

INDEX

Production Notes

The *Adobe Photoshop Elements 7 Classroom in a Book* was created electronically using Adobe InDesign CS3. Art was produced using Adobe InDesign, Adobe Illustrator, and Adobe Photoshop. The Myriad Pro and Warnock Pro OpenType families of typefaces were used throughout this book.

References to company names in the lessons are for demonstration purposes only and are not intended to refer to any actual organization or person.

Team credits

The following individuals contributed to the development of this edition of the *Adobe Photoshop Elements Classroom in a Book*:

Project coordinators, technical writers: Torsten Buck & Katrin Straub

Production: Manneken Pis Productions (www.manneken.be)

Copyediting & Proofreading: John Evans

Designer: Katrin Straub

Special thanks to Christine Yarrow.

Typefaces used

Adobe Myriad Pro and Adobe Warnock Pro are used throughout the lessons. For more information about OpenType and Adobe fonts, visit www.adobe.com/type/opentype/.

Photo Credits

Photographic images and illustrations supplied by Katrin Straub, Torsten Buck, John Evans, Han Buck, and Adobe Systems Incorporated. Photos are for use only with the lessons in the book.

Contributors

 Torsten Buck has been involved in the development of software for the design and desktop publishing industries in Japan, China and the United States for almost 20 years. A Masters in Computer Science combined with a passion for typography have shaped a career that took Torsten from the development of ground-breaking Asian font technology in Hong Kong to a position as Head of Type Development at Adobe Systems in the USA. Currently he is the Director of Manneken Pis Productions and has authored a wide range of design software training books including several versions of *Adobe Photoshop Elements Classroom in a Book* and *Adobe Premiere Elements Classroom in a Book, Creating a Newsletter in InDesign: Visual QuickProject Guide*, and more recently *Adobe Photoshop Lightroom 2 Classroom in a Book* and *Adobe Creative Suite 4 Classroom in a Book*.

 Katrin Straub is an artist, an MA in media studies, a graphic designer, and author. Her award-winning print, painting, and multimedia work has been exhibited worldwide. With more than 15 years experience in design, Katrin has worked as Design Director for companies such as Landor Associates and Fontworks in the United States, Hong Kong, and Japan. Her work includes packaging, promotional campaigns, multimedia, website design, and internationally recognized corporate and retail identities. She holds degrees from the FH Augsburg, ISIA Urbino, and The New School University in New York and has authored many books in the past 5 years, from *Adobe Creative Suite Idea Kit* to Classroom in a Book titles for Adobe Photoshop Lightroom 2, Adobe Creative Suite 4, Adobe Soundbooth, and several versions of *Adobe Photoshop Elements Classroom in a Book* and *Adobe Premiere Elements Classroom in a Book*.

 John Evans has worked in computer graphics and design for more than 20 years—initially as a graphic designer, and then since 1993 as a multimedia author, software interface designer, and technical writer. His multimedia and digital illustration work associated with Japanese type attracted an award from Apple Computer Australia and was featured in Japan's leading digital design magazine. His other projects range from music education software for children to interface design for innovative Japanese font design software. As a technical writer his work includes software design specifications, user manuals, and more recently copyediting for *Adobe Lightroom 2 Classroom in a Book* and *Adobe Creative Suite 4 Classroom in a Book*.

 Tao Buck and her sisters have been volunteering as photo models for the last three editions of *Photoshop Elements Classroom in a Book*. When she is grown up, Tao wants to work for WWF and make the world a better place, especially for all the cute animals.

 Zoë Buck loves to juggle with numbers, play chess, do gymnastics, and at this very moment is considering becoming a vet.

 Han Buck would like to become a painter (actually, she is one already) or else "work from home and do nothing like her parents."

 Mia Buck strives to become a great pianist (although she does not believe in practicing).